WILLIAM K. B. STOEVER

'A Faire and Easie Way to Heaven'

COVENANT THEOLOGY AND ANTINOMIANISM

IN EARLY MASSACHUSETTS

WESLEYAN UNIVERSITY PRESS

Middletown, Connecticut

The publisher gratefully acknowledges the support of the publication of this book by Western Washington University and by the Andrew W. Mellon Foundation.

Library of Congress Cataloging in Publication Data

Stoever, William K   B   1941-
    A faire and easie way to heaven.
    Bibliography: p.
    Includes index.
    1. Covenants (Theology)—History of doctrines.
2. Antinomianism. 3. Puritans—Massachusetts.
4. Massachusetts—Church history. I. Title.
BT155.S77   238   77-14851
ISBN 0-8195-5024-8

Manufactured in the United States of America
First edition, 1978
Wesleyan Paperback, 1988

'A Faire and Easie Way to Heaven'

Contents

Preface

Within seven years of its founding in 1629, the Puritan commonwealth of Massachusetts Bay was troubled by a sectarian outburst that focused the attention of the clergy, and then of the civil authorities, on the church at Boston. There certain of the congregation, led by Anne Hutchinson and abetted by John Cotton, teacher of the church, charged that the ministers of the Bay Colony, almost entirely, were a company of unregenerate "legalists," preaching a "covenant of works" instead of a "covenant of grace" and thereby hindering the work of redemption. The ensuing wrangle rent the religious and civil peace of Boston and threatened that of the whole colony. For two years the "Antimonian Controversy" clouded the radiance of John Winthrop's City on a Hill.

Studies of New England Puritanism sometimes imply that the antinomian incident of 1636–38 was largely a local phenomenon, generated by the interaction of basic Puritan impulses and conditions of settlement in the wilderness. This interpretation is partly accurate and partly an artifact of the interpreter's chosen width of field. Certain opinions voiced by the Massachusetts dissenters belonged to an English sectarian current already recognizable in the 1620s, and others are traceable in contemporary English nonconformist discussion about the precise nature of the central Protestant notion of "justifying faith." Anne Hutchinson enjoyed, for a time, greater freedom of action in new Boston than she had in old England, but the bent of her spirituality was apparently set, and the tendency of her theology acquired, before she emigrated. The issues disputed in Massachusetts, furthermore, were understood by the majority of the clergy in the context of a theological dialectic that was the common property of Reformed divines in the sixteenth and seventeenth centuries. This dialectic, which was held to be divinely ordained, sought to relate divine grace and created nature in the regeneration of sinful mankind in such a way that the gratuity of grace and the integrity of nature were each preserved. The "covenant theology" associated particularly with Puritan divines of the early seventeenth century was an important expression of this dialectic and a manifestation of the respect for the liberty and agency of reasonable creatures that appears in Protestant scholasticism. At moments of controversy, the theological dialectic and its covenantal expression could be invoked in restraint of apparent excess in the name of either divine power or human integrity, as was done on both sides in the New England dispute.

Though occupying a relatively minor place in the sweep of Puritan history, the New England antinomian incident, considered in its larger setting, may be viewed as a characteristic Puritan event. It involved a major issue of Christian theology and practice, to which Puritans, in consequence of their commitment to experiential religion, were especially sensitive. As the first encounter of a Puritan commonwealth with its own radical offspring, it revealed tensions inherent in the movement and foreshadowed the sectarian flowering of the 1640s in old England. It was also, in a sense, the opening round in a controversy over the precise nature of the "covenant of grace" that exercised English nonconformists until the end of the seventeenth century. Operating in the New England controversy, moreover, may be seen the theological dialectic of nature and grace that informed Puritanism's self-conscious attempts at social construction. This dialectic was doubly important, for it served not only to legitimate practical efforts to reorder earthly society according to God's will, but also to moderate such efforts, so that transformation of individuals and institutions, while earnestly pursued, was not simply equated with dissolution of worldly order in either church or society. In these respects the New England Antinomian Controversy exemplifies a considerable range of Puritan experience, on both sides of the Atlantic.

The following essay seeks to examine the substance of the ministerial debate in Massachusetts in relation to elements of its contemporary theological, controversial, and sectarian context, and to clarify the issues in dispute and the way in which the participants seem to have apprehended them. The appearance in modern editions, during the last decade and a half, of important source-material, previously difficult to obtain or available only in manuscript, suggests the timeliness of such an enterprise.

Many individuals have contributed to the personal context whence this study emerged. I am particularly indebted to Sydney Ahlstrom, Edmund Morgan, David Hall, David Little, George Lindbeck, and Gerhard Ebeling, who, at different times and in diverse ways, helped to stimulate and shape my interest in seventeenth-century Puritan theology. I owe special thanks to Professor Ahlstrom, for continuing encouragement and counsel, in this and other endeavors, and to my wife, Barbara Clement Stoever, who has seen the project through as both critic and companion. Thanks are due to the following libraries for assistance in obtaining source-material: the Beinecke Rare Book and Manuscript Library, the Houghton Library, the Folger Shakespeare Library, the Henry E. Huntington Library and Art Gallery, the Boston Public Library, and the British Library. I am especially grateful to the National Endowment for the Humanities and to the College of Arts and Sciences, the Bureau for Faculty Research, and the Department of Liberal Studies, Western Washington University, for financial support and technical assistance. I must also thank the editors of *Church History* for permission to use, in brief portions of Chapters 1, 3–6, and 9, material previously published in that journal (44, No. 1 [March, 1975]).

'A Faire and Easie Way to Heaven'

CHAPTER 1

The Dialectic of Nature and Grace

PLUM ISLAND AND THE CREATED ORDER

In 1697, six years after the arrival of the royal charter and five years after the affair of the Salem witches, in the midst of the struggle for control of Harvard College, two years before the Brattle Street Manifesto and three before the controversy over "Stoddardeanism," a pamphlet appeared at Boston in New England bearing the title *Phaenomena quaedam Apocalyptica ad Aspectum Novi Orbis configurata, Or some few Lines toward a description of the New Heaven as It makes to those who stand upon the New Earth.* The work was Judge Samuel Sewall's contribution to an already vast Puritan literature interpreting the Book of Revelation. The booklet concludes with what has come down in the tradition as the "hymn to Plum Island."

> As long as Plum Island shall faithfully keep the commanded Post; Notwithstanding all the hectoring Words, and hard Blows of the proud and boisterous Ocean; As long as any Salmon, or Sturgeon shall swim in the streams of Merrimack; or any Perch, or Pickeril, in Crane-Pond; As long as the Sea-Fowl shall know the Time of their coming, and not neglect seasonably to visit the Places of their Acquaintance: As long as any Cattel shall be fed with Grass growing in the Medows, which do humbly bow down themselves before Turkie-Hill; As long as any Sheep shall walk upon Old Town Hills, and shall from thence pleasantly look down upon the River Parker, and the faithful Marishes lying beneath; As long as any free and harmless Doves shall find a White Oak, or other Tree within the Township, to perch, or feed, or build a careless Nest upon; and shall voluntarily present themselves to perform the office of Glean-

3

ers after Barley-Harvest; As long as Nature shall not grow Old and dote; but shall constantly remember to give the rows of Indian Corn their education, by Pairs: So long shall Christians be born there; and being first made meet, shall from thence be Translated, to be made partakers of the Inheritance of the Saints in Light.[1]

This passage has been somewhat puzzling for scholars. The body of the *Phaenomena* is anything but poetical, and there is a persistent suspicion that conscientious Puritans were not really capable of lyricism or of sensuousness, save under pious disguise or via some complex sublimation. Could Sewall, who was both conscientious and a Puritan, really have written the "hymn"? Such reservations notwithstanding, one may suggest that in fact Sewall's paean, in its sensuousness and its cadences, is in harmony with the Puritan character. This essay is chiefly about Puritan theology. It may appropriately begin, however, with a notable literary illustration of an affirmation basic to Puritan life and thought, the affirmation, namely, of the essential goodness of the created order.

There is ample evidence of this attitude in Puritan literature. Richard Sibbes, for example, wrote that human "reason is a beam of God, . . . judgment is a spark of God, nature is but God's candle, it is a light of the same light that grace is of, but inferior. . . . Every creature has a beam of God's glory in it, the whole world is a theater of the glory of God." The editors of John Preston's *Life Eternal* observed that the human soul and its faculties bear the "prints and imitations" of the divine attributes. Preston himself declared that faith, though beyond sense and reason, is not contrary to them, "for sense and reason are God's work as well as grace, now one work of God does not destroy another." Richard Baxter insisted that the Holy Spirit "works on man as man, and causes him to believe nothing but what is credible," and he remarked that the Christian faith would not suffer had the Spirit guided the authors of scripture in the "matter" only and left them to their "natural and acquired abilities" in the manner of expression. Walter Craddock observed that we may learn of God by examining his creatures, and John Goodwin noted that right human reason is effective in the discerning of spirits.[2]

These phrases, in varying ways, express the underlying conviction of English Puritans that there is no *natural* hostility between the creation and the Creator. The substance of the cosmos, and mankind's participation in it, they believed, cannot be treated as essentially bad, because both are the work of God, who is essentially good, and are the expression of his sovereign will. Upon this premise rested the distinctive asceticism of Reformed Protestantism, which sought to encompass the full range of human social and biological life, and also the "Puritan ethic," as expressed in the doctrine of the saint's "particular calling" to worldly diligence in service of God and the common good.[3] Neither, Puritans believed, is there any inherent conflict between "piety" of the heart and human intellection; for the powers of reason and volition which distinguish human beings among the creatures are given them by God, and God treats with them via these faculties. An individual is brought into a state of grace in this life by the instrumentality of created things—by words heard and read, by experiences pleasant and painful—stimulating the senses, persuading the understanding, kindling the affections, moving the will.

The estate of grace itself, for Puritans, consisted in a special kind of knowledge and a special choosing, namely, in the ability and desire to order all worldly living, in thought and deed, to the divine will as set forth in scripture and interpreted by godly minds. Graciousness expresses itself not in withdrawal from "worldly" living, but in loving obedience to God in and through the daily work of this world. Accordingly, Puritans regarded formal theology as practical instruction for human action, rather than as a speculative exercise, which seemed to them a waste of time. In the now-familiar words of William Ames, New England's favorite theologian, theology is "the doctrine of living unto God." Ames's teacher, William Perkins, called it a "science of living well and blessedly forever." Typically, Ames's own *summa* was a monumental elaboration of the "observance" incumbent upon Christians, rather than a systematic exposition of articles of faith; and he construed "observance" as including domestic economy, personal morality, politics, economics, and lawmaking, as well as the practice of religion.[4] The "practical" theology of both men was predicated on the double affirmation that the world is susceptible of godly ordering and that human faculties, properly disposed, are capable of ordering it.

The urgent issue for Sewall's generation of Massachusetts Puritans was to define precisely and perform adequately the "observance" incumbent upon them under the "national covenant" that in their conception constituted the bond between God and their New England commonwealth and formed the foundation of their collective prosperity. Sewall ended his booklet with the affirmation that, until the Kingdom indeed came, Massachusetts, or at least Newbury, would remain faithful to her calling as a people in covenant with God, in accordance with which covenant she properly enjoyed the bounty of the land. The tone of the passage suggests pronounced personal fondness for the land itself, its creatures, and its seasons; one infers that the author would not be wholly displeased should the Lord tarry. A more rigorously ascetic nonconformist might complain that Sewall's affections were not sufficiently "weaned" from this world. Sewall, noting the futility of predicting the date of Christ's coming, and the ethical imperative to use the world for man's good in accordance with God's will, might have replied that too nice an asceticism is an offense against God's beneficence. There was ground for such a reply in the theological affirmation of the goodness of the created order, and one may wonder, accordingly, whether Sewall's feelings of affection were necessarily guilt-ridden.

There remains the matter of the "hymn's" sensuous imagery. This imagery, like Sewall's affection for Plum Island, is also in accord with the affirmation of creation's goodness, and with the canons of Puritan discourse and the epistemology underlying them. Believing that the mind is the avenue to the heart and the senses the gateway to the mind, Puritan preachers, in order more directly and powerfully to convince their hearers of divine truths, abandoned the ornaments of classical rhetoric in favor of the plain language of scripture and the imagery of familiar sensible things. The result, as articulated by a skilled practitioner, was a language of rich if humble metaphor. In this respect, the Puritan "plain style" was itself an expression of respect for the created order.[5] Whether a Puritan might revel in sensuous verbal images without conscious reference to divine things is doubtful—to see such connections was part of being a Puritan—but he had few inhibitions about employing them.

To say all these things is not to minimize the poignancy for conscientious Puritans of living in the world "with weaned affections," but rather to accent the value they placed on the worldly, and to suggest that the weight of the alternatives was rather nearly balanced.[6] Puritans believed that God gave them the good things of this world to serve their own well-being and to support their pilgrimage toward heaven. It was for them axiomatic that men need to know of much more than God's bountiful existence in order, in the words of the Westminster Larger Catechism, "to glorify God and fully to enjoy him forever." But God, they believed, by his word and Spirit has revealed "sufficiently and effectually" everything needful for salvation.[7] They knew that glorification of God is properly the chief end of all human activity and that love for Christ is the supreme affection. Known also were the means and avenues of preaching and discipline by which God brings his elect to the felicity prepared for them. Though they regarded the present world as transitory and "perishing," Puritans conceded that God alone knows the exact moment of its dissolution. In the meantime, true Christians are called to live responsibly in it, participating fully in social, political, and economic life. At the same time, all their worldly activity is to be conducted according to God's will for human action, as far as it should be revealed to them.

Individual Puritans might feel this tension between immanence and transcendence with great intensity. Puritan theologians, however, did not perceive the elements of the tension as strict opposites but rather as mutually implying each other. Everything in creation, one of them declared, comes from God and is governed by and serves the ends that God sets for it, and these ends ultimately coincide in God himself. All creation is thus at once a flowing out from and a flowing back to God.[8] Cognizant of God's revelation touching salvation and of the conformity of creation with the divine intent, and mindful of the ends for which God made the things of this world, the Puritan saint might embrace the creation with a good conscience. In Newbury, he might affectionately contemplate the perch and pickerel in Crane Pond, the barley harvest, and the rows of Indian corn, secure in the knowledge that they are things of God, given for his good, and properly to be enjoyed.

NATURE, GRACE, AND THE DOCTRINE OF THE TWO COVENANTS

The tension between Puritans' sense of divine order and their sense of divine immediacy corresponds in formal Puritan divinity to a tension between created nature and divine grace in the understanding of personal conversion, or, as they termed it, "effectual calling." In the Augustinian tradition, Puritans affirmed with equal seriousness that creation is the work of the good God and also that creation befouled by sin can be restored only by God's new creative act. In accordance with the latter affirmation they maintained the absoluteness of salvation by faith alone, the gratuity of regenerating grace, and the sovereignty of God's will in all phases of redemption. The former affirmation required them to conceive of regeneration in such a way that the ontological and moral orders established at creation were not violated by God's omnipotence. Thus, in Puritan divinity regeneration is approached through a dialectic of nature and grace that preserves the integrity of the one and the efficiency of the other. The emphasis on human activity in conversion, sometimes noted in Puritan sermons, is therefore not necessarily a departure from Protestant principles but may be viewed as an effort to uphold the "natural" element of this dialectic.[9] Puritans consistently affirmed that the corruption of human nature entailed by Adam's "fall" is pervasive and tenacious. At the same time they regarded regeneration as the renovation and reordering of human nature, as of a good thing gone foul; and they held that human faculties, thus reordered, participate legitimately in effectual calling.

In the late sixteenth and early seventeenth centuries, Reformed divines, especially in England, came increasingly to formulate the relationship of nature and grace in God's treatment of mankind in terms of a sequence of covenants. According to this "covenant theology," God originally entered into a "covenant of works" with Adam, promising mankind everlasting life in return for obedience to the divine law. After the fall, God entered a "covenant of grace" with Adam, which became fully effective when Christ's active obedience and atoning death fulfilled the requirements of the law. In the covenant of grace, salvation is offered mankind in return for sincere faith in God's promise to justify the believer in virtue of Christ's work, and God himself undertakes to enable the elect to believe. Adam's fall, Puritans held, destroyed mankind's ability to apprehend the ultimately true and to will the truly good, thereby rendering human beings incapable of achieving blessedness by their own efforts under the covenant of works. The fall, however, did not fundamentally alter human nature as such. Though injured, reason and will remain the faculties that distinguish mankind from other earthly creatures and fit them to enjoy union with God. The process of redemption necessarily takes these distinctively human capacities into account. Moreover, in promising Adam blessedness on condition of perfect obedience to the moral law, God was held to have bound himself to a moral order that defined mankind's relationship to him thereafter. Adam's failure to obey did not alter the significance of the law as the standard of human conduct, nor did it alter the terms of blessedness, which remains contingent upon obedience to the law. God's subsequent dealings with mankind concerning salvation, Puritans held, are governed by the conditions of his initial transaction with Adam and so are necessarily covenantal.

Puritan covenant theology may be viewed as an effort to formulate the mechanism of redemption in terms set by the dialectic of nature and grace. This theology presupposed God's sovereign initiative throughout and insisted that fallen man is entirely incapable, by himself, of satisfying the conditions of both covenants. At the same time, covenant theology upheld mankind's place in the created order by making the covenant of works paradigmatic in both form and content of God's redemptive activity. In the covenant of grace, blessedness is contingent upon willing obedience to God's command and upon man's act of faith. God, however, undertakes through Christ to supply the first condition and through infusion of supernatural grace into human faculties to enable individuals to fulfill the second. There is thus a "sweet concurrence" between divine grace and natural human activity in regeneration, such that the distinctiveness and proper function of each is preserved and the conditions of salvation established at the creation of the world are satisfied.

Within this theological framework, Sewall expressed his affection for Merrimack and Crane Pond. Within this framework, also, the theological arguments of the New England Antinomian Controversy were conducted.

John Winthrop, governor of the Bay Colony during the controversy, noted in his journal that the specific issues in dispute were whether the Holy Spirit dwells in believers bodily and whether sanctification may be evidence of justification.[10] These issues were part of a larger group of questions concerning the manner in which God actually effects regeneration, the nature of regeneration itself, and the relationship in it between divine omnipotence and human liberty and agency. In formal Puritan divinity the covenant *locus* is the medium by which the doctrines of God and man are related in the "application of redemption" to particular individuals, and it forms the context for considering the specific "means" by which individual regeneration is accomplished and revealed. Most directly, the New England controversy concerned the operation of these means, but it unavoidably concerned also the doctrine of the covenant and the fundamental question of the relationship of nature and grace in regeneration. Taken largely, the issue in Massachusetts Bay may be posed as follows. Does God, in regenerating individuals, employ instruments that belong to the created order— church ordinances, for example, and the words of scripture—and does he respect and work through the inherent capacities of human beings, empowering human faculties to perform holy actions? If so, there are objective criteria, given in scripture, by which the regenerate may recognize, by the power of their own enlightened consciences, the presence of sanctifying grace in themselves, and so may conclude that they are truly justified. Or does God act directly upon human beings, overruling their natural capacities and transforming them apart from or in spite of any activity of their own? If this is the case, then God himself, through his Spirit, must somehow "act" the regenerate in holy works, and saints-presumptive must wait until the Holy Spirit grants them "direct sight" of their justification.

Anne Hutchinson and her followers charged the elders of the Bay Colony, excepting John Cotton and John Wheelwright, with "preaching a covenant of works" instead of a "covenant of grace," and with being therefore unfit ministers of the gospel.[11] The elders, Hutchinson maintained, admitted human works and legal injunctions in the discerning of regeneration. She believed, on the contrary, that the gospel of free grace properly has nothing to do with works of the law, which are made superfluous by the Holy Spirit's direct activity. On the basis of this distinction between works and grace she and her followers drew another, with potentially serious social consequences, between people who are "in" and people who are "outside" Christ. Cotton also—though he did not draw overtly separatist conclusions—insisted on the priority of the Spirit's operation in all phases of regeneration, including the evidencing of it, to the point of seeming to exclude created nature from even an instrumental or mediatory role. Covenant theology specified the mode of God's redemptive activity as a mutually binding pact between two parties, in which God agreed to act in stated ways consonant with created human nature. To Cotton and the Hutchinsonians, this manner of speaking implied a commerce between God and creatures that they regarded as prejudicial to God's sovereign freedom and holy purity. God's treatment of mankind in the covenant of grace is altogether different, they insisted, from that in the covenant of works. From the elders' viewpoint, Cotton and the Hutchinsonians seemed to question the truth of God's self-accommodation in the covenant, to cast doubt upon the continuity of the ontological and moral orders established at creation, and to reduce the dialectic of nature and grace to its transcendent element.

EASING THE WAY TO HEAVEN

In 1644, when religious radicalism was beginning to abound in England and Parliament was taking steps to reorder the English church, the Hutchinsonian affair was recalled, to the embarrassment of the emerging New England ecclesiastical "way." In response, Winthrop caused a pamphlet to be issued in London, containing an account of the proceedings against the Boston "antinomians." Winthrop's presentation was less than lucid, and Thomas Weld, the colony's London agent, reissued the piece, adding a preface in which he sought to give a coherent account of the incident and to place it in perspective.[12] Weld maintained that the popularity of the antinomian gospel, in New England as in old, resulted from its intrinsic attractiveness, rather than from any irregularity of doctrine or church government in Massachusetts. "The opinions themselves," he wrote, "open such a faire and easie way to Heaven, that men may pass without difficulty."

> For, if a man need not be troubled by the law, before faith, but may step to Christ so easily; and then, if his faith be no going out of himself to take Christ, but only a discerning that Christ is his own already, and is only an act of the Spirit upon him, no act of his own done by him; and if he, for his part, must see nothing in himself, have nothing, do nothing, only he is to stand still and wait

for Christ to do all for him. And then if after faith, the law no
rule to walk by, no sorrow or repentance for sin; he must not be
pressed to duties, and need never pray, unless moved by the Spirit:
and if he falls into sin, he is never the more disliked of God, nor
his condition never the worse. And for his assurance, it being given
him by the Spirit, he must never let it go, but abide in the height
of comfort, though he falls into the grossest sins that he can. Then
is their way to life made easy, if so, no marvel so many like of it.[13]

Antinomianism, in short, took all the struggle out of religion by
absolving individuals from personal responsibility for the observance that God demands of Christians. By implication, it appealed to
people who were impatient of discipline, religiously lukewarm, or
in search of easy assurance of heaven. Weld had a point to make and
was somewhat sweeping in his judgment. In fact, the people to
whom he referred struggled rather earnestly with the tensions between assurance and doubt, and between obedience and failure of
obedience, that were inherent in the Christian life as defined in
Reformed Protestantism. Weld's characterization of their manner
of resolving these tensions was not, however, inaccurate.[14]

Thomas Shepard, minister at Newtown (later Cambridge) and
one of the leading participants in the New England controversy,
saw the Hutchinsonians in a similar light. He said they discouraged
people from earnestly using "all known means" of grace, by claiming that "Christ must do all" and by asserting that excessive concern with human "works" disparages divine grace. Shepard felt that
to make such assumptions was to turn a Christian's proper graces
into defects and subtly to appeal to the moral indolence natural
to the unregenerate. Holding that Christ alone is active in regeneration, and men entirely passive, the Hutchinsonians appeared to
say that God does not really change human *beings* at all, but only
some of their *actions*, and that, by implication, Christ "is a Saviour
... to save men and their sins." Such people, Shepard suggested,
were not improbably "evangelical hypocrites," who, though appearing outwardly to be under grace, were in fact under the law and
were, therefore—turning the Hutchinsonians' charge upon themselves—"under a covenant of works, ... and under the curse."[15]

Modern scholarship, in contrast, when it has considered the
theological dimension of the Antinomian Controversy, has tended

to support Cotton and the Hutchinsonians in their judgment of the other elders and to suggest that the latter, rather than the antinomians, were appreciably easing the way to heaven. Thus Perry Miller, in a classic instance, represented Puritan covenant theology as a more or less deliberate attempt to make a place in regeneration for the capacities of rational creatures and thereby to humanize what he regarded as the harsh and debilitating Calvinist doctrines of election and sovereignty. Miller strongly implied that the New England divines made sincere approximation of a moral life the condition of entry into the covenant of grace and strained in consequence to draw a doubtful distinction between Reformed heresy and their own doctrine of a conditional covenant. He also argued that covenant theology, by conceiving of regeneration as entry into a contract, implied an interval between complete deadness in sin and true conversion, during which men could deliberately prepare themselves to take up the covenant. The resulting "doctrine of preparation" asserted the ability of the unregenerate to act in ways significantly related to, if not actually productive of, conversion, which thereby became a gradual, largely rational process, rather than a sudden, unpredictable inbreaking of divine power. This doctrine was a further example of the "expansion" of the "limits of natural ability" at the expense of divine sovereignty that in Miller's estimation was taking place in New England; it was denounced as such, he argued, by Anne Hutchinson and John Cotton.[16]

This interpretation, while plausible in light of what has commonly been assumed about New England Puritan theology, is not without its problems. Miller's characteristic antitheses—between an arbitrary, overpowering divine sovereignty and a human ability to condition regeneration; between the "absolute moral impotence of the strict [Reformed] doctrine" and "enlargement of [man's] innate capacities"; and between conversion as "a sudden prostration, . . . a holy rape of the surprised will" and a "gradual process," comprising "negotiation" and "preparation," in which the will participates—have been quite fruitful for the interpretation of New England Puritan culture, and they have continued to inform interpretations of the Antinomian Controversy.[17] It is the contention of this essay, however, that they are overdrawn, and in important respects involve a misreading of seventeenth-century Reformed divinity and of the fundamental theological issues in the New England affair. Weld, one may suggest, was not wholly off the mark when he charged that antinomians offered an easier way to religious assurance than that commonly advocated by Puritan ministers in accordance with their understanding of covenantal doctrine.

Divine sovereignty and human inability to achieve salvation were indeed cardinal points of Reformed teaching. It bears noting, however, that acceptance of these tenets did not mean that human activity, as such, was excluded from regeneration. Nor did the doctrine of a conditional covenant of grace, as articulated in New England, fundamentally qualify the doctrines of divine sovereignty and election held by sixteenth- and seventeenth-century Reformed theologians. Close examination of the principal sources for the Antinomian Controversy, against the backdrop of contemporary Reformed divinity, suggests that the crucial theological issue in New England was the relationship between created human nature and the increated power of the Trinity in the regenerative transformation itself.[18] In part this was a question of the concrete means by which the sovereign God effects the regeneration of individuals, a theologically more fundamental and serious matter than the ability of an individual deliberately to "prepare" for conversion. Reformed divines, in the early seventeenth century, distinguished quite readily between the unconditioned operation of God's will in decreeing—the precise referent of the attribute of "sovereignty" —and the exercise of God's power in effecting his decree, which may very well be conditioned. They believed, also, that God ordinarily effects his gracious decrees through means belonging to and operating within the created order, including the human mind and will. Accordingly, these divines did not find conditional and covenantal formulations absolutely incompatible with the doctrine of the divine nature.[19]

We shall return to these issues after reviewing the course of the New England controversy and examining the arguments of both sides, together with elements of the theological and historical context of the dispute. At this point a word is in order about the theological frame of reference within which the examination is conducted, and about the warrant for conducting it in the first place.

PURITANS AND REFORMED ORTHODOXY

As theologians, English and New English Puritans belonged to the period of so-called old Protestant orthodoxy, extending roughly from 1570 to 1700, during which Lutherans and Reformed in their several ways labored to systematize the insights of the Reformation and to articulate them in the intellectual idiom of late scholasticism. In Reformed Protestantism this enterprise was international in scope, embracing a variety of regional churches distinguished by nuances of polity, liturgy, and theology. Despite internal variety, however, Reformed orthodoxy, except in extreme cases, comprised widespread consensus regarding the substance of doctrine that defined the Reformed position, even while allowing considerable latitude for individuality in ordering the theological system and in the treatment of particular elements of it.[20]

English Puritans shared both the doctrinal consensus and the theological individualism of Reformed orthodoxy. As suited their particular controversial and pastoral needs, they drew on all of the Protestant Reformers, on a host of later Continental theologians and exegetes, including Lutherans, on contemporary and medieval Roman Catholic scholastics, and on the church fathers. In logic, rhetoric, and certain aspects of theological method, especially in stressing the practical character of theology with the consequent focusing of the system on experience and observance, they tended to be Ramist. In psychology, metaphysics, and other aspects of theological method, especially regarding the relationship between faith and reason and the place of natural theology, they tended to be Aristotelian scholastics. If they did not often compose large, systematic treatises, they studied those of others, disputed in their schools after the scholastic fashion, and not infrequently preached their way through the entire "body of divinity."[21]

The characteristic literary expression of Reformed orthodoxy was the formal *loci communes,* treating the "common places" or "heads" of Reformed divinity, systematically arranged. Of examples by Englishmen, William Perkins's *Golden Chain* (1591) and William Ames's internationally popular handbook, *Medulla Theologica* (1623), are best known. Both were employed extensively in New

England, as was Johannes Wollebius's more abbreviated *Compendium Theologiae Christianae* (1626). New England's own contribution to the genre was John Norton's short but comprehensive *Orthodox Evangelist* (1654). On the whole, Puritans produced fewer and less substantial systematic works than their Continental brethren, their theological reflection tending, instead, to take the form of sermon-cycles on issues of current pastoral or controversial importance. These, subsequently published, became part of the standard theological literature. John Preston's *Breastplate of Faith and Love* (1630) and *Life Eternal* (1631), Richard Sibbes's *Soul's Conflict* (1635), and Thomas Shepard's *Sound Believer* (1645) are cases in point. These titles and others from the pens of what New Englanders called "our standard Reformed divines" form a major part of the backdrop for the following discussion.[22]

Examined in relation to this material, the chief New England elders appear less radical than sometimes supposed, and John Cotton, their colleague on the opposite side of the antinomian dispute, rather more radical than sometimes represented.

THEOLOGY AND ACTION

In an era of self-consciously post-Hegelian historiography, it is perhaps appropriate to comment on the propriety of undertaking a theological analysis of an event widely regarded as involving other, more fundamental human realities. This is not the occasion for extended exploration of the connection between "concrete" and "ideological" aspects of social reality. Yet it is fitting here to suggest that the relationship of these aspects is at least reciprocal, in that theological propositions, under certain conditions, may motivate human action and therein shape concrete institutional reality.

Religious representations, whatever their original relationship to economic function and class interest, belong to the socially objectivated universe of the group whose representations they are. To this extent they enjoy a degree of existence independent of individual believers, whom they confront as factual realities that must be taken seriously. As such, they are clearly capable, by shaping individual and collective behavior, of acting upon concrete social reality. In the process, religious representations may themselves be altered, or even superseded—as Wesley observed about the people of humble station who, becoming Methodists, became frugal, and then growing well-to-do as the result of their thrift, became less methodistical. That particular beliefs appeal in particular cases is not unrelated to factors of individual personality, family and educational influence, and religious tradition, which in turn are related to economic function, social class, and cultural milieu. Yet it is not historically incorrect to observe that abstract categories may elicit passionate action from people who believe them to express truth about the universe, however much such categories may seem to an observer to reflect material contexts, and however unconscious the actors may be of the less-than-ideal quality of their "real" motives.

It would be perverse, as well as false, to attempt to reduce the New England Antinomian Controversy to the theological language in which it was conducted. It would be inaccurate, however, in the case of a religiously intense and theologically alert community, to discount entirely the motivational significance of religious beliefs and theological concepts. The prominence of the doctrine of the Holy Spirit in English Puritanism is well attested, as is the challenge to Puritan societies, both civil and ecclesiastical, by people— not infrequently of Puritan extraction—who claimed greater than usual intimacy with the Holy Spirit. For particular strata of seventeenth-century English society, such protest was clearly social, economic, and political, as well as religious. At the same time, it must be acknowledged that in the religious climate of the period, beliefs about intimacy with the Spirit provided a singular charter for protest, and that religious radicalism seems in important respects to have been the mother of more socially concrete radicalisms.[23]

English Puritanism, whatever substructural tensions it harbored, sought at the ideological level to hold together a deliberately cultivated ardor for personal experience of divine grace and an intensely felt divine imperative to establish disciplined, godly collectivities in church and state. When, as in Winthrop's *Arbella* sermon, Puritans envisaged their societal objectives, both of these moments were implicit.[24] Puritan social ethics presupposed the reality both of personal regeneration and of the divine law and regarded both as dialectically necessary to the existence of the godly commonwealth. Regeneration hallowed the law, transforming it from the crutch of hypocrites and the terror of convicted sinners into the rule, guide, and mirror of saints. The law, as the expression of God's ordering intent for individual and collective action, channelled and controlled ardor for the Spirit, harnessing the energy of religious experience to the task of transforming the social order. The profound experientialism that distinguished English Puritanism within Reformed Protestantism included not only the affirmation that individuals may be taught by the Spirit in the word of scripture, but also the affirmation that they may be radically transformed in their own persons, becoming by the Spirit's work new beings. These two ideas, taken together, had great potential for disrupting established orders. At the same time, Puritans characteristically defined the "new being" of the regenerate as the capacity willingly to obey, and therein to seek the incarnation of, God's will in all aspects of earthly life. In doing so, they subjected regeneration to a pattern of order that, though mediated to individuals by the Spirit, was conceived as lying objectively beyond them. The worldly incarnation of this divine order depended upon the radical newness of spirit that God effects in the elect. The manifestation of this newness, however, was held to be ordered in particular ways, according to the divine intent disclosed in scripture and in the orderliness of nature itself.[25] The Spirit might "blow" when and where he listed; the person whom he encountered had less large a liberty.

The individual Puritan's life, like his formal divinity, moved back and forth between personal experience of gracious transformation and obedience to the order dictated by God's sovereign will. Both moments met in that devotion to conscience captivated by the word of God, with its attendant resolution and tenacity, characteristic of Reformed Protestants and especially of Puritans. Puritans disagreed over the precise shape of the new order—a circumstance that contributed to the fragmentation and eventual defeat of the movement. Yet they seem to have been generally agreed on the parameters of newness and order within which conscience must attain unto conviction. In Puritan precisionism the Reformed sense of order and orderliness—of God in bestowing grace, of the church in administering it, and of the Christian's participation, in virtue of it, in civil and ecclesiastical life—mingled with Puritanism's own peculiar sense of the Spirit's creative work in individual souls. This combination made innovation, separation, and revolution difficult and conscience-wracking matters for Puritans, even as the Spirit and events pressed them toward all three.[26]

This same combination of newness and order in his own life placed the conscientious Puritan in a situation of perennial tension, preventing him from single-mindedly pursuing either heaven or the world to the exclusion of the other, and demanding that he consciously maintain a balance between both. As determined a radical as Cromwell could not spiritualize the new order, as did George Fox and Roger Williams in their respective ways, nor could he preside over the inauguration of the Danielic Fifth Monarchy on English soil. Yet he must somehow seek an order at once new and English and godly, in the sense of conforming to God's will, and one to which he felt himself conscience-bound; and he must seek such an order, moreover, even if this pursuit meant committing acts of violent radicalism on one hand while restraining radicals of a different color on the other. At the ideological level (that is, at the level of conscious self-understanding), this felt tension between divine newness and divine order under the ontological and deontological conditions of creation—creation being viewed as now redeemed but not yet fully restored—may be regarded as in significant measure diagnostic of English Puritanism, properly so-called. Had Cromwell resolutely abandoned one side of the dialectic of order and newness for the sake of the other, he would have ceased to be a Puritan.

It seems indisputable that Puritan social ethics were conditioned by the concrete circumstances in which Puritans lived. Yet the concrete circumstances of Puritans, as well as their ethics, were also conditioned by their belief-system, which they regarded as a practical directory for "living to God" in the broadest possible sense. To the extent that they earnestly endeavored so to live, both individually and institutionally, they conferred legitimacy upon their belief-system; and their belief-system, by locating their mundane activity within a transcendent order, reciprocally legitimated that activity. Life was complicated for Puritans by the inclusion in their transcendent referents of both spontaneity and order: their "living to God" must therefore be a due mixture of each. This problem is reflected in formal Puritan divinity, and in covenant theology in particular. At the same time, as part of the socially objectivated religious world of Puritans, covenant theology provided a conceptual framework within which to integrate responsibility for order with yearning for spontaneity and newness. It also provided a standard with which to oppose excess of either. In this sense, it may be argued, Puritanism's concrete efforts to transform men and institutions radically, yet without thereby dissolving the social order, were both legitimated and moderated by the theological conviction that God, in attaining his ends, employs means that belong to the created order and employs them according to their natural capacities.

Both of these convictions lay close to the center of the New England Antinomian Controversy, which was also, in this respect, a controversy about the practical Puritan endeavor to establish an earthly community leavened by the presence of truly godly individuals. New England was unique in the Puritan enterprise, inasmuch as a godly commonwealth existed there for some thirteen years before the Puritan ascendency in old England and continued to exist, with considerable unanimity, long after the English Commonwealth had succumbed to exhaustion, disillusionment, and Toleration. The founders of the Bay Colony were deeply conscious of their plantation's exemplary role in what they hoped would be the Puritan future; and hardly anywhere else were English Puritans so successful in embodying their convictions in godly institutions of church and state. The antinomian crisis of 1636–38 is of interest in that it represented the first serious confrontation of an established Puritan society with its own radical offspring and therein heralded things to come. It is also interesting as an historic incident illumining the significance of the covenant-motif in Puritan life and thought, as Puritans strove to "work out" their salvation and to incarnate God's will, with what they regarded as due respect for divine grace and for created nature.

CHAPTER 2

The New England Controversy

The founding of Massachusetts enabled Puritans to put into actual practice the further reformation of the Church of England for which they had been agitating since the reign of Elizabeth. With the colony's charter safe in Boston, they could, without interference of king or prelate, enjoy all the ordinances that Christ intended for his church, and enjoy them "purely." Unencumbered by ceremonies of "mere human invention," they could make vigorous and learned preaching of God's word—which they regarded as the very means and instrument of regeneration—the proper center of their ecclesiastical life. Having gained the power of church discipline, they could protect the purity of their worship from defilement by the morally scandalous and, as much as was practically possible, might even restrict church membership to the truly regenerate. When they sailed from England, the founders of the Bay Colony knew that they were undertaking an exemplary errand. They were to build a "city set upon a hill," a beacon-light which would guide the eventual reformation of old England. They were to establish, even, a commonwealth of such singular holiness that Christ himself might fittingly descend there at his second coming. When they embarked, however, the practical details of this undertaking had not been worked out: having been continually hindered and harried, they had had little opportunity to make concrete plans. The initial years in the wilderness, therefore, were years of flux and experiment.[1]

Flux, however, was peculiarly troublesome for Puritans, for the absence of a standing order permitted the Holy Spirit to blow unimpeded, and in as many different directions as there were earthly spirits to receive him. Puritanism as a movement was inherently susceptible to sectarian proliferation. Its religious energy was focused upon personal experience of the Spirit's regenerating work, and it taught that individuals, unencumbered by ecclesiastical tradition, could discover God's will directly in scripture by the Spirit's illumination. In the theology of the principal Puritan divines, the fissive potential of this mixture was contained by the dialectic of nature and grace and by a highly developed sense of divine order. Among the less sophisticated, intimacy with the Spirit could be powerfully alluring, and, in the excitement and disarray of the Civil War, Puritanism contributed its share of enthusiasts to the congeries of sects then rapidly emerging.[2]

The eschatological urgency with which Puritans pursued their holy commonwealths and pure ordinances also contributed, under the right conditions, to sectarian enthusiasm. Toward the end of the fifteenth century all Europe seemed to fall under the spell of the Apocalypse. The peasant revolts, the upheavals of the Reformation, the wars of religion, even the outbreak of syphilis, acquired apocalyptic overtones, and the conviction was widespread that the world was drawing to its close. To Protestants, designation of the pope as Antichrist was not entirely metaphorical. During Elizabeth's reign, England emerged as the most Protestant country in Europe, locked in contest with Catholic Spain, whose avowed aim was to recapture the heretic island for the pope. In this contest, Protestant Englishmen perceived special significance. For them, the Reformation had begun with Wyclif, and now England had become the refuge of the true faith, beset by satanic forces. England's destiny, apparently, like Israel's of old, was to be an elect nation and "to lead the world back to God's true religion and end the tyranny of Antichrist."[3] After that, Christ would come. First, however, England must undergo further reformation, Elizabeth having stopped part way. After the Hampton Court Conference (1604), this English destiny became increasingly the burden of Puritans, who also became increasingly isolated and constrained, while time continued to run. There is an enormous Puritan literature devoted to interpretation of the Book of Revelation, and Puritan preaching is filled with allusions to the developing eschatological situation. To contemporaries it did not seem impossible for the advance of

Catholic armies on the Continent after 1618 to be the opening stage of Armageddon, in which case the Puritan program for completing the English reformation was not a matter to be tarried in.[4]

Beginning in 1629, the westward swarming of Puritans tapped a head of religious energy, pent up from two generations of earnest searching of scripture, listening to the Spirit, and reading the signs of the times, and let this energy spill out into the "free aire" of New England. It is in a measure surprising that in the early years of settlement Massachusetts Puritans were as restrained as they were. They seem, however, to have seriously regarded their mission as a trust both public and divine, and as a collective responsibility. Their sense of the positive relationship between divine and public order was pronounced, and they had able leadership. In John Winthrop they received a conscientious magistrate distinguished for moderation and common sense, who sought earnestly to maintain a due balance between worldly necessity and otherworldly purity in the conduct of public affairs. In John Cotton they acquired a zealous Puritan minister who, whatever his initial tendencies, was able eventually to institutionalize the drive for purity without unduly compromising it, while stopping short of separatism.[5] Yet it was apparent from the outset that not all those who came to the Bay Colony had been listening to the same spirit or brought the same notions about the nature of the New England enterprise. For good reason Winthrop, aboard the *Arbella,* insisted that their plantation, while it was to be a model of holiness, must also be "a model of Christian charity."[6] From the moment of settlement there was disagreement over church order, and shortly thereafter differences emerged about the nature of regeneration itself. In the first instance, Roger Williams vociferously pursued the course of separation. In the second, Anne Hutchinson raised the spectre of antinomianism.

Anne Hutchinson was born in 1591, the daughter of Francis Marbury, minister of the Church of England in Alford, Lincolnshire. Sometime thereafter, Marbury moved to London. Anne returned to Alford in 1612 to marry William Hutchinson, a local merchant. In the same year, the corporation of the port-and-market town of Boston, some twenty miles away, obtained the services of John Cotton, tutor at Emmanuel College, Cambridge, and already a Puritan of note, as vicar of St. Botolph's Church. Anne Hutchinson became one of his more earnest admirers. She was a woman of strong temperament, and was religiously inclined. Troubled about the validity of the Church of England, she found relief (she later claimed) when God, by an immediate voice of the Spirit to her soul, gave her the ability to distinguish true ministers of the gospel from those who, having the Spirit of Antichrist, did not teach the new covenant. Cotton and John Wheelwright, vicar at Spilsby, Lincolnshire, and married to William Hutchinson's sister, qualified.[7] When the authorities silenced Wheelwright in 1631, and Cotton fled to New England in 1633, Hutchinson was deeply troubled, there being none left whom she felt she might hear. Then the Spirit bade her follow Cotton. In May 1634 the Hutchinsons sailed from England. It was later reported that in London, just before departure, Anne Hutchinson confided to a fellow passenger that nothing important had ever happened to her without being revealed to her beforehand. On shipboard, she shocked a clergyman by predicting the time of arrival at new Boston, and on sighting the town observed that "if she had not a sure word that England should be destroyed her heart would shake."[8]

In November 1634 William Hutchinson was chosen deputy to the General Court from Boston. Anne moved among the women of the town in the capacity of midwife, finding therein opportunity to discuss their spiritual estates. She began holding weekly meetings for women in her home, at which she expounded sermons by Cotton, now the esteemed teacher of the Boston church. She began holding meetings for men, also, and shortly progressed from interpreting Cotton's remarks to criticizing those of other ministers. Anne Hutchinson's orthodoxy had been questioned briefly when she applied for church membership, but the elders had been satisfied and she was admitted. By the spring of 1636, however, Boston church members were voicing strange opinions, which were attributed to her, and the neighboring elders called the matter to Cotton's attention. He made inquiries, but Hutchinson was apparently circumspect, and he reported nothing amiss.[9]

When Cotton came to Massachusetts, in September 1633, he was forty-eight years old, a leader among his generation of Puritans, reputed for godliness, learning, and candor. Within a month he was made teacher at Boston, partly by local demand and partly at the wish of his Lincolnshire congregation that he minister to those of their number who had preceded him or might now follow. The result was a minor religious awakening, in which sixty-three persons joined the church in six months, something of a record. Cotton sought to repeat the performance three years later, with indifferent success, though Governor Winthrop found himself markedly stirred by Cotton's preaching of the "doctrine of free justification." By 1635, however, the religious excitement attending the initial settlement had cooled, and enthusiasm for the means of grace was giving way to anxiety about spiritual estates and hostility toward clergymen who seemed unable to provide "settled assurance."[10] In these circumstances controversy arose over the spiritual adequacy and doctrinal correctness of the preaching of certain ministers. Cotton, whose theology and style made him the favorite of a substantial part of the Boston church, found himself, along with Anne Hutchinson, a central figure in this dispute.

In May 1636 John Wheelwright arrived and was warmly received by the Boston congregation. His views were similar to Hutchinson's, though not in all points identical. By the fall of the year, their opinions had become sufficiently evident, and rumor of them sufficiently widespread, that the ministers of the Bay became alarmed. At the time of the General Court in October, they met at Boston to confer privately with Wheelwright and Hutchinson, and also with Cotton, whose sermons had begun to attract attention. The points at issue were whether the person of the Holy Spirit dwells in believers and whether sanctification can be evidence of justification. All agreed that sanctification helps to evidence justification. Cotton and Wheelwright insisted that the Spirit does dwell in, though he is not personally united with, believers. Shortly afterward, however, Wheelwright affirmed that the believer is "more than a creature" and that the Spirit and believers are personally united—views in which the governor, young Henry Vane, and apparently also Cotton were presently found to concur.[11] At another conference, in December, Cotton indirectly and Hutchinson explicitly "told the ministers . . . that many of them were preaching 'works,' not 'grace.'" About the same time, part of the Boston congregation met with members from the church at Newtown, each group seeking to discover the other's true views and to appraise the "soundness" of their respective "spirits."[12]

In the meantime, Hutchinson's followers in the Boston church sought to secure the appointment of Wheelwright as teacher along-side Cotton and John Wilson, the pastor. Wilson had come to Massachusetts with Winthrop in the great expedition of 1630 and had gathered the first church in the colony. He was noted for his hospitality, generosity to the needy, and compassion, and for his skill in exercising pastoral discipline (for the latter he was said to have enjoyed Ames's public approbation). The Hutchinsonians disliked him, because he made faith a condition of justification and because he insisted that works of sanctification might evidence justification. They said, in consequence, that he was a "legalist" and preached a "covenant of works," and they questioned the sound-ness of his calling. The appointment of Wheelwright was a calcu-lated affront to Wilson, and Cotton apparently supported it. Winthrop, however, who was Wilson's personal friend and who exercised considerable influence in the congregation, contrived to block it, protesting that they knew little of Wheelwright's spirit and that what they did know was unsound.[13] The Hutchinsonians were stymied, Wheelwright went to the church at Mt. Wollaston (later Braintree), and the affair became a public quarrel.

In December, at a special Court of Deputies, Governor Henry Vane asked permission to resign, being fearful, he said, of divine judgment upon the colony for the recent dissensions in religion and resentful of allegations that he was the cause of them. He also pleaded urgent affairs in England. A young, and an extreme, Puri-tan, Vane had come to Massachusetts in October 1635 and had joined the Boston church. The following March, aged twenty-three, he was made freeman and, partly because his father was an influ-ential officer in Charles I's government, governor as well. Since his arrival he had lodged with Cotton and had become identified with the antinomian party. The Court indicated its willingness to allow Vane's departure for the sake of business but not for his other anxieties, and then summoned the ministers to give advice about the sources and possible cure of the colony's religious troubles. Whereupon Vane took angry offense at an earlier, private meeting that the elders had held without his authorization. Hugh Peter, the minister at Salem, admonished him for his pique and reminded him that two years previously, before Vane came over, the churches were at peace. Vane replied testily that the "children of the bondwoman" would persecute those of the "freewoman," alluding respectively to persons under a covenant of works and those under a covenant of grace.[14]

At the same Court, Wilson delivered a lamentation on the state of the New England churches, in which he attributed the current dissension to opinions lately advanced in Boston. This allegation was ill-received by Cotton and by many of the Boston congregation, who moved formally to censure their pastor. Since the vote could not be made unanimous, however, Cotton staid them and gave Wilson a "grave exhortation" instead.[15]

With Wilson's speech to the Court the full scope of the suspected opinions began to be apparent. Wilson emphasized a point that Cotton had addressed in a sermon the same day, namely the value of sanctification as evidence of justification. The question thereupon arose whether any sort of sanctification could be evidence to a person "without a concurrent sight of his justification." Cotton and Vane denied it. In the uproar attending the admonishing of Wilson, Winthrop reported, other opinions came to light:

> as that the Holy Ghost dwelt in a believer as he is in heaven; that a man is justified before he believes; and that faith is no cause of justification. And others spread more secretly,—as that the letter of the scripture holds forth nothing but a covenant of works; and that the covenant of grace was the spirit of the scripture, which was known only to believers; and that this covenant of works was given by Moses in the ten commandments; that there was a seed (viz. Abraham's carnal seed) went along in this, and there was a spirit and life in it, by virtue whereof a man might have spiritual and continual communion with Jesus Christ, and yet be damned. After, it was granted that faith was before justification, but it was only passive, an empty vessel, etc.; but in conclusion, the ground of it all was found to be assurance by immediate revelation.
>
> All the congregation of Boston, except four or five, closed with these opinions, or most of them.[16]

From the ministers' viewpoint, these were thoroughly alarming ideas. Individually they were at variance with Reformed theology as held in Massachusetts. Together they tended to deny the constancy of God's action in the covenant as declared in the scriptures and the instrumentality of created nature in the work of regeneration; and they implied that the individual Christian, in his pilgrimage of faith, is dependent entirely upon the personal operation of the Holy Spirit.

The parties were now sharply drawn. Hutchinson and her followers in Boston, together with Vane, Wheelwright, and Cotton, faced Wilson and Winthrop, with whom the rest of the elders apparently sided in a body, and the majority of the magistrates. The controversy was confined largely to Boston and the immediate vicinity, and the elders labored in their respective congregations to ensure that it did not spread. Inasmuch as it concerned important differences in doctrine and—more seriously—issued in public alienation, the affair became the concern of the General Court.

The December Court had proclaimed a general fast for January 19, 1637, in order prayerfully to consider and lament the estate of certain of the Reformed churches, including those in New England. On the fast-day, Wheelwright attended church in Boston, and Cotton invited him to preach. Wheelwright proceeded to divide professing Christians into two classes, those under the covenant of grace, who are truly Christ's, and those under a covenant of works, who belong to Antichrist. Against the latter, as against mortal enemies, the children of God must take arms and fight courageously with all the weapons of spiritual warfare. The only reason for true believers to fast, Wheelwright declared, is the absence of Christ from them, as a result of their backwardness in doing battle with enemies. Christ's own differ decisively from their adversaries in that they base their "faith of assurance" on direct revelation to the soul of Christ himself and of his righteousness freely given. The "enemies" rest their assurance upon some work of sanctification in themselves. The implication was clear. All the ministers but Cotton, most of the magistrates, and "most of the people of God in these churches," Winthrop noted, were known to hold the latter view of assurance.[17]

Wheelwright's language was figurative, but his tone was inflammatory, and he did not shrink from practical conclusions. The spiritual difference between the parties, he observed, was infinite and could not stand with external peace. On this point, the Hutchinsonians needed little instruction. In April Vane and Wheelwright, together with Cotton and the Boston congregation, boycotted the ordination of Peter Bulkeley and John Jones at Newtown, because the principals and the participants were "legal preachers." In May, when the colony gathered an expedition against the Pequot Indians, the children of God at Boston refused to join, because Wilson, the chaplain, and most of the militiamen were "under a covenant of works," and because the magistrates who called them out were "enemies." The same spirit appeared in town meetings and between individuals. Members of the Boston church disturbed the services of neighboring ministers with questions about the soundness of their callings and their doctrine. They dissociated themselves from members of other congregations and would admit none to their own unless the candidate would renounce his sanctification and "wait for an immediate revelation of the Spirit." Every public affair, Winthrop wrote, had become an occasion for contention, "and it began to be as common here to distinguish between men as being under a covenant of grace or a covenant of works, as in other countries between Protestants and papists."[18]

At the Court in March Wheelwright was summoned to answer for his sermon. The majority of the magistrates proving "sound," he was declared guilty of contempt and sedition for having deliberately used a fast-day, intended as a means to reconciliation, as an occasion for fomenting further discord.[19]

In May 1637 the Court of Election for choice of a new government was held at Newtown, across the Charles River, where feeling was presumably less intense than in Boston. Governor Vane desired to consider a petition in Wheelwright's defense before proceeding to election but was defeated in a contest that nearly came to blows. Winthrop was chosen governor and Thomas Dudley deputy, and the Boston faction was left out entirely. New deputies from Boston were initially refused seats, and the Court, fearing an influx of sectaries, voted to prohibit new arrivals from remaining in the Bay for more than three weeks without the magistrates' permission. Wheelwright's sentence, deferred from the previous Court, was deferred again, in hope that further reflection on his part might bring reconciliation.[20]

The ministers, meanwhile, had not been idle. As early as June 1636 they began quietly sounding Cotton on his views, finding certain of them "offensive"; and they noted his apparent good opinion of, and his familiarity with, those of his church who were spreading strange doctrines. After the censuring of Wilson, they "drew out sixteen points, and gave them to [Cotton], entreating him to deliver his judgment directly in them, which accordingly he did." Winthrop recorded that "some doubts he well cleared, but in some things he gave not satisfaction." These "points" became the basis of a lengthy written exchange between Cotton and his colleagues, covering the nature and order in regeneration of faith, justification, sanctification, and assurance. The elders also met privately with Hutchinson, hoping to ascertain the exact content of her teachings, about which she had thus far been guarded. In their pulpits they sought to refute the dissenters' views, insofar as they knew or suspected them.[21]

The official opposition was led by Thomas Shepard, the Newtown minister, and by Peter Bulkeley, minister and planter at Concord. Shepard had come to Massachusetts in August 1635, after five years of flight and hiding in England. At Newtown his party bought out Thomas Hooker's company, on the eve of their departure for Connecticut, and in February 1636 gathered a church. On this occasion, Cotton, "in the name of the rest, gave [them] the right hand of fellowship." Chronically ill and unprepossessing in appearance—Edward Johnson called him "poor, weak, pale"—Shepard was nonetheless an affecting preacher and an effective pastor. In June 1636 he began a series of sermons on assurance of salvation, in the context of the problem of distinguishing the truly regenerate in the church from "evangelical hypocrites." In them he addressed both the opinions of the Boston "errorists" and the personal experience whence they sprang. Cotton Mather suggested that the decision to locate Harvard College at Newtown reflected Shepard's success in resisting the Hutchinsonians.[22]

Twenty-two years Shepard's senior, Bulkeley had slipped his family and then himself over to New England in 1635, stopping for a while at Newtown and then going on to Concord, whose founding he superintended. There he conducted a successful agricultural enterprise, out of which he set up a succession of his servants in farms of their own. Though physically infirm, he conducted also a vigorous and fruitful ministry, drawing his people to him, when he could not visit them, by the force of a winning personality. His catechism he based on that of William Perkins. He was noted for the gravity of his demeanor and for the strictness of his Puritanism, and his colleagues esteemed him as a scholar and treated him as a patriarch. Shortly after his arrival in Massachusetts, Bulkeley began a sermon-cycle on the doctrine of the covenant, which he regarded as the crucial *locus* in divinity, in the context of which he addressed the complaints of the Hutchinsonians.[23]

The Court in May, which returned Winthrop to the governorship, decided that a synod of the colony's churches should consider the differences now troubling them; and on August 30, 1637, an assembly comprising the teaching elders of New England convened at Newtown. Shepard formally opened the meeting; Bulkeley and Hooker—whose talent and eminence equalled Cotton's—were chosen moderators. For three weeks in open session the elders debated, and settled to their satisfaction, the questions of doctrine and church order that Cotton and the Hutchinsonians had raised. They identified some ninety "erroneous opinions" and "unwholesome expressions" abroad in the colony, refuted them, and condemned the lot. Faced with united opposition from his colleagues, Cotton dissociated himself from the followers of Hutchinson. A reconciliation was effected with him on the issues of union with Christ and sanctification as evidence of justification. Wheelwright, however, remained obdurate. On the final day, the synod formally disapproved private meetings in the style of Hutchinson, condemned the Hutchinsonians' practice of putting private questions after sermons, and recommended against dismission of church members over questions not fundamental. John Davenport, lately arrived from England but not yet situated, was deputed to deliver the mind of the assembly in a sermon after its adjournment. Thereafter, wrote Edward Johnson, the condemned opinions were no longer seen to go abroad "in a living manner," though "sometimes like wizards to peep and mutter out of ground."[24]

The synod at Newtown dealt only with doctrines and practices of church members. The General Court, in November, dealt with persons. The Hutchinsonians persisted in social disruption and disrespect of authority, there were rumors that a group of English sectaries were about to join them, and trouble with the Indians continued. It was clear to Winthrop that the dissenters' behavior was no longer compatible with public peace and safety or with the errand of Massachusetts Bay. The light of the City on the Hill was being dimmed, perhaps its very existence jeopardized, by discord among the inhabitants. Accordingly, the leaders of the Hutchinsonian party were summoned before the Court as troublers of the peace of commonwealth and church. Judged guilty of sedition and contempt of the magistracy, they were disenfranchised and banished. Lesser offenders received corresponding punishments. The Hutchinsonians in Boston were publicly disarmed.[25]

Then the Court turned to Anne Hutchinson herself. She was charged with having "a great share in the promoting and divulging of those opinions that are the causes of this trouble," with having said things "very prejudicial to the honor of the churches and ministers thereof," and with having continued the meeting in her house after the assembly of ministers had condemned it. She responded with some wit and much obstinacy, and with a degree of naiveté. Asked to answer the elders' allegation that she had said they preached a covenant of works and were not able ministers of the New Testament, she demanded that they be made to testify to the charge under oath. Owing to the seriousness with which oaths were then held, the ministers were unwilling to do so. The ensuing wrangle diverted the proceeding for a moment, but then Hutchinson interrupted it to volunteer a full explanation of her meaning. She gave personal revelations as her authority and warned the Court that calamity would befall the colony for the Court's mistreatment of her, "for the mouth of the Lord hath spoken it." This development put the case outside the Court's civil competence, while confirming the general suspicion that Anne Hutchinson was the fountain of all their troubles. Whereupon, being prepared in any event to proceed against her for slander and contempt, the Court found her "unfit for our society" and banished her from the colony.[26]

Wheelwright removed immediately to the Piscataqua River, beyond Massachusetts's jurisdiction to the north. Hutchinson was confined in a private house, where the ministers visited her in an earnest but vain attempt to reason her out of her errors. In March 1638 she was cited to appear before the Boston congregation. After some discussion with the ministers about her rather novel understanding of the resurrection and the soul's mortality, she was formally admonished by Cotton for willful and arrogant persistence in error. Cotton and Davenport made a final private attempt to secure her repentance, and she appeared once more before the church, on March 22. A written retraction was introduced, which she acknowledged and almost immediately withdrew. Then she claimed never to have held doctrines that she was publicly known to have held. At this point the congregation, exercising its disciplinary function, voted to excommunicate for recalcitrant and deceitful behavior.[27]

About the end of the month Hutchinson departed to Narragansett Bay, where members of her party had purchased an island from the Indians. She joined readily in the sectarian quarreling that distinguished early Rhode Island. After several removes, she was killed in August 1643, near what is now Rye, New York, by Indians. In Massachusetts, antinomian ideas continued to "peep and mutter," and ministers to preach against them, into the 1640s, but they disturbed the peace of the commonwealth no further.[28]

CHAPTER 3

The Preeminence of the Spirit: John Cotton

The immediate practical focus of the controversy between Cotton and the other elders was the problem of personal assurance of election. In the aftermath of Cotton's Boston revival, anxiety about assurance appears to have intensified among his parishioners.[1] Hutchinson, and Cotton also, responded to this anxiety with the affirmation that assurance must be founded upon some direct apprehension of justification or election. This was conclusive evidence of a hopeful saint's estate, though in practice it might be difficult to obtain, since it depended entirely upon the transcendent work of Christ and the Spirit. In contrast, Wilson and the other ministers counselled the hopeful to look for some "gracious work" on their part, which God had designated in scripture as the mark of a gracious estate. Such evidence did not immediately free an individual from all feelings of doubt, nor was its occurrence particularly dramatic. Its effect was cumulative, however, and the elders maintained that with time it might become a firm foundation for assurance. Cotton's colleagues considered his allegedly "immediate" evidence to be unduly subjective, and they wondered about the constancy, in the long run, of the assurance founded upon it. On his part, Cotton accused the other elders of transforming the covenant of grace into a covenant of works by making an individual's inclusion in it contingent on some human "work" of his own, therein offering a false, deceptive, and doctrinally questionable assurance.

This largely pastoral problem focused a considerable set of broader and more fundamental theological issues. In formal Re-

34

formed divinity, the *locus* on assurance occupies a definite systematic-theological position, in that what is said about evidencing election follows from what is said about the nature of God and the way in which he accomplishes regeneration.[2] It also depends on what is said about the nature of faith, justification, and sanctification, and about their relationship in regeneration. Accordingly, it may be asked, how did Cotton's understanding of these things differ from that of his colleagues, to the extent that his approach to assurance appeared radically different? And what larger theological resources did the other ministers employ in addressing the same problem? These questions are the primary subject of this chapter and the one that follows. Their answers, together with certain biographical and historical data, help to locate Cotton theologically in relation to the Antinomian Controversy and to the history of Reformed Protestantism.

THE PLACE OF COTTON

Cotton began on one side of the controversy and ended on the other, and his position during most of it was equivocal. His intellectual and professional qualifications were equal or superior to those of his colleagues, yet he sided in doctrine, and up to a point in practice, with the unlearned folk who found that Hutchinson "preache[d] better Gospel than any of your black-coats that have been at the Nineversity." He was not by temperament a sectary, as Hutchinson apparently was. Yet shortly after his arrival in Boston he revealed a theological spirit different from that of the other elders, which she, Vane, and sundry of the Boston congregation recognized immediately as their own. Cotton was not the source of all of Anne Hutchinson's ideas, either directly or by deduction on her part, yet on certain points the two were substantially in agreement, whatever the sources of their views. Cotton's colleagues continued to regard him as a brother, albeit coolly for a time, and his position as teacher of the Boston church was never officially questioned. Until the fall of 1637, however, he publicly sided with the Hutchinsonians in debate with the other ministers, and at Hutchinson's examination by the Court he sought to qualify both the testimony against her and her more extreme assertions.[3]

Faced with solid opposition at the Newtown synod, Cotton publicly conformed. His compliance, however, was regarded by some at the time as *pro forma* only, and when Hutchinson was before the Court he was himself closely questioned. The following March, he formally admonished her in the Boston church, the other elders—not without irony—having requested him to do so, "as one whose words . . . may be of more respect and sink deeper and so was likely to do more good upon the party offending than any other."[4] Ten years later, he still held his pre-synodical view of two of the five points on which he had professed agreement at Newtown.[5] He emerged from the controversy to become an important spokesman for the Bay Colony's church polity in the debate over ecclesiastical order occasioned by the summoning of the Westminster Assembly. This involvement, too, was touched with embarrassment, for the Presbyterians seized upon Cotton's support of "antinomian" and "familistical" errors as evidence of the heresy and disorder implicit in New England independency. For official apologetics the colony relied on Thomas Hooker and John Norton.[6]

Official Massachusetts opinion, beginning with Winthrop, explained Cotton's association with the Hutchinsonians by saying he was duped. Cotton, much later, laid the blame on his own temperament and the Hutchinsonians' cleverness. He was not, he said, naturally suspicious, and they were careful to say nothing unorthodox in his presence, while giving out publicly that they held only what Mr. Cotton held. He claimed that it was not until members of the Boston church defended some of the errors collected by the synod that he discerned "a real and broad difference" between himself and the Hutchinsonians. Robert Baillie, the Presbyterian polemicist, charged that Cotton was seduced by Hutchinson, becoming an eager supporter of her views, which was a less charitable way of putting it.[7] Modern opinion has tended to reverse the relationship, treating Hutchinson as Cotton's most apt pupil, who carried his distinctive teachings to extreme conclusions.[8] This view is not without foundation, since obvious continuities exist between Cotton's ideas about the passivity of faith, the incapacity of creatures, and the Spirit's witnessing and indwelling, and some of Anne Hutchinson's expressions. At the same time, Hutchinson's more extreme utterances about direct revelations, the soul's mortality, and the nature of the resurrection were clearly contrary to Cotton's judgment and spirit. Allowing for differences in sophistication, however, Cotton shared key theological views with the Hutchinsonians. It seems not unlikely that, when they arrived in New England, Cotton and Hutchinson were travelling in much the same theological direction, though along somewhat different paths.[9]

Cotton's reply to Baillie contains a clue to his doctrinal affinity with the Hutchinsonians and also reveals something about his personal style. In May 1637 the General Court voted to require official permission for new immigrants wishing to settle in the colony. When the law went into effect, Cotton recalled, "I was informed that some godly passengers who hither arrived out of England, were refused to sit down amongst us, because (upon trial) they held forth such an union with Christ by the Spirit giving faith, as did precede the acting of faith upon Christ: and such an evidence of that union, by the favour of God shed abroad in their hearts by the Holy Ghost, as did precede the seeing (though not the being) of sanctification." The new ruling, it seemed, would prevent people from joining the Boston church unless they held on these points the very opinions that Cotton regarded as false. "Besides," he went on, "I was informed that such a doctrine of union, and evidencing of union, as was held forth by me, was the Trojan horse, out of which all the erroneous opinions and differences of the country did issue forth." Fearful that his presence might breed further contention, and reflecting that he had come to New England to edify rather than disturb, he began to think of leaving the Bay Colony. On consulting the magistrates, however, he discovered that the immigrants in question had been refused "upon denial of inherent righteousness in believers, and of any evidence of a good estate from thence, first or last," rather than upon maintenance of the points he had taught about union and evidencing union. These opinions, the magistrates allowed were not so serious as to warrant separation, so he stayed in Boston.[10]

Cotton's understanding of the relationship between faith and union with Christ and the Hutchinsonians' denial of inherent graces in the regenerate were not, as will be seen, unrelated. The latter notion, however, was more immediately productive of antinomianism, especially in untutored minds, and also of civil and ecclesiastical disturbance. As long as Cotton remained a nonpolitical minority of one, the untutored being removed or restrained, his presence and his views were tolerable. That his doctrine of union and evidence was a Trojan horse in the sense charged was not untrue, and he himself came very close to denying the inherence of graces in the sanctified. He admitted "ingenuously" to Baillie that "there was some color of my leaning to one Antinomian tenet in one day of the Synod," touching the instrumentality of faith in receiving Christ's righteousness unto justification.[11] This admission was less than candid, in that it was understated and in that, considerably prior to the synod, Cotton had argued vigorously against such an instrumentality. Indeed, the "corrupt opinions" that the Boston members defended at Newtown—which Cotton claimed had first alerted him to the true state of affairs—were essentially those in which he had himself differed from his colleagues the year before, namely, "such as concerned union with Christ before faith, justification without faith, inherent righteousness, and evidencing a good estate by it at all, first or last." They were also substantially the same as those over which the Boston church challenged the church at Newtown in December 1636.[12]

Cotton published the defense of his conduct in the antinomian affair ten years after the fact, during a dispute in which the ecclesiological validity of New England church polity was a larger issue than his own reputation. He replied in detail to Baillie's charges about his "antinomianism," for Baillie had sought to make the issues one. Yet a slight disingenuousness in Cotton's rehearsal of the events of 1636–38 suggests that the Scot's barb had touched a tender place. In fact, Cotton had a reputation with which, for polemical purposes at least, he could be taxed. In the early years of his ministry at St. Botolph's he had accepted the ceremonial of the Church of England, and when he later opted for nonconformity, he admitted that his views on the matter were still tentative. About the same time he expressed ideas on the conditionality of reprobation that the irreproachably orthodox William Twisse subsequently felt compelled to refute.[13] By the time he left Lincolnshire, Cotton was firmly convinced that the liturgical forms of the English Church violated the third commandment, and, arrived in New England, he soon evinced a more radical conception of the nature and relationship of faith, justification, and sanctification, and of the Spirit's involvement in all three, than he had held during his English ministry.[14] His ideas about church polity also changed significantly during his life, a fact on which Baillie appropriately capitalized. Acknowledging one such shift in a sermon in 1636, Cotton gave his reasons for it and added that "if anything which I have since written or spoken, God give me to see it, appear different from the truth, I will retract it also." This willingness to follow further light was not untypical of the man, however tenaciously he might hold a particular position at a given moment. The same attitude made Puritans characteristically difficult to stop once they started on the road to truth, landing some of them, as seekers and tolerationists, at the end of a trail of cast-off convictions. Cotton travelled hardly so far, but he moved rather swiftly during portions of his career. Baillie said simply that Cotton was chronically unsettled in his mind.[15]

Another aspect of Cotton's personal style, namely his capacity for verbal obscurity, also bears on the ambiguity surrounding his involvement in the New England controversy. Already in England he was reputed for incisiveness and depth of scholarship, on the strength of which a Massachusetts colleague sagely suggested that he be commissioned, for the benefit of New Englanders, "to go through the Bible, and raise marginal notes upon all the knotty places of scripture."[16] Cotton had, however, another side and was capable more than occasionally of saying not quite what he meant, or of saying it less than clearly. William Twisse, analyzing Cotton's manuscript on predestination, complained repeatedly of "the miserable confusion that like a leprosy seizes upon your manner of expression . . . enough to make any intelligent reader despair to receive satisfaction from you."[17] Twisse had to do with a particularly difficult sample of Cottonian prose. During the New England affair, however, the ministers more than once pointedly requested Cotton to respond to their inquiries "by way of writing rather than speech" and then found the result sometimes disappointingly opaque and involved, and Mr. Cotton (adapting Twisse's phrase) "very close and reserved therein." When the controversy was over, Samuel Stone admonished Cotton for being so tender of himself as not to state his views at sufficient length and in adequate detail. Whether Cotton, in a given instance, was obscure because he was in an unsettled interval between convictions, because his position was insufficiently thought through, or because he wished to conceal something is difficult to say. Whatever the reason, the quality of Cotton's discourse in the spring of 1636 was such that people might readily hear things in it that were not explicitly there, and also sufficiently suggestive that his colleagues could well desire, as they put it, to "have from your own hand what you hold, whereby to stop the mouths that raise up any slander of you, or prejudice against the truth," in view of "sundry opinions ... going up and down as yours in repute of some."[18] That Cotton on certain points refused a straight answer only intensified their desire.

JUSTIFYING FAITH AND THE NATURE OF SANCTIFICATION

In his journal, Winthrop noted the five points on which, at the end of the Newtown synod, Cotton and his colleagues reached an understanding. The first four were central to the controversy.

> 1. The first was about our union with Christ. The question was, whether we are united before we had active faith. The consent was, that there was no marriage union with Christ before actual faith, which is more than habitual. 2. The second was, about evidencing justification by sanctification. The consent was, that some saving sanctifications (as faith, etc.) were coexistent, concurrent, and coapparent (or at least might be) with the witness of the Spirit always. 3. That the new creature is not the person of a believer, but a body of saving graces in such a one; and that Christ, as the head, doth enliven or quicken, preserve and act the same, but Christ himself is no part of this new creature. 4. That though, in effectual calling (in which the answer of the soul is by active faith, wrought at the same instant by the Spirit), justification and sanctification be all together in them; yet God doth not justify a man, before he be effectually called, and so a believer.[19]

Each of these points concerns the manner of God's proceeding in regeneration and also—especially items (2) and (3)—the nature of regeneration itself; and they all involve in varying degree the question of the proper relationship between divine power and created nature in the administration of the covenant of grace. The balance of this chapter is devoted to examination of Cotton's unaccommodated position on these issues.

Habitual and Justifying Faith

"Faith," in Puritan discourse, has at least four distinct senses: (1) "historical faith," which is intellectual apprehension of doctrinal truth, shared by the unregenerate and devils; (2) "miraculous faith," a temporary adherence to Christ wrought by God apart from ordinary means, which ceases when the extraordinary influence is withdrawn; (3) "faith of assurance," in which a person is convinced of his justified estate; and (4) "justifying faith," which unites to Christ and thereby justifies, and which, considering its form, may be called "faith of adherence and dependence." Only justifying faith is properly "saving," as it forms the critical link between the destitution of the humbled sinner and the fullness of Christ's riches of grace, and only justifying faith can be the foundation of true assurance. Puritans generally took Paul's phrase "A man is justified by faith" (Rom. 3:28) in a causal sense, treating faith as the condition of entry into the covenant of grace. As such, faith is necessarily a human act, man being by nature an agent. The act of faith is distinctive in that it is a gracious act. No one can truly believe from his own power, but only as the Spirit, infusing a supernatural principle, enables him to do so; and the act of faith does not merit justification but is merely an arbitrary condition imposed by God when he set up the system of covenants. Faith is, nonetheless, ontologically prior to union with Christ, as the movement of which union is *terminus ad quem*, and without it there is no union. At the same time, justification (which follows from union) is "by faith" and "by grace" alone, for the Spirit, who works gratuitously, is—in scholastic terminology—the "efficient cause" of union, faith being the "instrumental cause" of it. Crucial to this understanding was the scholastic distinction between "habit" and "act," the habit of faith being defined as the principle or power of faith freely infused into the soul, the act of faith as the motion put forth from the habit. In receipt of the habit the soul is passive; in virtue of it the soul actively believes in Christ. Both were understood to be antecedent conditions of entry into the covenant and of justification.[20]

Cotton approached the understanding of justification rather differently. He excluded by definition the possibility of a gracious

act prior to union with Christ and therefore reversed the relationship between faith and union, with the result that "justifying faith"
became equivalent to "faith of assurance." He retained the distinction between habitual and actual, or active, faith, but he made
habitual faith coincident with union and active faith subsequent
to it. By habitual faith he meant the passive faith by which the soul
is fitted to receive Christ; by active faith he understood the faith
by which the soul becomes aware of its justified estate and consciously believes in Christ. Such faith he included among the graces
of sanctification, describing it as a "condition consequent" to union,
meaning a state of affairs flowing from union, a somewhat different
sense of "condition" than was usual in Reformed discourse about
justification.[21]

Cotton's view of the nature and role of faith emerges in an
exchange with Peter Bulkeley, from about the middle of 1636,
when the ministers were probing Cotton's theological position.
Bulkeley proposed that faith wrought in the soul must be "effectual
faith, to make the bonds of union on our parts," that is, must actually bring us into union. Cotton replied that faith was indeed
effectual, but in the sense of rendering men capable of receiving
Christ "as an empty vessel actually [but not actively] receives oil
poured into it." Habitual faith, he declared, is "of an emptying
nature, emptying the soul of all confidence in itself and in the creature, and so leaving and constituting the soul an empty vessel . . .
but full of Christ."[22] Bulkeley responded that faith so conceived
gives no form to the union, "for it does nothing till the union be
made: which yet can never be true union without true causes."
Faith as a formal cause, he maintained, gives being to the union in
the same way that "anima rationalis gives being to the man." Cotton
responded that faith is active and a formal cause, but it acts on the
man himself, rather than on Christ unto union. Faith dwells in the
man as a form in the formatum, conferring on him capacity to receive Christ. Faith, so considered, is not the formal cause of union
with Christ, as giving being to the union, but is rather the formal
cause of the Christian. "As forma dat esse formato, so doth faith to
a true faithful Christian making him alive in Christ, and so a member of him."[23]

Here Cotton was employing an ambiguity in the definition of
the formal cause. It might mean, as it apparently did for St. Thomas,
that which "determines or completes in the sphere of essence,"

which is yet distinct from the act by which essence has being. Other scholastics treated existence as inseparable from essence, so that form could be regarded as conferring being as well as distinctiveness on matter, which apart from form is only potency.[24] It is in this sense that Bulkeley used the term in reference to union with Christ: faith gives being to the union, "as the reasonable soul gives the being to the man." Slightly but significantly, Cotton altered the terms of the discussion: "*Anima rationalis* makes a man to be what he is, a man. . . . So faith makes a Christian man to be what he is, a true Christian, and so united to Christ and a member and heir of his." The Spirit works faith and faith works an actual fitness to receive Christ, in which union consists, though faith is not yet "active to believe on Christ."[25]

Cotton would admit a habitual receiving of Christ by the regenerate but not an active going to Christ or taking of Christ prior to union. The latter, however, was precisely the point in dispute. It was, moreover, a point that went beyond the issue of the Protestant *sola gratia* to the question of the integrity of the human creature, as by nature a rational agent, vis à vis the creative power of the Trinity. This problem concerned Cotton less, however, than did upholding—in the language of a later era—the qualitative otherness of justifying grace.

> Though God has ordained faith to help the soul to close with Christ, yet not to make up our union with Christ by actual believing on him, but on our parts to say Amen to what God has done, and to receive what God has given and wrought in us. . . . We must be good trees before we can bring forth good fruit. . . . If then closing with Christ be a good fruit, we must be good trees before we can bring it forth. And how we can be good trees, before we be engrafted into Christ, we must look for it in Aristotles . . . : for it is not revealed in the gospel of Christ.

To hold as Bulkeley did implied for Cotton a freedom of the will to close with Christ prior to regeneration, and this allowance he was utterly unwilling to make, even if the will were felt to be liberated by infusion of a gracious habit and so a "good" will. Union with Christ must precede active closing with him; indeed it precedes all activity of faith. This was the premise of all Cotton's arguments respecting the place of faith in the order of redemption.[26]

Accordingly, active faith could not be for Cotton a proper instrument for the receiving of Christ in union or a proper condition of entry into the covenant of grace. Indeed, "justifying faith" is not properly the faith that justifies but is, rather, the faith that reveals to us that we are justified. It is related to justification not as antecedent cause but as something following from it. In effectual calling, the Spirit works faith in the soul to receive Christ passively into union. Thereupon the soul enjoys communion with Christ, receiving faith to believe in him and other spiritual graces. Faith is thus the first of the graces of sanctification and the root of all the others. From Christ "we receive grace for grace . . . : the like faith, hope, love, zeal, meekness, patience, etc." Faith, "as a qualification inherent in us and deriving holiness from Christ to all our duties, . . . is a part of sanctification," and the acting of faith and all the other graces is in no way necessary to union, which is constituted, rather, by the Spirit's working of them in us.[27]

The Power of Sanctification

In the handbooks of Reformed divinity, the regenerate are held to undergo a double alteration. In justification, they receive Christ's righteousness by imputation, so that God no longer regards them as under condemnation. Christ's righteousness is not subjectively in the regenerate—it remains in heaven in Christ—but the regenerate enjoy the benefits of it through their relationship to Christ by faith. In sanctification, in contrast, created graces, new principles of action, are positively infused into the regenerate, making them literally new creatures, able to act in obedience to God's will. The Spirit begets and preserves these habits of sanctification, and they derive their power from his continued sustenance, yet these habits are active in the saints themselves and enable them to act holily.[28] Cotton agreed that there is a positive change in the regenerate and retained the notion of infused habits of sanctification. But he so emphasized the dependence of such habits on Christ's power as to make their existence in the regenerate merely relative, and he flatly denied that gracious habits might work in the regenerate of their own power.[29]

As with faith and justification, so with sanctification, Cotton regarded Christ as the one true center of activity and efficiency. All spiritual gifts exist first and in their fulness in Christ, whence they are derived by the Spirit's agency to those who are in union with Christ. In spiritual things, including divine commands, activity in and from the creature is as inadmissible after regeneration as before it. Christ is the root of holiness, which has no life save as it flows from this root. Indeed, Cotton could speak of sanctification as something imputed to, rather than inherent in, the regenerate, as springing from "the imputation of Christ's righteousness" even as "corruption of nature springs from the imputation of Adam's unrighteousness." He meant that as men stand by nature in relation to Adam as head of the race, and thus share the consequences of Adam's sin without sharing in his sinning, so Christians, standing in relation to Christ as head, share Christ's righteousness without themselves acting righteously. That Christ's righteousness is imputed to men in this manner for justification was a standard Protestant affirmation. To speak similarly of sanctification was something of a novelty. Cotton, however, was so concerned to diminish creaturely activity that he would place the effective center of gracious action outside the regenerate: the righteousness of sanctification is primarily Christ's and is in the regenerate relatively, that is, as they stand related to Christ.[30]

The other ministers affirmed that the Holy Spirit is the "procreant and conservant" cause of sanctification, begetting and maintaining graces in the soul. Cotton agreed, but complained that they nonetheless allowed an excessively independent existence to graces. As the root of holiness, Christ is not only the procreant and conservant cause of sanctification but also the matter of it. The righteousness of sanctification is not properly ours but Christ's; indeed, it is Christ who (after 1 Cor. 1:30) is "made . . . our righteousness and sanctification." When his colleagues asked Cotton "whether a Christian be not further active after regeneration, than before it?" Cotton replied that a Christian is not at all active before regeneration but allowed that, after it, "acted upon we act." Graces in us "become active and lively not of themselves, but as Christ is active in them and puts forth himself in them day by day." So tenuously do graces reside in the saints that without Christ's continuous activity, their gifts would fly away as Adam's did and leave them naked, though Adam's gifts were perfect.[31] Without power from Christ to activate them, sanctifying graces are simply impotent, and there is, therefore, no possibility of any "active power in us of ourselves through gifts received."[32] With this assertion, Cotton distinguished himself from the tradition of Reformed orthodoxy as received in New England.

THE EVIDENCING OF JUSTIFICATION

Anne Hutchinson allegedly held that "union to Christ Jesus is not by faith," that "the first thing we receive for our assurance is our election," and that "we have no grace in ourselves but all is in Christ and there is no inherent righteousness in us." Urged to pray that graces of sanctification might be found in them, her followers replied, "We must not pray for gifts and graces but only for Christ." Exhorted to stir up and put forth such graces as they might have, they responded, "Here is a great stir about graces and looking to hearts, but give me Christ, I seek not for graces but for Christ, I seek not for promises but for Christ, I seek not for sanctification, but for Christ, tell me not of meditation and duties, but tell me of Christ."[33] These propositions, being intended by the ministers for public examination, were formulated more crisply than was perhaps the case among those suspected of holding them. They are, however, generally consistent with the five points in dispute between Cotton and his colleagues at the Newtown synod, and they reflect an understanding of the nature and order of regeneration essentially the same as Cotton's. Until the fall of 1637, Cotton had in effect been arguing that the elect are united to Christ and justified before active faith, that graces of sanctification are really in Christ and not in believers, and that in consequence Christ and not graces —that is, direct apprehension of "our election" in Christ—is the sole sufficient ground of assurance. These issues were gathered up in the question about evidencing justification.

The Priority of Absolute Promises

Cotton's colleagues maintained that graces of sanctification manifest themselves in the regenerate in empirically discernible ways, by means of which an anxious saint might conclude that he is truly justified even though he has not yet "seen his name writ in the book of life." Crucial to this view was the elders' understanding of the so-called "conditional promises" of the covenant of grace.

These were biblical promises of blessedness to "gracious qualifications" in Christians, such as "blessed are the poor in spirit" (Mt. 5:3), and to "evangelical obedience," especially love to the brethren (1 John 3:14). Such promises were contrasted with the "absolute promises" of the covenant (for example, biblical promises of redemption without mention of any condition, as Acts 10:43–44 and 16:31), where the listeners, "upon hearing the promise of remission (or justification) unto faith, . . . received both faith and justification, and the evidence of both altogether."[34] Cotton and the other elders agreed that initial closing with Christ is always in an absolute promise. His colleagues, however, maintained that God intended conditional promises as aids in discerning justification, and that individuals who discovered in themselves works of sanctification to which biblical promises were made or implied might take assurance therefrom of their justified estate. In so doing, the elders argued, a person was not "closing with Christ" as he does in entering the covenant of grace, but merely drawing a reasonable conclusion from empirical evidence interpreted in light of scripture.

Cotton rejected this line of argument, on the ground that it involved conditions, created works, and commands, which he held to be incompatible with the free grace of the covenant. In his view, daily works of sanctification depended on the presence of conscious faith, by which the saints derive power from Christ for such acts; and conscious faith depended on the Spirit's testimony that a person is united to Christ and justified.[35] It is not possible, therefore, to conclude from sanctification to justification; and since sanctifying graces do not really subsist in the regenerate, and so cannot be perceived by them, there is really no basis for such a conclusion. Cotton thus rejected the conceptual framework that underlay his colleagues' case for sanctification as an evidence of justification. He felt, in any event, that the evidencing of justification was really inseparable from the attaining of it, and so he tended to shift the discussion from an evidential connection between sanctification and justification to a causal connection, which permitted him to sound very Protestant while making the other elders sound less so.

Cotton allowed that conditional promises are useful for instruction and exhortation and for discerning sanctification.[36] They have no place in discerning justification, however, for it is impossible to come to Christ, that is, to come to believe that one is justified, on promises to conditions preexistent in us—conditions that, apart from Christ working in us, we cannot hope to attain. Conditional promises, indeed, are not made directly to elect individuals at all, but first to Christ. The conditions are fulfilled in him and the promised blessings accrue to him, whither the elect must go in faith to receive them. Gracious qualifications are truly gracious, not because God works them in the regenerate but because they are to, in, and from Christ, and only derivatively to and in the regenerate. Cotton's colleagues saw nothing amiss in taking active faith as a prior condition of the covenant of grace, since, they believed, it arises from a gracious principle freely infused by the Spirit. Cotton would not allow prior conditions in the order of redemption at all, not even gracious ones. At issue for him was not so much the freeness of the promises of grace, which the phrase "going on in a covenant of works" might suggest, as whether created graces have anything at all to do with either the being or the apprehension of justification.[37]

God gives himself initially, Cotton insisted, only in the offer of Christ "in an absolute promise of free grace, without any qualification mentioned." He comes by the promise declared in the gospel "and begets faith back again in the soul by the promise, whereby we receive Christ." God unites himself to the soul as a father to a child, or a husband to a wife, but "did you ever know a true real marriage made in a conditional promise? Does a man say to his wife, 'If you prove a loving and kind wife, then, I will be thine husband'?" The offer of Christ requires neither antecedent faith nor works, though it requires and will produce both as consequents. Those who are thirsty and poor and long for Christ are made so by some former assurance that all riches are unconditionally laid up in him, nor is their first assurance from their poverty, as a gracious qualification. Rather, their poverty directs them to go to Christ to receive satisfaction. Wherefore, "if you know that you are in Christ, you may know that the promises are yours, otherwise you shall not be able to know your right in Christ by your right in the promises."[38]

The Visibility of Saints

Cotton was committed by the Reformed theological tradition to belief in a positive change in the regenerate, by which they are distinguished from hypocrites, that is, from people who merely appear regenerate in outward behavior. Following his conviction about the Spirit's overruling operation, however, he rendered this change practically invisible. "To distinguish in men between that sanctification which flows from the law, and that which is of the gospel is a matter so narrow, that the angels in heaven have much ado to discern who differ: a work fitter for angels to cut the scantling in it, than for the ministers of the gospel, though indeed there be great difference of the one from the other."[39] Cotton's colleagues held that works of sanctification could be evaluated by the "root" whence they spring, the "rule" by which they are guided, and the "end" at which they aim—that is, by the basic disposition of the individual actor, it being assumed that a person could know his own disposition. Cotton accepted this triple standard, but he applied it in a distinctively Cottonian manner, leaving it useless as a guide to assurance.

The root of sanctification, Cotton argued, is faith, which—the individual being already united with Christ—the Spirit works in the soul. But both believers who persevere and hypocrites who fall away have this root to some extent, as do those who, terrified by the law, are moved to works of reformation. There is no perceptible difference in the root, and yet there is a difference, "but it is very hard to discern": it lies in the consciousness of the faithful, who, being apprised by God, know that God "work[s] all their works for them." As to the rule of sanctification, Cotton noted that both saints and hypocrites seek the word of God and delight in its commands. "Gross hypocrites," of course, will soon return to their favorite lusts. Yet others will so thoroughly appear to delight in God's commands, continuing in universal obedience until their deaths, that it is impossible to distinguish them. Respecting the end of sanctification, hypocrites aim at their own comfort, rather than the glory of God. Yet their own ends may long coincide with seeking God's glory, so that an honest Christian soul cannot, beside them, be any surer of his own devotion to God. In root, rule, and bent of holiness, hypocrites, therefore, "will carry all things in so fair a way" that a Christian will hardly be able to discern the difference, unless he "has his wits well exercised."[40]

But supposing his wits be properly exercised? Could not an enlightened conscience discover whether a person's sanctification was true? Cotton's colleagues believed it could and offered the anxious a "practical syllogism" of the form:

> He that is truly sanctified is justified,
> But I am such,
> Ergo, I am justified.[41]

Accuracy in the minor premise was critical. The elders held, however, that a regenerate conscience is able to perceive the soul's disposition in good works and is competent, by reflection, to draw appropriate conclusions from it. Cotton allowed that such conclusions by practical reasoning are valid, but only if the observation of conscience is based on the Spirit's testimony and only if the conclusion follows from "spiritual" sight of interest in Christ—which qualifications, in effect, denied the point.[42]

In explaining what he meant by spiritual sight, Cotton came very close to revealing the basis of his difficulty with the other elders' view. He distinguished between empirical "knowledge" of justification and "faith of assurance" of justification based on immediate divine testimony, and he added a corresponding distinction between "a created spiritual light abiding in the regenerate conscience" and "an immediate light of the Spirit of God above the letter of the word, and above the created light of the conscience." Knowledge of justification, he allowed, may be had from arguments founded on works of sanctification, such knowledge being a deduction from observable data, founded upon a proposition derived from scripture (for example, a conditional promise) and upon a judgment of conscience concerning a man's behavior—conscience being "enlightened with that created light which hath renewed it." A conclusion of *knowledge*, however, cannot yield assurance of justification, save as it follows from a prior conclusion of *faith*, in which the proposition from scripture must be "an absolute promise or some word of grace freely offering Christ and his righteousness without the condition of any works of ours to go before it"; and instead of the judgment of conscience there must be "an effectual application not so much of that proposition, as of Christ in it." This "application" is made only by the Spirit himself, without respect to the being or apprehension of any work in us. In other words, it is quite impossible for a hopeful saint to discover his estate by examination of his behavior, his motives, and the rule of scripture.[43]

Cotton argued that self-knowledge of the sort his colleagues proposed was entirely subordinate to, and dependent upon, the Spirit's role in "clear[ing] up to [us] all things pertaining to spiritual sight," including the presence of grace in us. There is no means under heaven for declaring these things "evidently unto the soul," save the Spirit acting immediately; and prior to the Spirit's witness a person's knowledge remains that of an enlightened conscience only—that is, knowledge based on the testimony of created things, which is, by Cotton's definition, incapable of ascending to things of grace. Though every regenerate individual has his mind and conscience in some measure enlightened with spiritual knowledge, yet more than this is necessary "to clear spiritual sight . . . , even the clearing of the object (our spiritual estate) and . . . of the scripture that concerns it, and of the works of God in us."[44]

The other ministers also regarded these things as the Spirit's work. The issue, however, was by what means of objective word and sensible work the Spirit in fact bears witness. They held that he accomplishes it through that gracious "created spiritual light" by which the regenerate are enabled to perceive the excellency of Christ the Savior, the truth of their own justification, and the soundness of their sanctification. For Cotton, such human perception, however enlightened by grace, was subordinate to a still higher, increated knowledge, given by the Spirit directly, which Cotton held to be alone determinative of true sainthood. "Evident sanctification," he allowed, may help to clear justification, but such sanctification is distinguished from works performed out of fear of the law—and thus made "evident"—solely "by the revelation or manifestation of the Spirit of God, both of the state and work of good Christians; and that ordinarily also."[45]

The elders inquired whether a Christian must necessarily have his first assurance from an absolute, in contrast to a conditional, promise. Cotton responded: If from a conditional, how, before we are assured of union with Christ, may we be sure that the condition is a saving grace peculiar to the elect?

> If it be said that any saving grace may be discerned to be peculiar to God's elect by some peculiar characteristics whereby it is dis-

cerned from the common graces of the forwardest hypocrites; I
answer, True, such peculiar characters there be, whereof this is
always one, without discerning whereof the rest can never be discerned, that, such graces spring from a lively faith, and do work
from faith in Christ, without which it is impossible to please God.

True sanctification is discernible only by the light of justifying faith
previously discerned, and by the Spirit's witness only. A person
is first in Christ, then the Spirit apprises him of the fact that he is
justified, then he has faith that he is justified in Christ, then the
Spirit shows him that his sanctification is true.[46]

"Going On in a Covenant of Works"

The Hutchinsonians justified their separatistic behavior on
the ground that the elders of the Bay Colony were "legal" preachers
and their hearers "legal" Christians, "preaching" and "being under
a covenant of works" instead of a covenant of grace. The ministers,
for their part, seem initially to have been somewhat puzzled by this
complaint and sought to draw the Hutchinsonians out. In the accepted meaning of the words, the charge made little sense. The
elders did not preach "do this and live" in the same way that it
was enjoined upon Adam as the terms of the covenant of works.
Wherein, they desired earnestly to know, did the Boston congregation find them to differ so greatly from Brother Cotton? Before the
Court, Mistress Hutchinson was pressed to state what she meant
by the distinction between the covenants of works and grace. She
intended, it appeared, that the ministers, lacking the seal of the
Spirit immediately in their hearts, were yet under the dispensation
of the law and not of the gospel.[47] This was a more sweeping judgment than that expressed by Wheelwright and Cotton, though not
an entirely different one. Wheelwright admitted that his fast-day
sermon against those "under a covenant of works" had been directed at people who made works of sanctification an evidence of
justification. Cotton, in response to the thirteenth of the *Sixteen
Questions*, developed the matter in terms of an illegitimate
"grounding" of justification on sanctification.[48] His handling of the
issue displayed the tendency already noted, namely, to subordinate
the activity and instrumentality of created things to the immediate
operation of the Persons of the Trinity.

Is it, the elders had inquired, "a building of my justification on my sanctification, or a going on in a covenant of works," if I evidence justification by my sanctification? Cotton allowed that "at first blush" the phrase seemed plain and familiar, but maintained that it was in fact ambiguous and obscure; and with unusual deliberation he proceeded to "clear" the expression. To offer sanctification for an "evident argument" of justification may mean, he said, to offer it as a cause or ground of justification, or to offer it as an evidence of justification, in the sense of a sign or effect. In the second case, sanctification may be adduced as the only evidence of justification (having nothing else to offer for it), or as "a concurrent sign, together with other signs and witnesses, which may make both my justification and sanctification clear" (Cotton's own position). The first case, in which justification is founded on sanctification as its ground, cause, and matter, is indeed to go on in a covenant of works. This much was agreed on all hands. In the second case, sanctification is offered not as the cause of justification but as the cause of *faith,* and in two possible senses: either as the ground of the faith by which one is justified or as the ground of the faith whereby one believes that one is justified. The first is also to build justification on sanctification and so to go on in the covenant of works: sanctification is not the cause of justifying faith, but vice versa. This point, too, was admitted by all. The second possibility may also be a building of justification on sanctification, in two ways: either (1) when a person has no evidence of dependence on Christ for righteousness or of effectual calling and faith in Christ, except a visible change in his behavior from a profane to a sanctified course; or (2) "when we shall give a man no other ground or evidence of his justification, but only from the evidence of sanctification." This distinction, though more to the point, was of Cottonian fineness, and its meaning remained somewhat elusive.[49]

On the first count the other ministers agreed: an outward change of behavior, by itself, evidences nothing; but they dissented on the second. Unlike Cotton, they regarded sanctification as both discernible and an adequate evidence of justification, and they did not consider the founding of "faith of assurance" on sanctification to be equivalent to founding justification on sanctification. They were concerned about the means by which a person might apprehend the prior fact of his justification, and they observed that "to give no other evidence of my justification but sanctification, at the most is but to build the assurance of my justification on my sanctification. And the being of my justification is much different from the seeing of it. Arguments from consequents (as effects and adjuncts, etc.) may ground my knowledge of a thing: whereas only causes, which are precedent, do make up the being of it."[50] Cotton, however, would not admit this distinction and in his "Rejoynder" replied at length and with a touch of asperity. If a man has only sanctification to give as ground of his justification, he declared, then his faith is not founded on Christ's righteousness, nor on the free promise of grace, but only upon his own works. Such a person does not believe "on him that justifies the ungodly (which is the faith of the Gospel, Rom. 4:5) but on him which justifies the godly; which is such a faith as Adam might have, and so belongs to the covenant of works." To give no other ground of justification but the evidence of sanctification "is not only, at the most, to build the assurance of my justification upon my sanctification, but it is also to build and ground my justification upon my sanctification for I have no other ground to give for the being of it." The sight of sanctification alone contributes nothing to assurance of justification, and to offer no argument for assurance save one's sanctification is to build both assurance and justification "either upon no foundation at all, or only upon such an one as works, which can have no place but if anywhere in a covenant of works."[51]

Cotton complained that the ministers changed his words and altered his meaning, "for I do not say, to give no other evidence, but to give no other ground of my justification."[52] This complaint was not entirely valid, for Cotton had seemed to use the terms interchangeably, as he had done with "justifying faith" and "faith of assurance." The ministers might fairly have responded that Cotton changed the question, for they were concerned with the apprehension of justification, not with the "ground" or causes of its being. As they put it initially to Cotton, works of sanctification were conceived as *posterior probatio*, proceeding from, and revealing, a condition previously existing. They did not argue that a person could claim a right *ex debito* to the covenant of grace on the basis of works in himself, but rather that if a person found gracious works in himself, he might conclude an interest in the covenant—which he already had in fact—in virtue of the arbitrary connection between justification and sanctification established by the divine will. If one was thereby claiming a right to the covenant of grace, it was only in the sense of personal awareness of one's interest in it, not in a causal sense, and certainly not *ex debito*. To put the matter in these terms, however, was for Cotton to use language that was not proper to the covenant of grace—language, indeed that was not Protestant.

Cotton professed himself unable to believe it possible for a person to maintain that grace works a condition in him, reveals it, makes a promise to it, and applies it to him, and still not to trust in the work. If a person did not trust in the merit of the work, he would at least be tempted to trust in the right of it to the promise, and he probably would not dare to trust a promise unless he could see a work. However it be stated, all such reasoning derogates from grace, and to it, Cotton declared, *Protestant* divines answer bluntly "that grace and works, (not only in the case of justification) but in the whole course of our salvation from election to glorification, are not subordinate one to another but opposite: as that whatsoever is of grace is not of works, and whatsoever is of works is not of grace." This antithesis applies not only to merit but to right, and not only to the being of justification but to the seeing of it. As God justifies without respect to works, so he will not declare justification "to us in the holiness of our works, nor in the promises made thereto. . . . Nor will it stand with the glory of grace to bring us to rest or assurance of peace in Christ, in the mediation of our works." To speak as the ministers do is wholly contrary to the tenor of the covenant of grace.[53]

At the conclusion of his response in the *Sixteen Questions,* Cotton affirmed that he who has "a clear sight of his estate in a free promise of grace in Christ" by the light of the Spirit shed abroad in his soul does "evidently" discern both his justification and his sanctification, each bearing witness to the other and the Spirit to both. Such a person neither builds his justification on his sanctification, thereby going on in a covenant of works, nor does he "go aside" to it by seizing prematurely on works to gain assurance of the justification he already has but of which he is temporarily unaware. The elders replied that Cotton here rendered vain the entire discussion of the question and subsumed all under a single conclusion: "that we can see neither sanctification nor faith no nor jus-

tification, before the witness of the Spirit; but all at once by it."
Cotton remarked wryly that when he read this statement he checked
over his manuscript to see what had suggested "such a vast conclusion." He proceeded to qualify himself, but without relinquish-
ing the point, and he admitted parenthetically that the ministers
had judged rightly.[54]

Fundamentally at issue between Cotton and his colleagues was
the nature of the evidence by which a person might be assured of
his union with Christ. For Cotton, only the testimony of Christ himself was sufficient. Neither faith in Christ, as a human act, nor free
and hearty obedience to divine commands is able to provide the
soul with settled comfort touching its estate, "until the Spirit of
Christ doth witness to the soul God's thoughts of peace toward
himself," and this "by immediate light from himself."[55] All six
witnesses of 1 John 5:7,8, which are given to beget and confirm
faith, are in fact witnesses "nextly and immediately only by the
testimony and efficacy of the Spirit," who, though himself a witness
in his own capacity, nonetheless also "applies and conveys the testimony of all the rest immediately to the soul. . . . Immediately I say
though not without the word of God nor without (sometimes in
some cases) the work of God, yet with his own immediate power
above the power which either the word has of itself, or the work of
any creature."[56] This distinction between the work of creatures and
the power of the members of the Trinity was crucial for Cotton.
Only the latter are able to bear witness to the bond arising in the
covenant of grace between sovereign divinity and impotent human-
ity. It is not within the capacity of any created thing, *qua* created
thing, including a gracious habit, in itself to reveal anything conclusive about this bond, until the Spirit illumines it directly. One
cannot argue to justification from acts of faith and sanctification,
as to a cause from its effects, because one cannot know, apart from
the Spirit's revealing, that one's faith and sanctification are true,
there being nothing distinctive about the works of either by which
to recognize them. True faith of assurance rests solely upon its
proper object—God's mercy and free grace offered in Christ—and
then only as "revealed to me in some divine testimony." The scripture is such a testimony in its content and origins, yet the application of its truths "is not of divine force, as a divine testimony unless
the Spirit breathe in them and apply them to me." Neither is an

enlightened—that is, regenerate—conscience of any help in judging the soundness of gracious works. To hearken to "the witness of our own spirit" will not serve, "for our own spirit is of itself but a creature, though a good creature." Prior to the Spirit's witnessing, to see by an enlightened conscience a work in oneself and a promise made to it in scripture, and to take confidence from thence that one is justified—such can only be to go on in the covenant of works; for "such a faith is not the work of God's almighty power begotten by the divine testimony and operation of the Spirit of God (for it is before it), but hammered it is and engendered out of the concourse of three creatures."[57] For Cotton, the operation of God's almighty power and the capacities of created things were incompatible, and the latter could not be the vehicle of the former, not even in a practical syllogism.

CHAPTER 4

The Objectivity of Regenerating Grace: Thomas Shepard and Peter Bulkeley

As Protestants, New England Puritans maintained that assurance of salvation may be had in this life, and they affirmed that God commands all human beings to labor to make their callings "sure." At the same time, as Reformed Protestants, they held beliefs that rendered the attaining of assurance relatively difficult. The decree of election, they insisted, is hidden in God's mind and is revealed to the elect only in God's good time. Hypocrites, they allowed, can counterfeit all the outward marks of grace. The remnants of sin, moreover, persist in the converted, so that their obedience and confidence often fail, and their ardor for Christ periodically cools. God, furthermore, in his sovereign wisdom chastens his own, in order to test and to refine them. He withdraws his favor and withholds his bounty and may be deaf to entreaty, as he wills. The most conscientious Christian, accordingly, may expect periodically to be assailed by doubt. It is not surprising that personal assurance of salvation became perhaps the chief practical problem of Puritan spirituality, or that hopeful but troubled Puritans should be tempted to seek easier and more direct routes to certitude about their estates.

In Massachusetts Thomas Shepard gave particular attention to this problem, and he was remembered as a preacher especially for his ability simultaneously to expose religious deceit and to comfort the spiritually troubled. "When Mr. Shepard comes to deal with hypocrites," Nathaniel Ward remarked, "he cuts so desperately that men know not how to bear him; he makes them all afraid that they are all hypocrites." Yet to the humble, downcast soul, "he gives comfort so largely that we are afraid to take it." As a young man, in the travail of his own spiritual awakening, Shepard was attracted to the security offered by perfectionist ideas, and he wondered if Puritans who wrote about the works and duties of the Christian life "were not all legal men and their books so." Throughout his life he was painfully conscious of the imperfection of the saints' holiness, and of the fragility of Christian assurance; and the pages of the journal that he kept in the early 1640s indicate that he understood the longing of those who sought assurance in immediate revelations. He took refuge, however, neither in perfectionism nor in personal intimacy with the Holy Spirit. Instead, he found comfort in, and bade his hearers trust in, the sufficiency of God to perform what was promised in the free offer of grace, as declared in the objectivity of the biblical word and as empirically manifest in gracious works in individual souls.[1]

In this advice Shepard articulated the accumulated wisdom of his generation of Puritan pastors, who sought to guide their flocks through the ambiguities of the Christian life as they perceived them, and in accordance with the standards of the Reformed faith. Concretely, Shepard counselled the hopeful and the troubled to look for specific occasions when God had acted graciously toward them, or when they had themselves acted in ways that could only be effects of grace. Both sorts of instances, he reminded his hearers, were marks of divine favor that could be identified on the basis of information God had disclosed in scripture, and both were guaranteed by God's promise in the covenant of grace, which was sure and indubitable. Ultimately for Shepard and his fellows, assurance of salvation rested on the conviction that God is able and willing to do what he has promised in the covenant and has therein bound himself to do, however frail and trembling the individual human object of his redemptive intent. The hopeful and the troubled, therefore, need initially only trust in the divine promise and put themselves in the way of the covenant.

In this approach to the matter of personal assurance the doctrine of the covenant was crucial. For the covenant, the New England elders believed, is the vital link between God's gracious intent toward human beings and their apprehension of that intent. "All deliverances and salvation which the Lord communicates to his people," Bulkeley declared, "he does by virtue of, and according

to, his covenant." The covenant is the comprehensive medium between God and his people, as both the meeting point of divine and
human action and the effectual instrument in the conferring of
temporal and spiritual blessings.[2] Shepard developed the same
theme:

> God the Father's eternal purposes are sealed secrets, not immedi-
> ately seen, and the full and blessed accomplishments of those pur-
> poses are not yet experimentally felt; the covenant is the midst
> between both God's purposes and performances, by which and in
> which we come to see the one, before the world began, and by a
> blessed faith . . . to enjoy the other. . . . For in God's covenant and
> promise we see with open face God's secret purpose from time past.
> God's purposes toward his people being as it were nothing else but
> promises concealed, and God's promises in the covenant being noth-
> ing else but his purposes revealed.

Accordingly, the covenant is also the ground of personal assurance
of one's estate. "Where then," Shepard asked, "is a Christian's
comfort, but in that covenant wherein two eternities (as it were)
meet together, and whereby he may see accomplishments (made
sure to him) of eternal glory, arising from blessed purposes of
eternal grace?"[3]

Shepard's conviction of the instrumental and mediatory role
of the covenant entailed three further convictions about the operation of regenerating grace within the covenantal context. First, the
elders affirmed, such grace operates regularly, according to a pattern rooted in God's will and declared in scripture, from which
God does not ordinarily deviate. Second, they maintained that such
grace is objectively discernible in its effects in human thought and
action. Third, they insisted that in justification, sanctification, and
the evidencing of both, God's activity is channelled through created
things, including human faculties, which operate according to their
own proper natures.

To this complex of issues we now turn.

THE PLACE OF CREATED MEANS

In their understanding of God's activity *ad extra*, New England divines were thorough voluntarists: what is, is, and is how it is,

because God wills it. The regeneration of particular individuals is grounded in God's secret choice, before time and for his own glory, irrespective of anything in them that might move him so to choose. This same decree, the elders held, also includes the means of its actual fulfillment: the redemptive work of Christ, the application of its benefits to the elect, and the preservation of the saints for salvation.[4] The order of salvation also encompasses the concrete instrumentalities of word and sacrament—the "means of grace" in the narrow sense—through which the Spirit works, and also the human faculties of hearers and recipients on which he works. The preaching of godly ministers and its effect in individual conversions are both grounded in the divine decree, as much as are the substance of the grace conveyed and the activity of the Spirit who effects the conveyance. Considered largely, the substance of saving grace is Christ himself and his benefits. But the sinner encounters Christ mediately, in the objective, created words of "poor, weak, pale" Mr. Shepard.[5]

The means of grace, moreover, operate in a manner that does not overrule man's nature as an intellective, volitional creature.[6] As Richard Sibbes observed, speaking for many of his generation of Puritans:

> We consist of body and soul in this world, and our souls are much confined and tied to our senses. Imagination propounds to the soul greater things than the senses. So God helps the soul by outward things that work upon the senses; sense upon the imagination, and so things pass into the soul. God frames his manner of dealing suitable to the nature he hath created us in. Therefore he used the word and the sacraments, and such things, whereby he makes impressions upon the very soul itself.[7]

Viewed in these terms, the problem of salvation was a problem of enabling an individual to apprehend communion with God as his greatest good, and of inducing him to "close" with that good. In the "faculty" psychology of the day, man's will is the seat of action, and his heart, or affections, the spur to activity. What the will chooses, the heart longs for, and its longings stir the mind to frame means to the desired end and stimulate the body to execute them. Yet the will chooses what the rational faculty, the understanding, values, and with an intensity proportionate to that valuation. Understanding is thus the avenue to the will and heart, and the senses are the way to all three. Though weakened and corrupt as a result of Adam's fall, these faculties were held to continue to perform their proper functions. Fallen man is no longer able to judge accurately in matters touching his salvation, and his will is so thoroughly twisted by sin that he is quite incapable of willing his salvation; indeed, he is unwilling to be made willing. Though he is at liberty to attend upon the means of grace, and though he is capable of obeying God's commands in a superficial way, he is unable to see in such attendance and obedience anything but a possible escape from God's wrath. He cannot seek God for God's own sake, nor can he see any reason to do so. Regeneration is thus a matter of persuading fallen man to judge differently.[8]

This alteration of judgment, the elders believed, is precisely what the Spirit accomplishes, via the ordained means. In the minister's plain, vigorous words, the Spirit propounds arguments to the understanding and thereby presents motives to the will. In the preaching of the law, he convinces a man of his own sinfulness, of the heat of God's just wrath against him, and of the utter insufficiency of his own righteousness to save him. In the preaching of the gospel, the Spirit presents God's offer of redemption to all who will receive Christ by faith, he reveals Christ to be a savior sufficient to cover sin however great, and he shows Christ yearning for and entreating the poor sinner to come and embrace him. The sinner need only be willing to come. Of his own power, however, the sinner cannot come. He sees all this and knows intellectually that it is true, but he is so wedded to his lusts and so conceited in his own righteousness that, if he cannot have these somehow, he will not have Christ.

When the elect have reached this point, God—according to his pleasure—gives them faith to receive Christ and actively to embrace him. There goes forth with the minister's words a power of the Spirit that overcomes the hindrances in the mind of the hearer. The conception, in effect, is sacramental: the audible, natural word is the vehicle of a hidden, supernatural grace.[9] In and through the preached word the Spirit conveys a new, spiritual light into the understanding, enabling it now to see God and Christ in their true excellency and to value them accordingly. Simultaneously, and by the same means, the Spirit infuses a new, spiritual principle of action into the will, enabling it to follow the judgment of the enlightened understanding and to choose Christ and his benefits as the greatest good. The result is that act of faith by which the soul goes forth to Christ, thereby entering the covenant of grace and partaking of its benefits. Faith in the heart, though its nature is spiritual and though its efficient cause is the Holy Spirit, is nonetheless a human act. Its "instrumental cause" is the word of the minister, and its form is that of a persuasion, which begins with cognition and issues in action.[10]

> We on the one hand [wrote John Norton] against the Enthusiasts affirm not only the power to use, but the duty of using the means; and on the other hand, against the Arminians deny that man before grace can do anything, having the power of a cause (so far forth as comes from them) in order to life; because we are reasonable creatures God proceeds with us in the use of means; because we are dead creatures, in respect of the efficacy of the means, we depend wholly and absolutely upon God.[11]

God does not operate directly upon human souls but normally employs means and instruments belonging to the created order, and he works in a manner appropriate to the distinctive natures of these means and instruments. Grace, the ministers maintained, is received mediately, through a chain of second causes (causes other than God, the First Cause), which forms the "middle term" between God's intent and man's condition. The regenerate sinner is in truth a "new creature," or he could not believe at all. Throughout, however, he remains fully a human being, and his spiritual rebirth is accomplished through created means, including his own distinctively human faculties.[12]

THE ROLE OF JUSTIFYING FAITH

As Protestants, the Massachusetts elders insisted that justification is "by faith alone," but they also held that a person is active in believing. Sinful man is incapable of raising a claim against God, that God should come to him; he can only go himself to God in faith, leaving all his works behind. Yet he must, in some sense, truly "go." In the gospel, Shepard noted, the life that Adam lost is declared to be now laid up in Christ, "to those who believe," and the sinner is informed that they who would have life "must go out of themselves to the Lord for it." A person must "flee to Christ," must "go to Christ," must "put forth his hand" and "take" Christ's righteousness. The figures are consistently active. A person must be able to "take grace and carry it away." He must will to receive it and behave accordingly. That corrupt nature can either so will or so do was not in question; the act of coming to Christ is a gracious act. Nonetheless, it is also a human act. It is, said Shepard, "the motion of the soul between those two extremes of emptiness and death here, to life and fulness there"; it is, Norton observed, the "direct act" of faith receiving Christ's righteousness "or relying on him for pardon, according to the promise."[13]

So understood, faith is what makes "effectual calling" effectual. The Hutchinsonians argued that people are entirely passive in re-generation and that talk of "taking Christ" is "legal" talk. The elders responded that faith is necessarily active and that "to sit still and see nothing, and do nothing, is not faith, but sloth." Neither, the elders argued, is faith "a passive possibility of the soul to receive Christ, though that may prepare for him." They con-sidered this one of Cotton's errors. In this connection Hooker likened faith to the stomach, which "receives not meat, as the dish or vessel doth, but . . . doth receive it and is fastened to it, and hath the sweetness of it, and is made one with it." Faith is properly active with respect to its object. It is, Shepard wrote, "that work of the Spirit whereby a sinner, sensible of his extreme nakedness, empti-ness, and want, being called of God, his whole soul comes out of himself to Christ, for himself." Or, as Bulkeley put it figuratively, "Faith is the hand of the soul, and the putting of it forth is the act by which we receive Christ offered." As such, faith is the necessary condition of entry into the covenant of grace. Though the elect, Shepard noted, are holy and sons of God in the divine intention since eternity, they are not actually justified or in Christ until they actively believe.[14]

Cotton would admit that the habit of faith, infused into the passive soul, is the necessary condition for union with Christ, be-cause it prepares the soul to receive him. However, objecting to the language of causality in relation to the covenant of grace, he pre-ferred not to speak of faith as a condition, at least not in the sense of "antecedent" condition. His colleagues agreed that the habit of faith is freely given while the soul is passive, but they insisted that the *act* of faith is what God requires as the condition of the covenant. Cotton conceived of Christ's entry into the soul as analogous to a form's entry into matter, which must be properly "disposed" before it can entertain the form; the habit of faith is a power disposing the soul to receive Christ, the act of faith (of adherence and dependence) being an expression of Christ's power dwelling in it. His colleagues treated the habit of faith as an infused potency which is perfected in act. Christ is the terminus of the act put forth from the habit, and faith is fully realized only in the soul's going forth to Christ. As part of his obligation under the covenant, God promises to supply the habit of faith. The condition of the covenant "required on our part" is "the acting of that faith received."[15]

At this point Bulkeley entered an important qualification. Men do not, he noted, first offer themselves to God, but God, at his own pleasure begins to stir his own while they are yet dead in sin. "In the making up of the covenant betwixt God and us, God is . . . the first mover, he begins with us before we begin with him." So also in the covenant itself, God first offers himself as a God of mercy and pardon, and it is faith's first work "to carry the soul towards the covenant," accepting God's offer. This, however, is the only work of faith: "Faith brings nothing to God of our own, it offers nothing to stand in exchange for the mercy offered; it receives a gift, but it gives no price. The Lord holds out and offers the free grace of the covenant; faith receives it and makes it our own." Herein, said Bulkeley, lies the meaning of Isa. 56:4, "where we are said to lay hold of the covenant."[16] Accordingly, it may be suggested, the frequent exhortations by New England preachers to seize, lay hold of, and take grace are properly to be read in light of this caution— which for Bulkeley was less a qualification than an affirmation of the gracious pole of the dialectic of nature and grace.

Reflecting on the phenomenon of spiritual rebirth, Puritan divines analyzed it into a logical order, and, on the basis of Rom. 5:1 —"Therefore, since we are justified by faith, we have peace with God"—assigned to faith the role of instrumental cause. In making active faith the condition of the covenant of grace, Bulkeley and Shepard considered it only in its instrumentality. The act neither creates man's justification as an efficient cause nor merits a reward as a good work. It is simply the ordained means by which the elect enter the covenant and receive its benefits. "Fides qua opus," Shepard once reminded Winthrop, is not part of the "matter of our justification."[17] The phrase "we are justified by faith," Norton observed, is a metonymy, "whereby that which belongs to the principal cause, is attributed to the instrumental cause. . . . Faith in the matter of our justification, is the instrument apprehending, and applying that which doth justify." Faith justifies neither for its own worth, nor as an act of ours, but for the worth of and in virtue of the object that it apprehends, namely Christ's obedience; nor is it faith apprehending that justifies, but Christ's obedience apprehended.[18]

Because they regarded active faith as the instrumental cause of justification, the elders distinguished "justifying faith" from "faith of assurance," that is, from the "reflex act of faith, whereby we are fully persuaded, and do believe that we believe." The latter act does not justify, but gives the believer a sense of peace. On this point they took issue with Cotton, who argued that faith is "justifying" in a declarative sense, in that by it a person apprehends the prior fact of his justification. Shepard responded that if this be true, then "a Christian is not justified by faith (which was Paul's phrase), but rather . . . [is] faithed by his justification." The elders agreed that one can speak of justification as existing before belief, inasmuch as it is purposed and determined in the divine mind and will and is already obtained by Christ's obedience. The point in dispute, however, was whether a particular individual "may be truly said to be actually just in the sight of God" before actually believing. The elders thought not, and argued that to make faith follow justification was to alter the order of redemption as given in Rom. 8:30, "Those whom he predestined he also called, and those whom he called he also justified."[19]

Bulkeley and Shepard also took issue with Cotton's inclusion of faith among the graces of sanctification, on the ground that faith, as the condition of the covenant, precedes sanctification as a benefit of the covenant. Cotton suggested that faith is "justifying" because it is wrought in a justified person. To which Shepard responded, "if that be the reason of the phrase, we may affirm our justification to be as well by love, and sanctification, and holy obedience as by faith, because these are wrought in a justified person."[20] Cotton's colleagues agreed that faith springs from a gracious habit infused,

as do works of sanctification, but they held that faith precedes justification in the order of redemption and so precedes sanctification,
strictly taken, also. Faith's distinctiveness, they maintained, springs
from its form as an act of adherence and dependence on Christ's
righteousness for justification, and from its place as the antecedent
condition of the covenant of grace. In contrast to Cotton, they
argued that a person is not first taken into union with Christ sec-
retly, and then informed of the fact, and that he is justified in consequence. Rather, a person is first informed that justification is to
be had only in virtue of Christ's righteousness, according to the
offer of the gospel, and seeing this to be the case, he willingly goes
forth in faith to receive it. "It is true," Shepard wrote, "God justifies the ungodly; but how? not immediately without faith, but
mediately by faith."[21]

THE NATURE OF SANCTIFICATION

The *locus* "of sanctification" in formal Puritan divinity is the
technical theological counterpart of the characteristic Puritan concern for spiritual rebirth and its effect in Christian life. Puritans
took seriously the affirmation that, in being translated to a state of
grace, a person is made a "new creature." A man under sin, wrote
Hooker, is so intimately wed to sin, it is so much a part of him, that
to separate him from it is to rend, almost, his very being as a person.
That someone should willingly obey God as his governor and delight in God's commands requires thorough renovation, if not re-
creation, of the person. Sanctification is part of this renovation. "By
it," Shepard wrote, "a man is morally made a new man—another
man. 'All things are made new': he has new thoughts, new opinions
of all things, new desires, new prayers and praises, new dispositions."
Justification is a legal transaction "in the court of heaven," in which
God pronounces the sinner to be righteous and free from condemnation. Sanctification, however, transforms the man himself, in-
wardly in his faculties and then outwardly in his behavior. The
pattern of this transformation is the image of God as it is in Christ
and once was in Adam, comprising those graces of wisdom and holiness that enable a person to know and judge of things as God does
and "to love and will holiness and the means thereto as God does."

Though this renewal is perfected only in heaven, in this life a Christian "at least has a holy disposition and inclination (the habits of holiness) so to do."[22]

Shepard and his colleagues maintained that sanctification consists primarily in habits infused, in powers enabling, and in a gracious disposition inclining to holy acts, rather than in acts *qua* acts. It corresponds minutely to its archetype in Christ, from whom it is derived, yet it belongs to the created order. It is wrought by the Spirit through hearing of the word through faith, yet it subsists in the person of the believer. Sanctification possesses objectivity. It is a presence and a power that can be discerned, and there are standards by which it may be judged. On all these points, the elders of the Bay found themselves in controversy with Cotton and the Hutchinsonians. Central to the dispute was the question of the location of the substance of sanctification—whether in the soul of the believer or in the exalted Christ—and the manner of its presence in the believer—whether inherently, or accidentally and immediately from Christ. The elders held the former. Christ is in believers, Shepard insisted, by the Spirit and in created graces. Unless Christ is personally present in believers, or acts them by his direct influence from on high, there is no other possible interpretation of biblical expressions of Christ's presence in his own.

The elders agreed with Cotton that the exalted Christ dwells in believers by his Spirit. They maintained, however, that Christ's Spirit is not in believers by immediate operations causing them to act, but mediately, by created graces infused into the soul, which empower the person himself to act. "The Spirit," wrote Norton, "is in the believer energetically, or operatively, by its effects." We are commanded, Shepard observed, to pray for grace, as David did: " 'Create in me a clean heart.' Now if it be a thing created in me, it is not the Spirit only in me, for that cannot be created."[23] If Christ acts upon the believer only by the immediate operation of the Spirit, Shepard declared:

> then there is seeing in a Christian without an eye, and hearing without an ear, and knowing Christ without an understanding, and loving without love, and living without life, and feeding without a mouth; and then, when these actings are over, a Christian is like another man; there is no law remains written on his heart, and so Christ should enter into his saints, like Satan into the ser-

pent, who only acts the serpent, and when that is done, he remains a serpent again. Know it, the Lord Jesus his greatest work is not only to change the acts, but to change the heart; not only to put new actions, but a new nature into men.

Gracious activity in believers springs from an inner abiding principle of life "received in us" and not from external influences whose effect is only temporary. "All strength is from Christ," but mediately, in and through created habits of grace, imparting new power to, and perfecting, human faculties.[24]

The Hutchinsonians agreed that all strength is from Christ and drew the corollary that the believer can do nothing until Christ moves him. The elders replied that Christ is indeed the source of a Christian's power, but the Christian acts nonetheless from a power within himself. Graces of sanctification depend for being and activity upon continued communion with Christ; a Christian must continually "go to Christ" for renewed strength, humbly on account of his faulty performance of duties, and thankfully that he has been able to perform them at all. This dependence, however, does not mean that a Christian is powerless in himself or must refrain from exercising such power as he has. "Adam had a law of divinity, whereby he, being a cause of counsel, was enabled by God to carry himself towards his end"; and in that measure in which Adam's image is renewed in them, believers are enabled to carry themselves toward their own proper end. If there really are no distinctive graces in saints, Shepard agreed, then a man may well say, I must do nothing and see nothing, but look to Christ for all, whether to believe or to love. This conclusion, however, Shepard would by no means allow.[25]

THE EVIDENCE OF JUSTIFICATION

To the Massachusetts elders, the ways of God in regeneration were not mysterious but plain and perceptible. The sinner does not encounter Christ in his heart directly, in a pure intuition or a spiritual rapture, but in the objective, audible, visible "means." Neither does Christ, in his free and gracious omnipotence, disregard or overpower man's created nature; rather, a person enters the covenant of grace by an act of consent and receives from Christ power

to act obediently according to the moral law. Because of this exchange, and because of the orderliness of God's activity, the regenerate are able to discern the presence of saving grace in themselves
without waiting for direct testimony from on high. In the New
England controversy, the concerns treated up to this point were
brought together in the question about evidencing justification by
sanctification.

The Place of Conditional Promises

Shepard and his colleagues located the biblical charter for
their position in the "conditional promises" of the New Testament.
Both sides in the controversy agreed that the covenant of grace is
dispensed in absolute promises founded exclusively on the divine
good pleasure (having the form, "For mine own sake will I do thus
and thus to you"). However, the ministers argued, such promises
in themselves are only general; they show the cause of salvation but
do not describe the particular persons to whom salvation is promised. This office belongs to conditional promises (of the form, "I
will do it to them that do believe"), which are included in scripture
as the most "direct, evident, and certain" way to try one's interest
in the covenant.[26] How is a person to apply to himself the blessings
of the promise when he is uncertain that the covenant belongs to
him, and how is he to be assured that his faith of adherence and
dependence is sound? Shepard answered:

> Let him so sue and seek for the good of the absolute promise, until,
> by reflecting upon his own acts, herein he perceive himself adorned
> and dignified with the qualification of some conditional promise;
> and then if he can find the condition or qualification within him-
> self, then . . . he may conclude that the conditional promise belongs
> to him; and if one promise, then all God's promises; and therefore
> that absolute promises are his own, because at least one conditional
> promise is.[27]

Neither Shepard nor Bulkeley meant that the "qualification" in
this instance merits the promised blessedness, or is the efficient
cause of it, or gives a right to a gracious reward. Life is indeed
promised to works, Bulkeley noted, but such promises "are not
causal, but declarative, making manifest who be those true believers
to whom the life promised in the covenant does belong." Absolute

and conditional promises both flow from God's same gracious intent, and in each case the condition itself is wrought by God, being included under God's covenant obligation. Both sorts of promises are given in the gospel, which is by definition "a doctrine of free grace"; and the nature of the conditions presupposes that a person is already in the covenant by faith.[28]

In the elders' view, conditional promises did not apply to gracious acts simply as acts, but to such acts reflected upon by enlightened consciences, in the knowledge that sanctifying graces inhere in believers and manifest themselves in distinctive ways. Though the conditions are given by Christ, the promises themselves are made to believers as individuals, to whom "all God's promises are and will be yea and amen." Cotton, who was unable or unwilling to distinguish between the declarative and the causal functions of works, held that conditional promises are made exclusively to Christ and fulfilled only in him, and that such promises in scripture are merely invitations to "go to Christ" to receive the condition indicated. The elders agreed that the promises of the covenant are made to Christ on behalf of the elect, but they insisted that there was nothing to prevent such promises from being made to particular persons, also. For the declarative function of gracious conditions they appealed to Christ himself in the Sermon on the Mount and in the Fourth Gospel, and to Peter and Paul, none of whom, they suggested, could be dismissed as "legal preachers." The two sorts of promises, they argued further, are specifically suited to the varying situation of Christians. Absolute promises, Bulkeley observed, give comfort in time of trials, scruples, and doubts; conditional promises stir up, in time of security and complacency, to search for the qualifications expressed. To the Hutchinsonians he suggested that "though the comfort tasted [in the absolute] be more sweet and delightful while it is felt, yet the assurance which we have by the trial of our graces [by the conditional], is the more constant and durable."[29]

Evidence from Sanctification

The covenant of grace, as the elders conceived it, contains a double promise, corresponding to the double plight of fallen man, who is both guilty and subject to punishment and also injured in his own nature. In justification, God pardons man's iniquity; in sanctification, by infusion of gracious habits, he restores fallen nature. Sanctification, as the second benefit of the covenant, flows from union with Christ, and in it God "writes his law in our hearts." The result is a disposition willingly to obey God's command in all things. By introspection the saints may know their own true motives, and so, by reflection on their behavior in light of the rule of scripture, they may perceive the presence of grace in themselves. In virtue of the covenant's double promise they may conclude from works of sanctification to the blessedness of their estates. Such a conclusion, the elders maintained, is not a "going on in" or a "going aside to" a covenant of works, but merely the proving of one benefit of the covenant of grace by another benefit of the same covenant.[30]

Crucial to the elders' position was the assertion that works of sanctification are characteristic of the regenerate and are empirically discernible. The true believer, Shepard declared, may know the blessedness of his estate "by the peculiarness of a work within him." The elect are distinguished by certain kinds of acts that are the effects of the Spirit's work; and through these acts, judged according to the revealed word, the Spirit's work can be known, even as God's power, wisdom, and goodness are known by their effects in creation. Though hypocrites may go far to counterfeit saintliness, there is an essential difference between them and saints, which the latter may perceive in themselves by a threefold "light," namely of scripture, of the Spirit interpreting scripture, and "of experience and sense. . . . For saints," Shepard wrote, "have an experimental knowledge of the work of grace, by virtue of which they come to know it as certainly . . . as by feeling heat, we know fire is hot; by tasting honey, we know it is sweet."[31] Cotton agreed about the first two "lights" taken together, but he denied that regenerating grace could be known empirically by its effects. For Shepard and Bulkeley, however, this proposition was fundamental.

Sanctification, they maintained, is positive evidence at the present moment of those whom God has redeemed.[32] Bulkeley noted that the work of election remains hidden until the Son lays down his life, revealing the Father's intent to save some; who they are remains unknown until the Spirit comes and sanctifies them. In this way the very individuals whom God intends to save are "singled out and marked." Some men, Shepard observed, would make the free offer of grace to sinners, with no work of grace in them, the ground of faith and assurance, and so declare that to look to works of grace is to make works the ground of faith or the cause of assurance. He replied that the free offer of grace cannot by itself be such a ground, for it indicates only that a sinner may be beloved; nor is the receiving of this offer by faith entirely sufficient, for it only shows why a person is beloved. Rather, "the work of sanctification (which is the fruit of our receiving this offer) is the first evidence showing that he is beloved." All three testimonies, he noted, are mutually related; all three are valid and to be sought for; and the order in which they are experienced is not crucial.[33] Sanctification, however, objectively identifies the elect, revealing that they are actually redeemed.

It was in this sense of an objective identifying mark that the elders regarded sanctification as the "seal of the Spirit." The Hutchinsonians construed this "seal" as the immediate witness of the Spirit, to the exclusion of "any thing in our selves, whether by faith or by any other grace." Yet if this construction be correct, Shepard declared, then the Spirit witnesses an untruth; for, according to the order of redemption ordained by God, a person is first a believer, and then justified, called, and sanctified in fact, before the Spirit witnesses it. The question was not whether the Spirit clears a person's estate, "but whether by seeking nothing, or showing something."[34]

To Cotton's dismay, the elders argued that sanctification could be taken as a first evidence of justification, and often must be so taken, because it is most readily manifest. Justification, Bulkeley noted, is the divine sentence of pardon from sin and is pronounced in both the court of heaven and the court of conscience. "By the first we are justified indeed from personal guilt, by the second we feel ourselves justified by the removal of conscience guilt." The former is instantaneous, complete, unchangeable, and transcendent. The latter may not be felt for some time and is not constant when it is felt. In any case, justification pertains only to a person's relationship to God. Sanctification, however, is a positive change in a person himself; it is immanent; and by its very nature it is more readily perceived. "Our justification is an act of God without us, God not imputing to us our iniquities; but our sanctification is an inward work wrought in a man's own bowels, of which he has (and can not but have) a sensible feeling in himself." How shall we know with certainty that "we have passed from death to life"? The Spirit in the word is plain: "Because we love the brethren"—from 1 John 3:14, the *locus classicus* for the doctrine.[35]

True Sanctification and the Visibility of Saints

In Cotton's estimation this urging of sanctification as evidence of justification merely begged the further question how sanctification could be known to be true; and he argued that sanctification may be an evidence only if the Spirit has validated it by previously revealing justification, and then it may be only a supporting evidence. His colleagues agreed that works of sanctification, as works, are deceptive. Bulkeley acknowledged "a kind of outward sanctification (improperly so called)," an external reformation to which a person may attain under constraint of the law but which is qualitatively different from true sanctification. "For though this reformation does and may come from some inward work of the Spirit of God upon the spirit and soul of man, as namely to convince and terrify the conscience, to stir the affections, and to awe the will also, so that a man dares not commit the things he would, yet the mind and will is still the same as it was before."[36] For the elders the decisive element in sanctification was the new "frame and disposition of the heart" underlying specific holy acts. *That* a person obeyed the commandments meant little; *how* and *why* he obeyed them were the vital points. Right, sincere, sound sanctification, Bulkeley declared, involves the entire man, body and soul, substance and faculties. It frames the heart to close with the whole will of God and to refuse comfort from anything apart from God. It makes the sanctified wary of sin and desirous of living wholly for God. True sanctification disposes a person to seek the society of those who are truly holy and to aspire after communion with God himself; and it makes him keenly aware of his own want of grace and of his dependence on Christ for strength.[37] Those who have passed from death to life may know it, if not intuitively then by reflective examination of their behavior. The truly sanctified render universal obedience to God, simply because they delight to do so. The end of their obedience is God's glory, and its source is the power of grace. Though outwardly a man may deceive the keenest observer, these are the touchstones by which he may know whether he is only "a close hypocrite."

To be in covenant with God, Bulkeley continued, is to be under the government of God's law as the rule of new obedience incumbent on Christians. God, on his part, undertakes to enable his own to obey; "he frames [them] . . . into a willing and voluntary subjection unto him." If, therefore, a person can be moved to good actions only by constraint, it is a sign that he is not subject to God's gracious government. Moreover, if we are governed by God, "we must yield him universal obedience in all things"; God's government cannot coexist with "some darling lust" of man's. "If thou hast thy exceptions, and reservations, and wilt not yield universal obedience, then art thou an alien from God and his covenant." True sanctification "forms the heart" to embrace the whole will of God. The truly sanctified labor willingly in duties of holiness towards God and in duties of love and righteousness towards men; the two realms are inseparable, and there can be no distinction between "saints" and "others" in duties owed.[38] In a passage on the relationship of holiness and duties, Bulkeley indicated what he meant by "universal obedience":

> Holiness of disposition, will as naturally put a Christian upon duties of holiness, prayer, and meditation, and other spiritual exercises, as a sinful disposition doth put us upon acts that are sinful. . . . Holiness planted in the heart will cause holiness to shine forth in our actions of common life, so that though the things we deal in be but outward and civil; yet our manner of dealing in them shall be spiritual and holy. . . . Whom God has sanctified, they do sanctify to themselves the common and ordinary actions of this life, by using them not in an ordinary profane manner, but holily. . . . If we eat, holiness causes us to eat before God, and to eat for God. . . . If we exercise ourselves in our calling, holiness directs a Christian to refer it to the glory of God.[39]

He meant, in effect, that comprehensive "art of living to God" which Ames treated, under the heading of "observance," as the substance of a blessed estate in this life.

In a similar vein Shepard declared that true sanctification is discerned not only in willing acceptance of the whole moral law as the rule of life, but also in the end for which the law is accepted. Indeed, the change wrought in sanctification may properly be defined as "the change of a man's utmost end."[40] As the pollution of fallen man, and of all his civil, moral, and religious actions, consists in self-seeking and in making himself his chief end, so sanctification "consists chiefly and . . . appears in making the Lord our utmost end of all we do." Hypocrites and saints are infallibly distinguished by the ends they serve. Hypocrites perform duties ultimately to ease their own consciences and to escape the wrath of the law, and thus please themselves by seeking to please God. When Christ was on earth, "some did receive [him] to be king, but it was that he might be their cook; he provided loaves for them; so here." The regenerate, in contrast, love Christ "for himself, whereby the Lord only is exalted." God, said Bulkeley, causes his own to seek the same ends that he in governing his creation propounds to himself, so that "God's ends and our ends meet in one, which is the glorifying of his Name." If a person closes with the whole law as his happiness and chief end because it is God's will and because God is glorified in such obedience, then that person is "a man after God's own heart," and his obedience is a pledge of God's grace towards him.[41] Cotton found the difference between saints and hypocrites too tenuous to be practically useful. To Shepard and Bulkeley the difference was readily detectable by the individual concerned.

The Power of Godliness

True works of sanctification, the elders argued, are distinguished not only by their ends but fundamentally by the power from which they are wrought. A man's lamp burns in profession, prayers, and moral reformation, but what, Shepard asked, feeds the flame? The case, he said, is similar to that of Christ's own mighty acts. Others besides Christ did miracles. How is it proved that he is Christ?

> It is answered, in all his miraculous works we are to consider not only *quid fecit*, i.e., what he did, but *qua virtute fecit*, from what power he did. The apostles and others did miracles, but it was *aliena virtute*: Christ did them, but it was *propria virtute*. So many an unsound heart, he may do greater works than saints, and his lamp burn brighter. Therefore, in this case, we are not to look so much to what is done, as from what power and principle it is done; for therein the best hypocrite ever fails.[42]

Fallen men, Shepard noted, naturally seek to have a righteousness of their own to carry before God; they characteristically "glory in" and "go in the strength of" their own powers and performances and comfort themselves that they "do as much as they can." They may be stimulated by outward example, by public applause, by the prospect of material blessings, by the desires of natural conscience, by fear of death and hell. They may strive by the power of created nature, of immediate and transitory actings of the Spirit, and of gifts of common graces. In all these motives, however, there is no abiding gracious "spring," no new, inherent power of life. Believers, in contrast, are actuated by the life of Christ as an inward principle. They share in this life mediately by faith, and it subsists in them by the Spirit's power working mediately in created graces; and by it believers are enabled to live unto God in all things. If a person has made a good profession, therefore, and has "a name to live in the judgment of all the church," still he must search his heart "and see from what principle it proceeds; for, if this be wanting all is nothing. As he that had beer given him, when milk and wine and sugar were put into it to mend it, said, the wine is good, and the milk is good, but the beer is bad; so profession, affection is good, but the heart, the man, is bad."[43] In judging the soundness of works of sanctification, the elders maintained, the crucial question is "from what power" do they spring; and they believed that human conscience, which is privy to the springs as well as the ends of a person's actions, is competent to answer truthfully.

THE OBJECTIVITY OF REGENERATING GRACE

The Hutchinsonians complained that the elders of the Bay Colony subverted the gratuity of the covenant of grace by urging people to take comfort from sight of gracious works in themselves. The elders rejoined that the Hutchinsonians, by limiting the ground of assurance to the immediate witness of the Spirit, left would-be saints dangerously at the mercy of feelings, fancies, and excited states of the natural affections and ignored altogether the objective means to assurance ordained by God and plainly declared in scripture. Natural affections, it was recalled, may readily be excited by such natural means as eating and drinking; people may

be stimulated by the novelty of the gospel or a "thundering
preacher" without any increase in grace. Ames was supposed to
have remarked, Shepard noted approvingly, that "Arminian universal grace ... may be the effect of a good dinner sometimes." A
man may have sudden pangs of feeling and flashes of affection for
Christ and still not be sound in the bent and disposition of his whole
soul. A carnal heart may turn old affections to a new object, even
as "the same eye may see the sun and a dunghill, and the eye [be]
not changed." If faith of assurance depends on feelings of "such and
such graces and heavenly impressions of God's Spirit," and "assurances of favor" in oneself, then assurance is no more constant than
such feelings are.[44]

The elders consented with Cotton that the Spirit's witness enables a person to know whether his justification is sure and his
sanctification sound. At issue was the manner of the Spirit's witnessing. In the case of justification, the ministers insisted, it is by
the call of Christ in the biblical word. Subjective feelings inevitably
are prey to the vagaries, doubts, fears, and presumptions of the
human spirit; but God's call, command, and invitation to come to
Christ is clear, sure, unchanging, and objective as the biblical text
is objective. "If God should speak from heaven to you to come to
his Son, it is not so sure a ground as the call of God from out of
the oracle of his word." The same is true of sanctification. To ascertain whether it be true, "you need not go to heaven for it: 'the
word is nigh thee.' Those that love Christ: who are those? 'Those
that keep his commandments.'" The Spirit alone seals the elect,
but he also "commands the elect not to sit idle and dream of the
Spirit" but with all diligence to make their election sure. Dream
they may, but at the risk of confounding assurance and fancy.[45]
"Would we then know," Bulkeley asked,

> whether we be of the number of those that are saved by the blood
> of Christ? we need not for this ascend up into heaven, to search
> the book of God's election, nor need we go down into the lower
> parts of the earth, for any there to tell us that we are delivered
> thence; but go down in to our own hearts, and if we find this work
> of sanctification there wrought, then what Moses said of Israel,
> "Blessed art thou O Israel, a people saved by the Lord," the same
> may be truly said of us; Our salvation is begun, we have the seal

of it, the earnest, the first fruits, which shall at length bring the full possession of the whole harvest.[46]

At the time of the Antinomian Controversy, John Cotton's theological posture was governed by a conception of the order of regeneration in which union with Christ was the primary, overruling moment. Transition from apostasy to grace begins with, and is effected in, the operation of the Spirit by which the passive sinner is brought into union; and personal apprehension of union, after the fact, is contingent on the same operation. Such apprehension is equivalent to conscious faith and arises solely on the Spirit's testimony. Creaturely agency and the mediation of second causes, in accomplishing and evidencing regeneration, are wholly subordinate if not irrelevant. Cotton was hostile to any suggestion that human agency might fulfill a condition or perform an obedience that might be related causally, in any sense, to justification. Unlike his New England brethren, he was suspicious even of the language of law, command, and condition in connection with regeneration. He treated the covenant of grace as, by definition, excluding creaturely works, not only of merit but also of sincere obedience. Any reference to works implied for him recurrence to the first covenant with Adam.

The same principle, Cotton thought, governs human activity in the salvific transaction. Justifying faith can only be the infused capacity passively to receive Christ, and not an active consent to the terms of justification. Cotton tended to disregard entirely human capacity as a rational agent, and to that extent he abandoned the conditionality of the covenant of grace, even while continuing to talk in covenantal terms.[47] Similarly, he felt that sanctifying grace could only be the work of the exalted Christ, discernible by the Spirit's direct light alone. Though Cotton sought to maintain an absolute distinction between saints and hypocrites, his treatment of sanctification rendered this difference extremely elusive and implied that the objective marks of godliness given in scripture are to no real purpose. Throughout the debate, Cotton tended to subordinate both the capacity and the integrity of human creatures to the increated, unconditioned operation of the members of the Trinity.

For Bulkeley and Shepard, on the other hand, the order of redemption necessarily included created instrumentalities, operating according to their distinctive natures toward the ends eternally intended by God, including the regeneration of particular persons. In this order, man's natural faculties of intellection and volition participate, and sinners are graciously reborn in empirically ascertainable ways. The covenant of grace is made with individuals, who enter into it knowingly and willingly in the act of faith and who are renewed in their own natures according to the terms of the covenant. Sanctification inheres in the regenerate, and, under the double promise of the covenant—to pardon and to renew—the soul may derive assurance of its justification from the sincerity of its religious and ethical observance. "Sincerity" is the crucial term in the syllogism. However, all the relevant data for trying one's estate fall within the human capacity for perception and reflection; and conscience, instructed by the biblical word, is competent to draw appropriate conclusions. To this extent, within the context of the covenant, certainty of salvation is objectively possible.

This possibility, for Bulkeley and Shepard, was ultimately founded on confidence in the abiding sufficiency of God's power to accomplish what he intends, in the constancy of God's will to complete what he has begun, and in God's willingness to channel his power through known means appropriate to the objects of it. The order of redemption, they insisted, in both the effecting and the discerning of an individual's rebirth, is reliably regular and is accommodated to the nature of reasonable creatures. There is thus in it a genuine, gracious—and therefore legitimate—commerce between man and God. The medium of this divine-human commerce, as noted above, these New England elders understood to be the covenant of grace. Their conception of this covenant presupposed that regeneration in the time of the gospel is accomplished in accordance with the moral order established by God in the covenant of works at the beginning of the world, and that between covenant of works and covenant of grace there is necessarily a continuity of both form and substance. This continuity is the subject of the next two chapters.

CHAPTER 5

The Doctrine of the Two Covenants: I

The "federal" or "covenant" theology, which sought to comprehend God's salvific relationship to mankind in covenantal terms, took shape among Reformed orthodox divines in the later sixteenth century, and became widespread in the seventeenth, though it was employed with much variety and not at all universally.[1] Among Puritans it was especially popular, and, in the formulation of William Ames (1576–1633), it belongs to the immediate intellectual context of the New England Antinomian Controversy. In this chapter and the next we shall consider the shape of Puritan covenant theology, examining in particular the relationship between the two covenants of works and grace and, in the latter, the relationship between divine grace and human agency.

THE EMERGENCE OF FEDERAL THEOLOGY

The critical place in the history of Reformed federal theology belongs apparently to Zacharias Ursinus (1534–ca. 1583), professor of theology at Heidelberg and principal author of the Heidelberg Catechism. Zwingli's successor at Zürich, Heinrich Bullinger, and John Calvin had both employed the covenant-motif in order to establish the unity of the biblical testaments and the identity of the faith of sixteenth-century Christians with that of the Hebrew patriarchs. Law and gospel, Old and New Testaments, they held, embodied different expressions or dispensations of God's single salvific covenant with Abraham.[2] Ursinus took a more speculative step and distinguished a covenant with mankind before the fall, contained in the natural law engraven on man's heart at creation. Following Melanchthon, he identified this natural law with the divine law revealed in the decalogue, thereby establishing an essential connection between the covenants before and after the fall. This formulation made the distinction between "old" and "new" covenants no longer simply equivalent, as it was for Bullinger and Calvin, to that between old and new biblical testaments, or to that between the "legal" and "evangelical" character of the Mosaic and Christian dispensations.[3]

In his *Summa Theologiae,* a catechism composed prior to the Heidelberg, Ursinus treated the difference between law and gospel in terms of the respective covenants that are the content of each. "The law," he wrote, "comprises *foedus naturale,* made by God with man in creation." It is known to man by nature and requires perfect obedience to God according to the law, promising eternal life to those who perform it and threatening eternal punishment on those who do not. "The gospel comprises *foedus gratiae,* that is, not at all known to exist by nature." It reveals that the righteousness required by the law is fulfilled in Christ and promises eternal life freely to those who believe in him. The covenant of grace is a mutual agreement, made possible by Christ's intercession, in which God pledges to be a gracious father and to give eternal life, and men in turn promise to accept these blessings by faith and to glorify God forever. The covenant of grace is one from the first promise in Paradise (Gen. 3:15) to the end of the world, differing only in certain "circumstances and mutable signs," in view of which it is called "old" or "new."[4]

According to Ursinus, the ground of blessedness in both *foedus naturale* and *foedus gratiae* is obedience to the divine law. Man is created in the image of God, which consists in "true knowledge of God and of the divine will, and in the inclination and zeal of the whole man toward living according to this alone"; and man is created for the purpose of "worshipping God with his entire life in eternal blessedness," which worship consists in "obedience to God according to his law" for the principal end of honoring him. The sum of this obedience is given in the commandment to love God with one's entire mind, soul, and strength, and one's neighbor as oneself. Since Adam's fall and consequent loss of the divine image, no man is, or ever shall be, able to perform this obedience.[5] It was for precisely such obedience, however, that God covenanted with man in creation, and God's immutable justice requires satisfaction for man's failure, before any reconciliation is possible. Satisfaction, accordingly, must be performed by a mediator who is capable of it and whose proper office is precisely "to restore the covenant between God and men, who have fallen away from God." Christ's mediation, therefore, is the indispensable foundation of the covenant of grace, inasmuch as "God, who is unchangeably righteous and truthful, wishes to receive us into the covenant of grace in such a way that he nonetheless does not act contrary to the covenant entered in creation; that is, in such a way that he neither regards us as righteous, nor grants us life eternal, except his own law be entirely satisfied, either by us ourselves, or, when this is impossible, by another in our behalf." Justification of individuals is solely by faith in Christ and concretely by gracious imputation to believers of Christ's righteousness and satisfaction.[6]

In his catechism Ursinus recurred to the covenant-motif throughout the treatment of the administration of grace after the fall. Though he did not employ the concept to any extent in his published writings thereafter, and does not seem to have mentioned the *foedus naturale* again, the substance of the broader conception remains evident in his work.[7] The *Summa*, moreover, contains the essential elements of the later federal theology: the covenant of grace, understood as *mutua pactio*, in which man is obligated to faith and obedience, and as *correlativum mediatoris*, is regarded as encompassing the salvific restoration of mankind required by Adam's lapse under the initial covenant at creation. The terms of salvation, understood as universal obedience to the divine law, are the same under both covenants, with the difference that since the fall the law requires satisfaction as well as obedience.

A similar conception of the covenants, set in the context of the divine decree, appears in a little work from 1592 by Franz Junius, Ursinus's younger colleague at Heidelberg. Junius's formulation exhibits the parallelism characteristic of Reformed federal theology between *foedus operum* and *foedus gratiae*, as they came to be called. Both covenants stem from the same divine decision to beatify men, both are mutual agreements, both involve a condition on man's part that is fulfilled in virtue of a gracious capacity, both are accommodated to man's created nature as affected by his estate before and after the fall, and the divine moral law is integral to both.[8]

On the Continent, Reformed federal theology attained its basic form, until the contribution of Coccejus, among theologians who either had reached or were entering upon professional maturity during approximately the decade before 1600.[9] About the same time it appeared among English theologians, notably in the works of Thomas Cartwright (1535–1603), Dudley Fenner (1558?–1587), and Robert Rollock (1555?–1599). Rollock, professor of divinity at Edinburgh, published a treatise on it in 1592, in which the covenant-motif, defined in essentially Ursinian terms, provides a comprehensive framework for considering the order and manner in which salvation is accomplished.[10] Rollock's contemporary, the prolific and influential Cambridge theologian William Perkins, also made use of the covenant-motif, which he introduced in the context of God's decision to glorify himself through the manifestation of justice and mercy in the reprobation and redemption of certain men. Predestination, creation, fall, incarnation, and covenant are all means toward this end—a conception echoed in later Puritan references to the covenant as the principal "means" between God's decree and its concrete fulfillment. In treating the covenants, Perkins agreed essentially with Junius and Rollock about the terms of the covenant of grace (faith and obedience) and its foundation (Christ's active and passive obedience), and also about the terms of the covenant of works (obedience to the moral law) and its foundation (the integrity of the image of God in Adam).[11]

In the work of Perkins's friend and independent pupil, William Ames, the covenant-motif appears in its full and characteristic Puritan form. God's relationship to mankind is represented as being specifically covenantal, as peculiarly suited to man's nature as a reasonable creature; the covenant appears as the chief "means" by which reasonable creatures are directed toward the end God has ordained for them; and the specific "means of grace" through which regeneration of individuals is accomplished are held to operate within the context of the covenant. In addition, the Perkinsian ordering of theology around the execution of the divine decree is overshadowed by concern for the divine sufficiency and efficiency in bringing the whole creation to its ordained end and, especially, in bringing man to that felicity toward which he naturally tends.[12]

Ames introduced the covenant in the context of God's "providence," that is, of "that efficiency, whereby he provides for his creatures now made, in all things, according to the counsel of his own will," and, more narrowly, in the context of God's "special government" of intelligent creatures. Inasmuch as such creatures are in some respect immortal, and being made after the image of God "have an inward principle of their own actions proceeding from counsel," God directs them toward an eternal estate of happiness or unhappiness in a manner agreeable to their nature. This special government or direction is "in a moral way" and consists in "teaching and in fulfilling" according to what was previously "taught," that is, according to the revealed will of God, which is the rule of moral life for reasonable creatures. From this peculiar mode of governing such creatures "arises that covenant, which is between God and them" and which is a "sort of transaction of God with the creature, whereby God commands, promises, threatens, fulfills, and the creature binds itself in obedience to God thus demanding." This covenant, identified by Ames as the covenant of works, is not between equals but between master and slave, as it were, and is called accordingly the covenant "of God" and not "of man"—though it is nonetheless a mutual agreement. In virtue of the covenant the moral works of the creature are related either to final happineses as reward or to unhappiness as punishment; and from it conscience acquires the power and standard by which to judge of the creature's subjection to God.[13]

The terms of the original covenant, Ames maintained, are given in the moral law, which is summarized in the decalogue and "written in the heart by way of a habit." The covenant's foundation is the natural ability of man as created, and its condition is "perfect obedience of works . . . to be performed by man of his own strength," prior to the conferring of any reward. Because human cognition begins with sense perception, outward "symbols and sacraments" are added to the purely "spiritual" law, to illustrate and confirm it, as in the case of the two trees in the Garden, in relation to the promise of continued life and the threat of bodily death, respectively. Accordingly, "the law or covenant of God with man in creation was: 'Do this, and you will live; if you do it not, you will die the death.' "[14]

God's special government of reasonable creatures includes not only moral direction but also the ordering of events toward the fulfillment of what is directed, and in this respect it encompasses man's apostasy and restoration. The latter comprises Christ's work of redemption and its application to men. As mediator between God and men and as the surety for the elect—as Adam was the common head of mankind—Christ became subject to all the laws of God, performing that obedience required of man "by the law of creation" and suffering punishment for the breach thereof.[15]

The covenant of grace Ames introduced under the rubric of the "application of redemption" to particular individuals, which is now accomplished in a "new covenant, . . . whereby God with greatest firmness performed that, which was contained in a covenant formerly made and broken." This new covenant is for the reconciliation of enemies (the old being between friends, as it were), and God alone covenants, man being utterly dead in sin and unable to enter into relationship with him. In extent the new covenant is limited to the elect, and its foundation is Christ alone. It promises not only life but also righteousness and, most significantly, all the *means* of restoring to life. It not only shows what righteousness is, but actually bestows it, and with it assurance of salvation. The new covenant requires no antecedent condition properly so-called, "but only following or coming between, and that to be communicated by grace, that it might be a means to perfect the same grace: which is the proper nature of faith." The covenant of grace is one in substance from its inception with Adam in the Garden, though differing in the clarity of its subsequent administration. From consideration of the covenant of grace, Ames turned to predestination, as the reason for the covenant's limited extent and on the ground that the decree of election is evident only in the actual regeneration of particular human beings.[16]

By about 1630, Puritan theology had accepted as a commonplace the notion that the basic means of bestowing eternal rewards upon men is God's covenant, established in creation and fulfilled in the application to the elect, through the covenant of grace, of Christ's redemption. Under this dialectic of covenants might be ordered all the theological system respecting man's fall and redemption, the calling and conversation of the saints, and the constitution of the church, and by it a substantial amount of biblical material could be expounded. The conception was dogmatized, in 1646, in the Westminster Confession.[17]

THE IMMUTABILITY OF THE COVENANT OF WORKS

In Reformed covenant theology the covenant of grace, while differing in important respects from the covenant of works, was understood to be nonetheless an extension of it. Though the two covenants in a sense balance each other and serve as contrasting foci for organization of theological material, the covenant of works remains primary, as the paradigm of God's salvific relationship with mankind. In form and substance, the two covenants are largely continuous, and the second is related to the first as means to end. This understanding of the relationship between the two covenants emerges from examination of the theological *loci* that treat of God as he is in himself and as he is related to creatures, and also of those that treat of the moral law and the mediatorship of Christ.

The Constancy of God's "Ordinate Power"

God's essence absolutely considered, John Norton wrote, is "that one pure and mere act, by which God is God." Men necessarily apprehend God in many acts and think of him as having multiple attributes, but these distinctions are merely apparent. The attributes are in truth one and the same divine perfection, and the acts one and the same divine act. In himself, as perfect and necessary being, "God is pure and simple act, without all composition." From the oneness and simplicity of the divine essence it follows that whatever is in God is God, that whatever God wills he wills from eternity and always wills, and that he wills "simply, absolutely, and independently." In his being, God is without beginning, succession, or end and is utterly independent of anything outside himself. There is no necessary connection between the being of creatures and the being of God. Likewise, in his will, God is unchanging and altogether unconditioned by anything extrinsic to himself. Strictly speaking, he wills everything *ad extra* in a single, comprehensive, constant, eternal volition. Conversely, all created things are entirely dependent for their possibility and their actuality upon God as Necessary Being and First Cause and as Supreme Volition. Considered in himself, God may be said to *be* everything, containing all things actually and potentially: "that which is increated, essentially; that which is created, to be created, or possible to be created [immanently]."[18]

God as creator has power sufficient to effect anything that he may conceive, as long as it is not logically contradictory. Yet the actual creation, including the order of redemption, does not exhaust the logically possible. God might have done things differently: that a particular set of possibilities was in fact realized results not from any inherent impotency in, or external constraint on, God but solely from his own free determination. All things outside God exist only by his "mere good pleasure" and, in creation, God's power follows his will.[19]

Reflecting on the divine activity *ad extra,* Puritans (and nominalist theologians before them) subordinated God's power, as manifest in the actual order of things, to his will and distinguished between *potentia dei absoluta* and *potentia dei ordinata sive actualis*.[20] The first refers to God's power considered in itself as unlimited, the second to his power as "ordinate, and limited by his decree, and revealed will: according to which God having freely bounded himself, [he] changes not, being immutable." Considered in itself, God's power is such that "he is able to do all things that are possible, though he never do them." In fact, however, Norton observed, "though God be omnipotent, yet he is not omnivolent; . . . God is not pleased to do whatsoever he can." It must be added that God's will is constant: having once determined to act in a manner appropriate to his intended end, and having once declared himself, God does not deviate from his course, nor, given the unity of his nature, can he. "There can no more be a new thought, a new intent, or a new purpose in God," Norton declared, "than there can be a new God."[21]

The ultimate end of the eternal, comprehensive decree is God himself, as his glory is to be manifested "in a way of justice upon the reprobate, [and] in a way of justice tempered with mercy upon the elect." The proximate object of the decree is the creation in its condition of possibility, as falling within the compass of the divine sufficiency. God's actual bringing-forth and working of what he has willed, as he has willed it, is, in the language of formal divinity, his "efficiency." It is the carrying-into-effect of the single immanent act of the eternal decree, in a series of "transient" acts, extrinsic to himself and having duration in time. In his efficiency God proceeds as he has previously determined, and so his efficient power is said to be "ordinate." This ordination, moreover, includes the means through which he exercises his power as well as the ends toward which he exercises it.[22]

When they referred to God's "efficiency," Reformed divines intended God's power in its limited, ordinate aspect. Strictly speaking, therefore, God's actions in time are not expressions of his omnipotence, which pertains only to possibility. In actuality, omnipotence is channelled in determinate ways through a series of intermediate causes, toward particular ends, some in time and some beyond time. Thus John Forbes observed that though scripture speaks of infinite wisdom, omnipotent power, and infinite goodness as fountains of God's working, these superlatives are not properly applied to God's actions outside himself; for "the will of God . . . limits the infiniteness, both of his wisdom, power, and goodness, in all his actions outward toward the creature: both in their creation and government, and dispensation of all blessings toward us, both bodily and spiritual."[23] This is true of regeneration, as well as of other divine acts toward creatures, so that regeneration is properly defined not as the impinging of omnipotence directly upon created human nature, but rather as the operation of God's efficient power through means appropriate to human capacity, including mental faculties and other created instruments.[24]

The concept of the ordinate-ness of divine action in the world provided Puritans with a theological base, within the context of the doctrine of God, for asserting the constancy of God's action in the details of regeneration and also in the whole scheme of redemption. The specific steps God follows were held to fall within the compass of his efficiency. So, also, were the covenant of grace, and the covenant of works of which it is the reflection, together with the work of Christ that unites them both. Thus, in the *Medulla*, Ames treated the covenant of works under the heading of God's "special government" of reasonable creatures, which is "special" because it is peculiarly suited to the created nature and appointed end of thinking, willing agents. The rule of this government is the moral law given at creation, and the instrument of its exercise is the covenant of works. These, together with the Incarnation and the covenant of grace, are the major links in the succession of ordained "means" leading to the grand end for which God undertook the creation in the first place.[25]

Within this succession, the covenant of works is crucial, for in it were established the terms of God's government of mankind and, thereby, the subsequent form of his redemptive activity. God agreed with Adam to reward perfect obedience with eternal bliss and to punish the contrary appropriately, in a transaction suited to Adam's capacity as created—suited, that is, to Adam as a perceptive, reflective, consenting being, with the moral law "written in his heart."[26] The moral law is God's perfect and universal rule for human behavior, and in the covenant of works mankind acquired an unalterable obligation to fulfill it. Having once ordained this means to his self-glorifying end, God is unalterably committed to it by the simplicity of his nature and the consequent immutability of his will. Considering the divine power as ordinate, the form of God's salvific relationship with mankind remains necessarily a covenant, and the moral law continues as the standard by which God is bound to reward or to condemn mankind.[27] The balance of the order of redemption, encompassing the restoration of fallen man, unfolds accordingly.

The Continuity of the Moral Law

The passion for an order rooted in and conforming to the divine will, characteristic of Reformed Protestantism, is evident in Ames's definition of "providence" as God's government of creatures according to an appropriate rule, in the case of mankind according to the moral law. It is also reflected in the insistence of Reformed divines, Puritans included, that in the moral law God's particular will for mankind is most nearly revealed and that the law, therefore, remains valid for the duration of the world, incumbent alike on elect and reprobate, regenerate and unregenerate. The law, strictly taken, is, in Norton's words, "that universal and perpetual rule of manners teaching how man should be ordered, disposed, qualified, conformed, and (if we may so speak) mannered towards God and men." It specifies the substance of that holiness which constitutes the image of God in which man was created; it is the standard of that conformity to himself which God requires of reasonable creatures. The renewal of the divine image in the saints, moreover, expresses itself in universal obedience to the moral law considered as God's commanding will.[28] Indeed, the whole course of salvation, including the Mosaic code and Christ's redemptive work, unfolds in positive relationship to the moral law.

The covenant of grace, accordingly, cannot be hostile to the law, but encompasses it as a condition. Thus Norton observed that until the completion of Christ's satisfaction, the second covenant was administered, though imperfectly, through the Mosaic law and ceremonies. The Mosaic law, of course, contains the substance of the covenant of works: the decalogue in essence is the same law Adam received in integrity as the rule of universal and absolute obedience and as the condition of the first covenant. Yet the decalogue was given to Israel, which included those who, by faith in the promise, were spiritual children of Abraham and were under the covenant of grace. Accordingly, Norton noted, the moral law republished through Moses may be understood in three senses:

> either as a law of works obliging man unto a pure legal obedience, and accordingly to expect life or death: or as a rule of universal and absolute obedience, obliging man not only to what was commanded at present, but also unto whatsoever should afterwards be required. Or as the covenant of grace itself, though dispensed after a legal manner, comprehending the law as a perpetual rule of righteousness, freed from its pure legal nature of coaction, malediction and justification by works.

The first sense includes all who have not heard or responded to the call of the gospel. The second applies to those who have heard the call and therefore stand obliged to believe in Christ. The third sense, which presupposes faith in the heart, is realized in the lives of the regenerate.[29]

One reason for reissuing the law through Moses, Norton observed, was to restrain wickedness and to preserve some semblance of moral order in a world disordered by the fall. Another was to apprise fallen human beings of their sinfulness, which they are characteristically disinclined to admit, to convince them that justification is impossible by works, and thereby to prepare them to receive Christ. In this respect, the moral law, in Old and New Testaments, is subservient to the covenant of grace, though the covenant of grace is, itself, subservient to the covenant of works as the instrument of God's providential government.[30]

After Christ's coming, and the full revelation therein of the covenant of grace, the moral law remains in force as the universal rule of manners and as the substance of the covenant of works; and its "pedagogical" function *ad Christum* continues. In addition, the law acquires a "third use" as the rule of the new obedience by which the regenerate are to walk.[31] The saints are freed from the law as covenant, that is, as the means of their justification. Though they transgress the law they are not for that reason cast out of the covenant of grace. They are, however, none the less bound to the law as rule, for at least two reasons. In the first place, sin, Shepard noted, is by definition deliberate transgression of the moral law as universal rule for mankind, so that "of necessity a believer is bound to attend the law as his rule, that so he may not sin or transgress that rule." In the second place, the law defines that holiness belonging to the image of God as it is renewed in the regenerate. All creatures, Norton wrote, inasmuch as they exist, resemble God as he is a being, but they do not all resemble him *"sub ratione boni moralis,* i.e., as he is holy, just, and good, in himself, the rule of which resemblance is the moral law." As rational creatures, moreover, believers are capable of acting in accordance with a rule, and, being sanctified and freed from the dominion of corrupt nature, they "have some inherent power so to act, . . . according to the rule of life." Those under the gospel, Shepard observed, are not therefore "under no law of doing," nor are they to "cast off all attendance to the directive power of the law." Law and gospel, indeed, require the same perfection of holiness of doing, inasmuch as both command that we be perfect and holy, as God is perfect and holy.[32]

For Shepard and his New England colleagues, as for their Reformed orthodox brethren, the moral law is fundamental throughout the order of salvation. Though the covenant of works was broken in the fall, it was not abrogated. The law, though violated, was not annulled. Both remain in force to the end of the world; and the law, understood as divine injunction for human action, continues beyond the end. Satisfaction of the covenant of works remains the condition of man's salvation. Everyone outside the covenant of grace, both reprobate and elect (until conversion), is under the covenant of works and obligated to perfect obedience to the law. Had Adam personally performed such obedience, he would himself have been just. After the fall, the covenant of grace replaces the covenant of works as the instrument of God's salvific government. Christ's legal obedience abolishes the law as covenant for those who share his righteousness by faith. It does not, however, free the faithful from the law as rule. The same law written in Adam's heart, delivered by Moses, and preached and fulfilled by Christ becomes incarnate in the sanctified lives of believers, who incur under the covenant of grace an obligation of thankful obedience to God's will as the standard of human action. To this extent, Shepard declared, the Kingdom of God is present in the visible church, for the very "laws of heaven . . . are not only here promulgated, . . . but accepted and received also." And, he observed, even in the state of glory, though "the external letter and scription both of law and gospel shall be abolished, . . . yet the living rules of both, for substance, shall remain."[33]

The Nature and Necessity of Christ's Obedience

The necessity of Christ's suffering is a perennial question for Christian apologists. If God is omnipotent, could he not redeem mankind less painfully? The distinction between God's absolute and ordinate power opens the way to one possible answer, which Norton articulated with characteristic succinctness:

> Though God by his absolute power might have saved man without redemption wrought by Christ: yet having constituted that rule of relative justice, "In the day that thou eatest thereof, thou shalt surely die," Gen. 2:17. He could not [avoid] in respect of his power now limited to proceed by this rule, so that man having sinned, man must die, and satisfy the law that man may live. Justice requires the surety should die, that the debtor may live. . . .

In the covenant of works God established obedience to the moral law as the standard of "relative justice"—that justice obtaining between God and creatures—by which he is bound to recompense men. Having freely determined to proceed with mankind in this way, God also "freely obliged himself to the observation thereof; and can now no more fail to execute justice according to this rule, than he can be unjust."[34] It follows, from the nature of God, that the law concerning punishment and obedience must be satisfied if men are to attain blessedness.

Here, however, is a difficulty. Fallen mankind are quite unable to render the obedience required, and if the elect undergo sentence of death in their own persons, election is frustrated, and with it God's intent to manifest "the glory of his mercy in a way tempered with justice." If they do not die, the threat of punishment is false, God is unjust, and the law is void. The covenant of works, however, does not prohibit God from accepting satisfaction from someone other than the proper debtors, provided the payment is sufficient to cover the debt owed. Accordingly, it is Christ's office, as "surety" for the elect, to suffer the punishment due mankind for breach of the law and to render the perfect obedience required by the law for eternal reward. It is unnecessary to enter here upon the substance of Reformed orthodox Christology, beyond the observation that Christ, because he is both God and man and is inherently righteous, is alone capable of satisfying the law in all respects. Puritans defined Christ's mediatoral office primarily as one of fulfilling the requirements of the law under the covenant of works, the "mystery" and "metaphysics" of the Incarnation being of interest chiefly as they established the fitness of the God-Man for this office. As God-Man, Christ's obedience was more acceptable to God than Adam's disobedience was detestable; and it is only in virtue of the sufficiency of his mediatorship that the covenant of grace, as the means of restoring the elect, is possible at all.[35]

Christ's obedience, Puritans held, corresponds exactly to the double misery of fallen mankind, who are under sentence of condemnation for breaking the law and who lack the righteousness demanded by the law. Restoration to felicity requires death in punishment for sin and perfect legal obedience performed in one's own person in satisfaction of the terms of the covenant of works. Fallen mankind must rely wholly on Christ for both, and Christ's obedience is therefore twofold: active, in fulfillment of the command, and passive, in the suffering of punishment.[36] "Mediatorly obedience," Norton wrote,

according to the received doctrine of the orthodox, is the inherent
conformity and whole course of the active and passive obedience
of Christ from his conception to his passion inclusively, performed
by him as God-Man Mediator, unto the law, in the way of covenant, whereunto the whole good of redemption was due unto the
elect for Christ's sake, according to the order of justice, though
conferred upon them in a way of mere grace.[37]

In so doing, Christ rendered in his own person the legal obedience
prescribed in the covenant of works in "habitual conformity unto
the law, and in a way of merit." As such, his obedience is the
"meritorious cause" of the justification offered the elect in the covenant of grace. Indeed, it makes possible the offering of the covenant
of grace altogether. The substance of justification is the same in
both covenants, namely, legal obedience, and in both cases it is the
reward of merit. But whereas under the covenant of works justification is by righteousness personally attained, under the covenant of
grace it is by righteousness freely and vicariously enjoyed. Christ
personally fulfilled, and therein upheld, the law of works. Believers,
by faith, in and through him obey the law legally in respect of both
precept and curse and benefit accordingly. Justification is by merit,
as it can only be, but it is not by our merit. The covenant of grace,
Norton noted, "denies merit in the debtor proper, but not in the
surety. . . . Our salvation cost Christ the full price, though it cost
us nothing at all."[38]

Christ's work as mediator between God and man, not unlike
that of Moses, looks backward toward the covenant of works and
forward toward the covenant of grace, and it unites the two. The
first covenant, however, remains primary. The covenant of works,
Bulkeley observed, is in substance "unchangeable and everlasting.
. . . None but the righteous ones saith justice, shall have life, the
reward of righteousness: This justice in God is unalterable, and
changes not, and thus far there is little or no difference between
the one covenant and the other, but both are alike." In the same
vein Norton observed that the Son was sent expressly to fulfill the
law of works "as a proper condition of his mediator's office."[39] The
covenant of *grace* is, in effect, *correlativum mediatoris,* whose distinctive office consists in restoring the covenant-bond between God
and man that was first entered in creation.

In Puritan covenant theology, the terms and the form of God's dealing with mankind for salvation are established in the covenant of works at the foundation of the world, and the covenant of grace functions as a means of applying to the elect the righteousness obtained by Christ, who satisfies the conditions of the first covenant. Under the covenant of grace, obedience is performed for men by Christ, the resulting righteousness belonging personally to Christ and being imputed to men by God. The *condition* of this imputation, however, is a human act: namely, willing acceptance of the offer of Christ's righteousness, together with a vow of renewed obedience to the moral law. In this respect, the covenant of grace takes its form from the covenant of works, as a mutual transaction involving a willing act on man's part. Thus, the moral order established at creation is sustained throughout the history of salvation; and the ontological order is preserved also, in that the divine power is held to be accommodated, in the application of redemption, to the nature of reasonable creatures. On both counts the covenant-scheme is referred back to its source in God's unconditioned will, in the execution of which he is held freely to have limited and bound himself to a particular method of operation. In this manner Puritan covenant theology sought to hold together both poles of the theological dialectic of created nature and divine grace.

CHAPTER 6

The Doctrine of the Two Covenants: II

THE CONDITIONALITY OF THE COVENANT OF GRACE

It was a commonplace among Reformed divines that the chain of events encompassing regeneration begins with God's decision, before time, to glorify himself in the manifestation of his justice and mercy toward certain men, and ends beyond time, in the eternal felicity of the elect in glory and the eternal infelicity of the non-elect in reprobation. Between these two eternities, federal theologians held, stands God's covenant with mankind, as the concrete, historic instrument by which God executes his decree respecting human destinies. As the vital meeting point between God and man, the covenant reflects the nature of the creature covenanting, as well as the nature of God who covenants. The covenant of grace, accordingly, is properly conditional, partly because that is the nature of a covenantal transaction and also because, as an expression of God's "ordained power," the transaction is suited to man's capacity as a rational agent. The absolute decree concerning mankind, covenant theologians held, is *dispensed* under a conditional form because God freely elects, in accomplishing his ends, to respect the integrity of second causes, including the human mind and will.[1] In the covenant of grace, as in the covenant of works, human beings are invited to consent to an offer of terms from God. This understanding of the conditionality of the second covenant emerges from examination of the systematic *loci* treating of the dispensation of grace under the decree, of the liberty of the human will, and of the agency of second causes.

The Conditional Dispensation of Free Grace

By definition a covenant, Bulkeley noted (echoing Rollock), is *promissio sub certa conditione*. The "proper nature" of a covenant requires "a mutual obligation and binding of the parties one to another by condition." This requirement is as true of the covenant of grace as of the covenant of works. God not only binds himself to men in the second covenant but also binds them to himself, in dependence and obedience. Not only does he promise to establish his covenant with Abraham (Gen. 17:7); he commands Abraham (v. 9), "Thou also shall keep my covenant." Scripture, in any case, expressly mentions the condition upon which the promise of life is made, "as in Acts 16:31, 'Believe on the Lord Jesus and thou shalt be saved.' Rom. 10:9, 'If thou believest, thou shalt be saved, etc.'" The promises of life and peace, Bulkeley emphasized, are "not made but upon condition of faith and obedience, not to the unbelieving and profane."[2]

This last point was quite important for Bulkeley. Salvation, he insisted, is offered to sinners freely, but not absolutely: God will not save them while they continue unbelieving and impenitent and walk at liberty after their own hearts and not under God's government. God, rather, "commands and works us to repent and believe, and then promises that in the way of faith and repentance, he will save us." On God's part the covenant of grace is absolute, but on man's it is conditional. Though the act of fulfilling the condition is itself the fruit of grace, and in no way merits justification, insofar as the transaction is covenantal, this act is the *sine qua non* of justification on man's part. Neither the covenant of works nor the covenant of grace leaves man at liberty; neither promises life without some correlative obligation incumbent upon him. The conditions of the respective covenants differ, but they are nonetheless genuine conditions.[3]

The essential gratuity of both covenants derives from their foundation in the free will and absolute good pleasure of God. That God condescends to treat with mankind at their own level and in their own way, covenantally, is solely the result of God's own free decision. Between the condition and the reward in each covenant, moreover, there is no inherent proportionality. Obedience merits eternal bliss, and faith issues in justification, only because God has arbitrarily established a connection between them.[4] The respective acts of obedience and of faith spring from habits that are themselves gifts of grace. Adam's ability to obey the law was a gracious endowment, "superadded" to his natural endowment, and the same may be said of the habit of faith by which the elect are enabled to fulfill the condition of the covenant of grace. The existence and the execution of both covenants, Norton allowed, are willed absolutely by God, and in this respect both are properly said to be "of grace." At the same time, however, the *execution* of both, in form, is conditional. In the covenant of grace, therefore, the indefinite proposition in the gospel, " 'Whosoever believes, shall be saved,' " is "equipolent unto that condition, 'If you believe, you shall be saved.' " Faith and salvation are so connected in the decree that one infallibly follows from the other, whence follows the general proposition, the conditional, and also the imperative, " 'Believe and you shall be saved.' "[5]

The covenants of works and grace differ in that God himself, in the latter, undertakes for the fulfilling of man's condition. In integrity Adam had power sufficient to obey the law, but no assurance from God that he would obey it. In performing the condition he was left entirely to himself. In the covenant of grace, however, God "does not only promise the good, but to begin, and perfect, and fulfill the condition absolutely." Men are assured that God himself will enable them to perform the required condition, in addition to conveying the blessedness promised to the condition. Herein lies the unique security of the covenant of grace.[6] The giving of first grace in vocation *precedes* "our personal covenant betwixt God and us, by which we bind ourselves unto him to take him for our God, to depend upon him, and to submit our selves unto his will." God infuses habits of grace, beginning to renew a man, and then "propounds" to him in and through preaching the blessings of the covenant and commands him to depend on God by faith for performance of them. Thus the man is enabled to walk in the "way" of the covenant. The answer of faith, which springs from the gracious habits, is the man's answer. Yet, wrote Sibbes, "the power by which we answer is no less than that whereby God created the world and raised Christ from the dead. The answer is ours, but the power and strength is God's whereby we answer."[7]

In Puritan covenant theology, the gratuity of the covenant of grace is rooted in the fact that God's willing of it, together with the application of it, is absolute. "Faith," Norton wrote, "is the condition of salvation, . . . yet both faith, and salvation by faith, are willed absolutely." At the same time, the integrity of the human creature is upheld in that God "so administers his absolute decree, as that there is as much place left for an efficacious conditional dispensation, as if the decree itself were conditional."[8] God chooses this manner of administering his decree, Norton observed, for reasons that in effect reflect his willingness to respect the created nature and capacities of mankind and to employ created means in regeneration. Grace is administered covenantally in order: (1) that the elect and reprobate, being ignorant of their estate until actual regeneration, may look upon themselves as equally under wrath and be encouraged thereby to attend upon the preparatory means and to hope for effectual vocation; (2) that all men, whether elect or not, may be admonished of their duty to believe; (3) that men may know what to do that they may be saved; and (4) that God may proceed as is most suitable to reasonable creatures, that is, by persuasion and the proposal of arguments. The covenant of grace is conditional, in other words, because man is by nature a "cause by counsel."[9]

This observation is supported by the *loci* treating of the natural liberty of second causes, including the human will.

The Autonomy of Second Causes

The specific question at issue in Reformed discussions of the freedom of the human will was, as Perkins put it, "whether a natural man or an infidel, can by the freedom of his will, without faith, and without the help of God, do any work morally good, that is, a work in which there is no sin."[10] Reformed Protestants answered in the negative: the will of fallen man, being corrupt, can only will corruption. This bondage of the will, however, pertains to the quality, particularly the ends, of human willing, rather than to the power of willing itself. "We grant," Perkins noted, "that liberty of will is not abolished, but wounded: because though liberty of grace to will well be lost, yet liberty of nature to will, still remains."[11] The notorious doctrine of the bondage of the will concerns man's power sincerely to obey God's commands, not the power of the will to perform its natural office of willing. It is this "natural liberty" of the will that God respects in determining upon covenantal means for the execution of his decree.

Perkins's definition of the human will may be taken as representative of early Puritan opinion on the subject. The will, he wrote, is a "power"—that is, "an ability or created faculty"—"of willing, nilling, choosing, refusing, [and] suspending, which depends on reason." It is that faculty of the human mind that elects or rejects a given course of action presented to it by the understanding. By definition the will is free from constraint and external compulsion. It is not, however, free from all necessity, inasmuch as it unavoidably acts in accordance with the antecedent determination of the divine decree. Nonetheless, the certainty of God's decree does not abolish the proper operation of man's will, "but rather order[s] it, and mildly incline[s], or draw[s] it forth.... [I]n the doing of a voluntary action, it is sufficient that it proceed of judgment, and have his beginning from within the will, though otherwise, in respect of God's will, it be of unchangeable necessity.... [T]he thing that is directly contrary to freedom of will, is compulsion: because it abolishes consent." The liberty of the will, considered as a natural faculty of the human mind, consists in its ability, of itself and without external compulsion, to consent to the determination of the understanding respecting a particular object, all the while retaining the power to nil what is willed and to will the contrary of what is willed.[12]

In the state of integrity, before the fall, mankind was capable of choosing either good or evil. This capacity sprang from two principles in Adam's soul, one gracious, the other natural. Adam's ability to will the good was founded in the "holiness" of his will, that is, in the gifts of grace superadded to his natural endowment, which equipped him to keep the divine commandments if he so willed. As part of his natural endowment, Adam possessed a liberty of will inherent in the faculty itself: the power of willing, nilling, or suspending. After the fall, mankind's "liberty of grace" is altogether lost, but his "liberty of nature" remains. Fallen man can and does will in all his actions, as is evident from "common experience." The natural liberty of the will, Perkins maintained, extends to all of man's physical, economic, political, and social activity, and also to the practice of religion. "Corrupt and sinful man, has power and liberty to think of God, and to think many things of him, good in themselves: power to read and search the Scriptures: power to speak and talk of the word of God: power to come to the congregation and hear a sermon, . . . : power to conceive a zeal (I say not a good zeal, but only a zeal I say) for the maintenance of outward duties of religion."[13] Though Adam's lapse extinguished utterly man's power to will *well,* to will God as last end and highest good, his natural ability to *will* continues; and God, in regenerating fallen men, proceeds in accordance with this natural liberty, as something integral to a created faculty proper to mankind.

In the accomplishment of regeneration, Reformed divines maintained, as in the ordinary execution of all determinations of his will, God respects and employs the agency of second causes. In the case of the human will, inasmuch as it is a second cause, God determines it in accordance with its nature as a free agent—he determines it, that is, so that it determines itself. "The efficiency of God," Norton noted, "offers no violence, nor changes the nature of things, but governs them according to their own natures." To say that God compels the will, either in its natural elections or in regeneration, is a contradiction, for it is to say "that which is willing is unwilling."[14] Rather than overpowering the will, God transforms it and orders its actions so that the will moves itself as he intends. God guides creatures, Sibbes affirmed, "sweetly according to the instincts he has put into them"; he supplies them with a power and a manner of working suited to their respective natures. In accomplishing his intent for creation, God "maintains both the [creature's] power and manner of working, and perfects and accomplishes the same by acting on it. . . . He applies and stirs up our abilities and actions to this or that particular. . . . He suspends or removes the hindrances of all actions, and so powerfully, wisely, and sweetly orders them to his own ends." Norton, with a characteristic taste for paradox, put it more succinctly: "The liberty of man, though subordinate to God's decree, freely wills the very same thing, and no other, than that which it would have willed, if (upon a supposition of impossibility) there had been no decree. Man acts as freely, as if there were no decree; yet as infallibly, as if there were no liberty."[15]

For Reformed orthodox divines, conversion was hardly "a forcible seizure, a holy rape of the surprised will."[16] It was, rather, a divine ordering of human action, in conformity with the natural character of human faculties. In the work of grace, John Preston declared, God does not move us by "a violent impression" by his own "immediate hand," as men do when they shoot an arrow or throw a stone. God moves us, on the contrary, "as he does in the work of nature," by "caus[ing] the creature to go on of itself, to this or that purpose . . . ; he changes a man's heart, so that he is carried willingly to the ways of God." In the same vein, Thomas Shepard, echoing Ames, wrote that God does not "work upon believers as upon blocks or brute creatures." Rather,

> believers are rational creatures, and therefore capable of acting by rule, and they are also sanctified and delivered from the power of their corrupt nature, and therefore have some inherent power so to act. . . . And therefore although God works in us both to will and to do of his good pleasure, yet this hinders not but that we are to work out our salvation with fear and trembling, by attending the rule, by virtue of which we are bound to work.[17]

Conversion is thus a consent, and the life of faith is a series of holy consents toward holy ends.

The Instrumentality of Creatures

In executing his decree regarding creatures, Reformed divines argued, God proceeds mediately, via the instrumentality of second causes. Second causes cannot produce an effect without the First Cause, for they depend upon him for their being and are subject to the divine decree determining the ends of all action whatsoever. However, Norton insisted, the First Cause will not produce a given effect without the appropriate second causes. God exercises his efficiency by "an external transient influence" upon the creature in time, exactly corresponding to the decree before time, "moving upon, co-working with, and assisting of the second cause in its operations. . . . [T]hough (as the beings, so) the operations of the second causes, are from the first cause efficiently, yet they are from their next causes formally. God causes the burning of the fire, yet we do not say God burns, but the fire burns. God works repentance in the soul, yet it is not a truth to say God repents, but man repents; God is the next efficient cause, but not the next formal cause."[18] The power producing a particular effect derives ultimately from God, and the existence of the effect depends upon God's willing of it. However, the form of the effect, *what* it is, is determined by the created agency that produces it.

What is true of fire's burning is also true of a man's believing. As fire burns from an inward power of burning, so a man believes from an inward power or "habit" of faith. The cases differ in that fire's inward principle is natural to it, whereas man's power to believe is infused by grace. The cases are alike in that the respective ends for which a given fire burns and a given man believes are determined by the divine decree, and are achieved through created means acting according to their proper natures. In and through the hearing of the offer of grace and the promise of the covenant, God implants gracious principles in the soul, which enable its natural faculties of perception, reflection, and volition to work together in their normal fashion toward the divinely intended end. So empowered, the soul comes to sense the value of grace for what it truly is, and to sense the misery of the absence of grace. Inasmuch as "desire naturally springs from the apprehension of any good made known," there arises from this esteem and misery a longing for grace. "Faith is both in the understanding and in the will; as it is in the understanding it opens the eye to see, and clearly to discern the blessing of the covenant, and then stirs up the will to pursue and desire the attaining of grace revealed." Sooner or later, sometimes forcefully, sometimes but haltingly, the soul goes forth in faith to embrace the promise and to receive Christ, giving him "the hand of faith" in covenant.[19] In the same manner, Christ, in and through the work of the ministry, writes the law, as an inward disposition, upon the hearts of the regenerate. Preston observed that "though the minister be the immediate writer of these laws in the heart, yet the ink is the Holy Ghost. . . . We are but coworkers with [the Lord], he holds our hands, as it were, when we write the epistle in any man's heart, it is he that guides the pen. . . ."[20] Yet the minister is in truth the pen; he is verily the "instrumental cause" of the writing.

In regeneration, as in all his ordinary actions *ad extra*, God works through created means, without doing violence to the natural constitution of the creatures involved. He does this, Ames declared, "not because of any lack of power, but because of the abundance of his goodness; he communicates a certain dignity of efficiency to his creatures and in them makes his own efficiency more perceptible."[21] Regeneration, Perkins observed, "is not in respect of the substance of body or soul, or in respect of the faculties of the soul, but only in respect of the goodness thereof, which is a conformity to the will of God."[22] This conformity is a matter of the quality and direction of a man's willing, in particular his ability sincerely to will as God wills, not of his ability to will, as such. God renews the corrupt will by "healing" it, by restoring its former ability to will well, and thereby attains the result he intends. To say that a man is converted against his will, or in spite of his will, is true regarding man's will as fallen and corrupt but not as volitional faculty.

The affirmation of the natural liberty of the fallen will and of the liberty and co-agency with God of second causes is the metaphysical foundation of Puritan exhortations to attend upon the means of grace. Said Perkins:

> In that the new birth and regeneration of a sinner, is not without the motion of his own will, we are taught, that we must, if we desire our own salvation, use the good means, and strive against our own corruptions, and endeavor earnestly, by asking, seeking, knocking. It will be said, that faith, repentance, and the rest are all gifts of God. I answer: there is no virtue or gift of God in us, without our wills: and in every good act, God's grace, and man's will, concur: God's grace, as the principal cause; man's will renewed, as the instrument of God. And therefore in all good things, industry and labor, and invocation on our parts is required.[23]

The doctrine of the "pedagogical use" *ad Christum* of the law, or of "ministerial preparations" for conversion, as articulated by English and New English Puritans, is also to be understood in light of Perkins's affirmation. The same is true of the constant appeals, from Puritan pulpits on both sides of the Atlantic, to be diligent in seeking and in exercising the gracious gifts of the Spirit. God's efficiency, in the accomplishment of spiritual as well as natural ends, proceeds in and through the normal activity of created instruments.

The Necessity of Consent

"The condition of grace and God's offer," wrote Hooker, "is this, that a man must *will* to receive Christ and grace, before he can receive Christ and grace." Though the offer of grace is freely made, yet "God will not save a man against his will." A man must first will to have life, before he can have it. The will "is the great wheel that turns all, and the power of the soul, that works all in this case." Sibbes sounded the same theme. "Divinity," he noted, "rules the will especially." The change wrought in regeneration affects the will most of all, and it is the will that determines the character of a man. "For the bent of the will makes a good or a bad man; and the desires of the will carry the whole man with it. We are as the bent is of our will. We are as the choice of our will is. . . . Though all grace come in through the understanding enlightened, . . . yet it goes into the will." In the same vein, Ames characterized faith as "an act of choice, an act of the whole man," in which the will, moved by the understanding, reaches out and embraces the good offered. "Only through a consent of the will" can a man "surrender himself to God in Christ as a sufficient and faithful Savior." Justifying faith, Preston reiterated, is not only an act of the mind assenting to the truth of the offer of grace; it is also and necessarily an act of the will, consenting to the offer, laying hold of the promises, and applying them to oneself. Puritans, in concert with Reformed orthodoxy generally, insisted that the crucial aspect of faith, as the soul's movement into union with Christ, is an act of will, carrying with it the whole man, soul and body.[24]

Entry into the covenant of grace requires an act of consent from man because such an act belongs to the nature of a covenant. That God *covenants* with man for salvation, however, reflects man's created nature as a cause by counsel. Man's uniqueness among the creatures springs from his nature as a purposive being. Stones, plants, and beasts work blindly or by reflex, whereas man moves by propounding to himself ends and framing means to achieve them. The will is the faculty moving the soul, and with it the man, actually to pursue a given goal. Apart from its agency, the understanding is powerless to move the man toward, or away from, any object. This distinction holds, moreover, for spiritual as well as for natural goods: though the understanding may discern the excellency of God, it is proper only to the will "to relish and receive the goodness or the mercy of the Lord. . . . [T]he will is the queen of the soul, that takes all that good which the understanding sees and discerns, and which is offered and tendered to it."[25]

Accordingly, to deny that the will is active in closing with Christ is to suggest that the covenant of grace is not truly a covenant, inasmuch as that denial deprives men of a proper consent. It is also to imply that that faith by which, alone, a person is justified is not an act of his own, is not his own faith.[26] These implications suggest, in turn, that God in regeneration disregards the efficiency proper to the will as a second cause. Those who argued, with the Hutchinsonians, that in respect of saving and sanctifying grace a person must "do nothing" but only "wait for Christ to do all" seemed to reject the proper activity of second causes altogether, as they are ordained instruments in the application of redemption. Therein they implied that God's ordinary efficiency is insufficient to the task before it, and that God must in consequence act "extraordinarily" and save men in spite of, or apart from, created means and natural faculties.

Such a view of God's salvific activity, however, was contrary to a basic conviction of Reformed divinity. Thus, to Norton, rejection of the efficiency of man's will as a second cause, logically extended, had enormous consequences. It called into question, he declared, the conclusions of common human experience and overthrew "the whole order of nature." It was to say, in effect, that the sun does not truly shine, or fire truly burn. If second causes have no proper efficacy, then creatures both animate and inanimate have no active principles in themselves. Fire has neither inherent ability to burn nor inherent tendency to ascend. If second causes are in fact incapable of producing effects, then it is impossible, by observation and reasoning, to conclude from effects to causes or to infer effects from causes, in which case it no longer makes sense to say that fire is hot from its burning or burns things because it is hot. Further, denial of inherent active principles removes all significant difference between living creatures, inasmuch as it denies the existence of the respective souls, vegetative, sensitive, and rational, by which such creatures are distinguished; and it also eliminates the difference between living and lifeless creatures "in respect of their formal, and most noble difference, which is a principle of action, with the operations thereupon ensuing." In the absence of an inner principle of action, living creatures differ only in outward shape, and action is in fact "only the first cause in the presence of such a creature."[27]

Denial of the efficiency of second causes, Norton felt, had unpleasant consequences not only for the order of nature but also for the order of redemption. If man is in fact incapable of understanding, willing, remembering, or being affected—all of which are actions—then he is incapable of blessedness, which consists in the intellectual vision and spiritual enjoyment of God as chief good. Moreover, if there are no actions, the human creature is incapable of proceeding in the revealed "way of heaven," that is, incapable of obedience; for if there is no action at all, there can be no good or evil action and hence no obedience. In this case, the obedience of Christ himself is called into question, and the Saviorhood founded upon it. Thus, by logical implication, denial of the efficiency of second causes means denial of salvation altogether. "Nay, if there were no actions of man (the very reasonable soul by just consequence supposing action) it would infer, that there were no man, and consequently no Christ, Christ being both God and man." All these conclusions, Norton allowed, are completely contrary to experience, and to scripture, which plainly ascribes efficiency to second causes: "So doth God administer all things which he hath created, as that he also suffers them to exercise and act their proper motions."[28]

Norton's representation of the consequences of denying efficiency to second causes was rhetorically inflated, but, considering the theological and philosophical ground on which he stood, it was basically accurate. The thorough subordination of created nature to the operation of increated grace, advanced by English and New English antinomians, had sweeping implications not only for theology and ethics but also for physics and epistemology. Were these implications followed to their logical extremes, a great wedge would be driven between God and his creation, with disturbing consequences for human social and intellectual life. Reformed divines were quite unwilling to allow such a rupture between Creator and creatures, and they looked with suspicion on anyone whose passion for the gratuity of grace or yearning for intimacy with the

Spirit tended in that direction. The normative position is accurately summarized in the sentence, last quoted above, from *The Orthodox Evangelist.*

DIVINE SOVEREIGNTY, HUMAN AGENCY, AND THE PROBLEM OF THE CONDITIONAL COVENANT

Twentieth-century students of New England Puritanism have on occasion assumed that the Reformed doctrines of divine sovereignty, unconditional election, and the bondage of the human will necessarily excluded any human participation in regeneration and, accordingly, that conversion for Reformed Protestants must be sudden, instantaneous, and entirely the work of divine power. Since Reformed Protestantism insisted that salvation is by grace alone, the individual, it has been reasoned, must be passive in the salvific transaction. Arminianism, after all, made justification explicitly contingent on the individual's consent to it, and Arminianism was the great Reformed heresy of the seventeenth century. From this perspective, the assertions of certain English and New English Puritans that the vigorous preaching of the commands and penalties of the law, together with the redemptive promises of the gospel, could effect in hearers certain spiritual conditions "preparatory" to effectual calling appeared doctrinally questionable; and the notion of a conditional covenant of *grace*, as articulated in New England, seemed to some interpreters not only to involve outright contradiction but also to constitute a significant departure from normative Reformed doctrine.[29]

Such a reading of the issues, however, in light of the foregoing consideration of Reformed covenantal doctrine, seems incorrect. It involves misapprehension of the dialectical relationship between nature and grace in covenant theology and of Reformed views about the relationship of divine and human activity in the created world. It overlooks the distinctions that sixteenth- and seventeenth-century Reformed divines commonly made between God's will and his power, between God's decree considered in itself as unconditioned and the conditional means decreed for its execution, and between mankind's natural ability to will and corrupt mankind's congenital inability to will well. In particular it seems to depend upon what

Reformed orthodox divines would have considered improper identification of divine sovereignty with divine omnipotence. These distinctions were not perceived by contemporaries as being at odds with the standards of the Reformed faith, nor was covenant theology felt to be the straining paradox that modern interpreters have occasionally found it.

This matter warrants attention here, since it bears closely upon analysis of the New England controversy and upon assignment of its principals to their proper locations in the history of Reformed Protestantism.

For Reformed divines in the early seventeenth century the really crucial theological distinction, it may be argued, did not lie between human activity, on the one hand, and divine activity, on the other, with the consequence that man must literally be passive in conversion. The crucial distinction lay, rather, between *merit* and *grace* in human action relative to attainment of justification, and also between the inability of corrupt man and the ability of gracious man to "close with" the offer of justification.[30] The Protestant *sola gratia* excluded the possibility that any human act could merit pardon from God. Exclusion of merit from justification, however, was not quite the same thing as exclusion of human faculties from participation in conversion. The scholastic doctrine of multiple causality, which was the common property of Reformed theologians during the orthodox period, enabled them to conceive of a concurrence of divine and human activity in conversion and of gracious and natural human agency in the individual's act of faith that did not violate the integrity of grace or nature. This seems to be a more difficult problem for post-Newtonians, who tend to conceive of causality exclusively in terms of efficiency.[31] In the scholastic conception, human will and the grace infused by God's Spirit may consist as the "formal" and "efficient" causes, respectively, of the act of faith, and as the "instrumental" and "efficient" causes of the individual's justification.[32] Divine and human activity are both ingredient in conversion, and both are "causes." Their respective causalities differ, however, and in the causal hierarchy God, as "final" and "efficient" cause, remains qualitatively primary. Moreover, their coincidence in any particular conversion and its effects is attributable solely to God's gracious will. The fundamental question, accordingly, is not whether man does or does not act in conversion, but rather *how* he acts, in terms of the will's disposition and in relation to other participant causes.

The Synod of Dort (1619), which condemned the doctrines of the Arminians, insisted that prior to infusion of grace fallen man is helpless to alter his disposition because his will is perverted by sin.[33] The synod affirmed, however, that both depraved man and converted man, as part of their human nature, are able to will and to do. The former is unable to will and to do the *good*—he cannot love and desire God for God's own sake—save as he is enabled by grace, save as his will is empowered to will the truly good—which is in fact what it means to be converted. Dort's formulation is instructive.

> Just as man by the fall assuredly did not cease to be man, endued with understanding and will, nor did sin, which spread through the whole human race, destroy the nature of mankind, but corrupted and spiritually slew it: so also this divine grace of regeneration does not work in man as in stocks and posts, nor abolishes the will and its properties, or forces it violently against its will, but spiritually vivifies, heals, corrects, sweetly and at the same time powerfully bends it: so that where formerly the rebellion and resistance of the flesh domineered entirely, now ready and sincere obedience of the Spirit begins to reign; in which change consists the true and spiritual renewal and the freedom of our wills. For which reason, unless that admirable worker of all goodness should act with us, there were no hope of man arising from his fall by his free will, through which, when he stood, he cast himself headlong into destruction.[34]

Both the converted and the unconverted are able to will concerning things propounded to them as objects of choice. Both obey the moral law, the unconverted reluctantly because they fear hell, the converted readily because they love the law's author. Both possess the natural human capacity for acts of obedience. But there is an eternity of difference—which is doctrinally the decisive point—between their respective abilities to "close with" divine things, and the difference is attributable solely to grace.

Dort's affirmation of the power of human willing presupposed the systematic-theological distinction between the absoluteness of God's decree considered in itself and the non-absolute character of the manner ordained for its execution. Though it was sometimes forgotten in the seventeenth century by especially zealous champions of "free grace," this distinction was generally allowed in Reformed dogmatics. Nor was it an invention solely of the orthodox period, still less of English Puritans.[35] Calvin himself noted that while God is the efficient cause of salvation, he is not prevented from, in certain respects, "embracing [human] works as inferior causes." The idea that second causes concur with the divine efficiency appears to have been first formally articulated in the Reformed tradition by Bucer. Among the generation of divines spanning the opening of the seventeenth century, a species of "secondary indeterminacy" of the sort represented by Perkins, which allowed substantial liberty to second causes, was fairly common. Indeed, it has been suggested that by 1600 this notion was sufficiently widespread among Reformed theologians that the inclusion of conditions in the covenant of grace appeared neither striking nor offensive. Even Franciscus Gomarus, who was one of the more rigorous predestinarians at Dort, was in certain respects a covenant theologian.[36]

The systematic distinction between the decree itself and the manner of its execution, moreover, appears in the theological handbooks precisely at the exalted level of God "considered as he is in himself." It appears, that is, in the *loci* treating the divine attributes and the divine decrees, where the emphasis on the unconditioned sovereignty of God's will is most explicit. In a number of instances the rubric of the decrees (including predestination) also encompasses the contrast between the object of the decree as end (God's glorification of himself) and the object of the decree as means toward this end (creation, temptation and fall, Christ's atonement and its application to the elect, glorification of the saints, damnation of the reprobate).[37] The assertion that God wills the creation as a means to the supreme end of his willing altogether is significant in this connection, for it means that God also wills the manifold world of second causes acting according to their distinctive natures. Such autonomy is implicit in the affirmation that God created an order of being genuinely separate from himself, and is likewise implicit in the Augustinian affirmation that Adam, though created in the image of God, was also created capable of supremely willing a lesser good than God, and so *posse peccare*. Otherwise, it is patently false to say, "The fire burns," and not, rather, "God burns," or to say, "Man wills," and not simply, "God wills." To be sure, the creature does not enjoy an absolute liberty of indifference, for in acting according to its own nature it simultaneously fulfills the divine decree; but it does so according to its own nature, and to this extent there is no inherent contradiction between the sovereignty of God's will in its absoluteness and the activity of creatures.[38] The Synod of Dort declared affirmatively on this point. Reformed orthodox divines, including some who were quite insistent on the matter of divine sovereignty, were also willing to allow that the Protestant *sola gratia*, while rigorously excluding human activity as meritorious of justification or as the efficient cause of vocation, does not exclude human activity, as such, or creaturely agency from among the ordained means by which God works in vocation.[39]

This point is important for proper understanding of the frequent exhortations of English and New English Puritans to attend diligently upon the means of grace, especially meditation and the ordinances of the church, and to cultivate the "preparatory" spiritual states of "conviction" and "humiliation" in the hope thereby of attaining to regeneration.[40] Neither predestination nor the *sola gratia* nor the doctrine of total depravity were understood by Reformed divines as excluding human action in the use of the created means ordained for the dispensing of grace, as themselves instrumental in the application to the elect of the redemption wrought by Christ. If justification is by faith, and if faith comes by hearing the preached word, then it is only by going to meeting and attending on the minister's words that a person may be saved. The preacher possesses no supernatural power to convert, nor does diligent hearing in any way merit saving grace. Yet preaching and hearing are, *potentia dei ordinata*, the normal instruments by which the Spirit works faith in the heart. Paraphrasing Thomas Hooker, a man has liberty to go to the church or to the tavern, and he is to be urged to choose the former for the safety of his soul.[41] That, in doing so, a person might be assailed by a conscience sharpened by the preaching of the law and drawn to Christ by the promise of grace in the gospel was not regarded as detracting from the efficacy of supernatural grace. For in neither case was the individual seen as compelling God to work further upon him toward justification; and neither experience could be taken as ground for hope of such future work, save as it belongs to the ordained means by which God prepares those in whom he intends to work vocation. That, and when, in a given case, he does work vocation effectually is entirely contingent upon his own will and power. *Potentia dei ordinata* there is a probable connection between conviction and humiliation and effectual calling, in that God ordinarily proceeds through them to vocation. There is, however, no automatic connection, such that attainment of the one insures the fruition of the other.[42]

Reformed divines noted, moreover, that the normative Protestant doctrine of justification by faith alone made justification contingent upon an individual's *own* faith, not on someone else's. This is clear, since *fiducia*—that trusting faith in Christ as savior which Protestants believed to be alone saving—can only be, properly speaking, an act of the *believer's* will, even though the act is contingent upon infused grace. Thus John Ball wrote: " 'The just' is said 'to live by his own faith,' and faith is called 'ours, or our own': not that we are the authors, cause or workers of it; but because we possess it, and are the special objects in which it is wrought by God. And also because it concerns ourselves in particular. . . ."[43] Without individual human activity—though wrought of God—there can be no justification of particular individuals. The crucial point, which distinguished "orthodox" Reformed Protestants from Roman Catholics and from Arminians, was whether faith or any other human act *merits* or is the *efficient cause* of justification. "Standard Reformed divines" answered unequivocally in the negative and dogmatized their answer at Dort. The connection between faith and justification is entirely gratuitous, and the power to believe is equally so, inasmuch as the depraved are utterly incapable of believing by their own power.[44] The act of belief, furthermore, even considered as a gracious human act, is incapable of covering their sinfulness, original and actual, in God's sight.

A John Cotton might argue that to make justification contingent on the human act of faith is to compromise the gratuity of grace and true Protestantism, too, and might cite Calvin for support. To do so, however, was to imply that faith does not come by the natural hearing of the preached word but by the supernatural whispering of the Spirit directly to the soul, a suggestion about which Calvin would have had serious reservations. To persons less sophisticated than Cotton, the assertion that a person is passive in conversion might suggest that God could as readily whisper in the tavern as in the church, and that it was relatively indifferent where one went, a suggestion Calvin would have found abhorrent.[45] In the orthodox view, however, the effectual activity of grace in vocation does not exclude human participation in the event, and human participation implies the instrumental use of created means, including human faculties. The effectual element in calling is indeed a supernatural power infused, but the effect of it is to enable the natural faculties of intellect and will to act fiducially. The effect of *gratia infusa* is conceived positively, not as overwhelming and coercing the natural capacities of the recipient but as renewing the human creature, whose nature, though corrupted by sin, is not destroyed and, though injured, remains susceptible of repair. In this connection it is not insignificant that, in Puritan and Reformed orthodox discourse, the prevailing metaphor for what occurs in conversion is "rebirth," in the sense of thorough renovation of human nature, rather than its violent destruction and creation *de novo*.[46] The relationship between divine sovereignty and the liberty of second causes, as expressed in covenant doctrine, was fraught with tension. At the same time, it may be suggested, a significant dialectical balance was achieved in it between divine and human autonomy.

Such balance appears, notably, in the pastoral writings of early New England Puritans. This literature, embodying the characteristic Puritan concern for religious experience, is addressed overwhelmingly to the two paramount questions generated by that concern: How may I come to have an interest in Christ? and How may I know that I truly have such an interest? A great portion of it is devoted to "marks" of a blessed estate and ways of knowing if one's faith is true, to assurances that God is faithful and will perform what he promises and complete what he begins, to warnings against despair if the Lord seems to tarry, and to counsels of patient and hopeful waiting upon him. One suspects, because much attention is given to these things, that the frequent exhortations diligently to use the means, actively to seek and take grace, and thereby to make one's calling sure—which also loom large in Puritan practical discourse—were more than adequately balanced by trenchant reminders of the inscrutability and absolute autonomy of the divine will, of the deviousness of the corrupt human will, and of the utter helplessness of fallen man either to compel God or to merit his favor for salvation.

One side of this pastoral dialectic—which is also the dialectic of covenant theology—appears in Hooker's remark about the choice between going to church and going to the tavern and in Shepard's and Bulkeley's insistence that faith is an active fastening upon the offer of grace. The other side is expressed, for example, in Hooker's pointed reminder to his congregation that the believing soul does not come to "close and become one with the Spirit of Christ in the promise" because "nature, or your wits, or parts [are] able to do this for you," but only because "the good Spirit of the Lord wrought upon, and fitted, and framed the heart hereunto"— something the Spirit does, moreover, according to his good pleasure and in his own good time.[47] Both sides of the covenantal dialectic are brought together in Bulkeley's sermonic "use," drawn from consideration of the role of active faith as the condition of the cov-enant of grace.

> This may let us see the kindness and love of God toward us, in that he has appointed such a condition of life unto us, as through his grace is possible for us to fulfill. To fulfill the righteousness of the law is now become impossible, through the infirmity of our flesh; but it is not impossible to believe on him who has fulfilled all righteousness for us. Here is grace in appointing such a possible condition; . . . If we had been held close to this condition of fulfill-ing the law, we should have missed of life for ever. The Lord therefore seeing and pitying our infirmity, was pleased to propound unto us another condition, saying unto us, only believe; believe on my son, trust on my grace, and thou shalt be saved; herein the Lord has condescended to our weakness, taking compassion of our infirmities, laying upon us no other burthen but this: Believe my promise, accept my grace, and rest upon it, and this thy faith shall save thee, Thou shalt never perish.[48]

In contrast to Bulkeley's effort to balance created nature and divine grace in the work of salvation, the Arminian variant of Re-formed Protestantism developed the natural side of the dialectic and made the covenant of grace correspond even more closely in substance to the covenant of works. Seeking to uphold the integrity of the creature and, in particular, human liberty of choice and action, Arminianism treated the act of faith required by the covenant of grace as equivalent to the obedience required as the condition of the covenant with Adam. God, having been disposed by Christ's meritorious sacrifice to look favorably upon mankind, now accepts man's imperfect faith in place of perfect obedience to the moral law, and reckons it to the believer as righteousness. The act of faith, moreover, is regarded as a natural act, inasmuch as, after God has done everything necessary to enable a person to believe, it remains up to the person whether to assent to the offer of grace. From the "orthodox" Reformed viewpoint this was to say that we are justified by faith "properly," as a righteous act of ours that God credits as such, rather than "metonymically," in the sense that "Christ's righteousness believed in by faith, is imputed to the believer for righteousness."[49] The Arminian formulation also made man's will the efficient cause of justifying faith, rather than the Holy Spirit acting through grace infused; and it made faith the antecedent condition of regeneration rather than the first effect of it. In both respects Arminianism appeared to allow undue advantage to fallen mankind and so to "derogate from grace." In the covenant theology of Ames and Bulkeley, however, the claims of nature and grace appear more equally poised. Thus Bulkeley insisted that while the elect are passive in receipt of the habit of grace, the covenant of grace requires the acting of the habit as its condition, as did the covenant of works.[50] The difference lies in that, with faith, the act springs from a gracious inclination to which corrupt nature by itself is unable to attain, and the relationship between the human act of faith and the divine act of justification is neither legal nor condign but entirely arbitrary.

It may accordingly be argued that, for those Puritans who were able to sustain the tension inherent in it and avoid excessive simplification, covenant theology succeeded rather well in maintaining a balance between divine efficacy and creaturely integrity, with important consequences for Puritan life and without loss of doctrinal correctness. The distinction between the divine decree and the means of its execution, which covenant theology presupposed and scholastic metaphysics sustained, made a place within the context of the divine sovereignty for the activity of second causes according to their own natures, including human faculties. The distinction between divine efficiency and creaturely instrumentality in gracious acts, including the act of faith—a distinction derived partly from scholastic philosophy and partly from St. Paul's "I worked . . . , yet not I, but the grace of God which was with me" (1 Cor. 15:10)—secured the Protestant principle that salvation is by grace alone.

In its dialectical character, moreover, covenant theology opened the way to a more-or-less objective assurance of salvation, founded on the orderliness of God's working and the prescriptions of the biblical word, on one hand, and on works of sanctification and the perceptions of a renewed conscience, on the other. This aspect of Puritan divinity and the more specific theological ingredients in the New England elders' approach to the problem of assurance are the subjects of the next two chapters.

The Order of Redemption and the Ground of Assurance

In opposition to Roman Catholics, who rejected the possibility of assurance of salvation in this life, and to Arminians, who implied that the converted could fall from grace, Puritans insisted that personal certitude of salvation is attainable short of heaven. The intense, characteristic Puritan concern for knowledge of one's estate in grace, which appears in the New England Antinomian Controversy, was founded on this confidence in the possibility of assurance. This conviction, in turn, was based on another, touching the order in which redemption is accomplished and the nature of the God who established that order. For Reformed orthodox Protestants, the ultimate ground of assurance of election was confidence in the immutability of God's determination to save and in the sufficiency of God's power to accomplish his intent, in both respects quite independently of fallen man's power of cooperation or resistance. The possibility of *knowing* one's estate was held to reside in the orderliness of God's use of particular means in effecting what he intends and in the constancy of the sequence of causes in the "golden chain" leading to the glorification of the elect. Herein lies the "practical" significance of the doctrines that treat of God as he is in himself: both the divine faithfulness and the divine constancy are rooted in the nature of God as one and unchangeable.

From the individual's viewpoint, the immediate problem of assurance was that of ascertaining the divine intent toward himself, in order to invoke the divine faithfulness and sufficiency in his own case. This requirement raised the question how God's will *pro me* is to be known, to which Puritan divines routinely answered, By means of the works of the Spirit in thine own soul. Their answer, however, prompted two further questions: what, concretely, does the Spirit work and how may his works be recognized? Both questions were crucial in the New England controversy. Cotton and his colleagues responded to them rather differently, and their respective answers reflected different theological understandings of the relationship, in regeneration, among faith, justification, sanctification, and personal assurance. Further, the clash between them was part of contemporary controversy among English nonconformists over these issues.

THE SPIRIT'S "WITNESS" AND THE EVIDENCE OF ELECTION

The Seal of the Spirit

Puritans agreed that personal assurance of salvation derives from the testimony of the Spirit, who is the divine agent in regeneration. The Father elects, the Son redeems, the Spirit applies redemption to individuals, calling, working faith, and sanctifying. The Spirit also "seals" the regenerate, confirming that they are beloved of God, that they truly believe, and therefore are justified and saved. In his witnessing function, he is called, after Rom. 8:15-16, the "Spirit of Adoption." "The Spirit of God," Sibbes wrote, "which knows the deep things of God and the depths of our hearts, doth reveal this mutual interest betwixt God and those that are his. . . . The Spirit of God, that reveals God to be ours, and stirs up faith in him, both reveals this trust to our souls, and the interest we have in God thereby."[1] The ordinances of the church, especially the sacrament of the Lord's Supper, are "the common broad seal of God," which outwardly confirms and declares the faith of true Christians. This is, however, only an outward seal, and excessive reliance upon it may delude with a false sense of security. More certain, Sibbes emphasized, is God's "privy seal," the inward witness of the Spirit to the soul, which cannot be mistaken and which is conclusive.[2] This private seal is the true foundation of assurance.

The doctrine of the Spirit's personal witness to the saints was highly suggestive, and its fruitfulness within the Puritan movement may readily be traced.[3] It expressed the essence of Puritan experiential piety. At the same time, as experience demonstrated, it could be a source of confusion in both doctrine and practice. Accordingly, while Puritan divines earnestly affirmed and emphasized the doctrine, they tended to qualify it in ways that reduced its suggestion of an immediate, transcendent encounter. This effort at qualification is evident, for example, in Sibbes's handling of the topic, which is characteristic of a considerable segment of Puritan opinion.[4]

Sibbes identified four principal ways in which the Spirit of Adoption provides believers with "superadded confirmation" of their faith. In the first place, the Spirit witnesses "by a secret whispering and intimation to the soul (which the believer's heart feels better than I am able to express), saying 'Be of good comfort, thy sins are forgiven. . . . Because thou believest, behold thou art honored to be my child.' " In the second place, the Spirit stirs up the heart, in prayer, to fervent and familiar supplications to God as Father. In the third, he stamps the soul, in sanctification, with "some lineaments of the heavenly image of Christ." Finally, as a foretaste of heavenly glory, he works a sense of joy in successful performance of "holy duties" in triumph over "old lusts." The first of these witnesses, as Sibbes acknowledged, is essentially ineffable, but the other three include elements of disposition and behavior in the individual and so possess a degree of objectivity. Sibbes was convinced that the Spirit sometimes witnesses "most sweetly" to the soul in a manner intuitive and beyond the categories of ratiocination. He noted, however, that this witness is in practice quite intermittent, and he took for granted that the more direct and intuitive testimonies from the Spirit are frequently, even usually, lacking from the experience of believers.[5] The same is true of the experience of heavenly joy, though to a lesser extent. In practice, therefore, Sibbes's emphasis falls on behavior in prayer and on sanctification understood as conformity in disposition and action to the image of Christ.

Even while expounding the doctrine of the Spirit's sealing, Sibbes and his colleagues reminded their hearers that the Spirit, in witnessing, is not *personally* present in or to the regenerate. On this point they shared the perspective Perkins had earlier articulated, in reply to the Catholic assertion that special revelation is necessary for assurance in this life. They held, namely, that the

Spirit witnesses not extraordinarily but by applying the promises of the gospel particularly in the heart, as they are propounded in the ministry of the word. The Spirit, Perkins had maintained, seals adoption in moving understanding and will to embrace the promises as our own; he moves us "by begetting a special trust and confidence" in us. The Spirit's sealing is thus mediated through the biblical word and the actions of human faculties spiritually transformed.[6] Similarly, when Sibbes came to specify concretely how the Spirit witnesses to the regenerate, he tended to speak most fully of actions of human faculties that were held to reflect the altered disposition wrought by the Spirit in regeneration. Considering the question whether the Spirit himself is the "seal" mentioned in 2 Cor. 1:23, or the graces wrought by the Spirit, Sibbes responded that the seal is *the Spirit present in his works.*

> [W]hosoever has the Spirit of Christ, the same is his. He is the author of our sealing; so that, except you take the Spirit for that which is wrought by the Spirit, you have not the comprehension of sealing, for that which the Spirit works is the seal. The Spirit goes always with his own mark and impression. . . . [T]he Spirit of God dwells and keeps a perpetual residence in the heart of a Christian, guiding him, moving him, enlightening him, governing him, comforting him, doing all the offices of a seal in his heart, till he has brought him to heaven.

The Spirit's presence is known by its effects, and his witnessing is discerned by and in them, even—the metaphor is almost routine— as smoke and heat disclose the presence of fire as yet unseen.[7]

The Spirit's sealing, therefore, is neither mystical rapture nor direct insight into the divine mind. It may be an intuitive apprehension—though Sibbes's ineffable sealing was to a degree tied to consciousness of the prior act of faith. Most frequently it consists in the discovery in oneself of distinctive persuasions, desires, and endeavors held to disclose the Spirit's regenerating presence. Such effects are likely, in any case, to be more constant, and they are more readily perceptible, than the more intuitive or strictly affective seals. The Lord knows who are his, but how shall we? Sibbes answered, in effect, By the seal of sanctification: " 'Let everyone that nameth the name of the Lord depart from iniquity,' not only in heart and affection, but in conversation, and that shall be a seal of sonship to him."[8] The quest for assurance thus became a matter of searching one's actions and motives for signs suggestive of regeneration, and sanctification became, in practice, a major evidence of justification.

At this point two questions loomed. First, by what means might a person know and judge the signs of regeneration? Then, on what basis might he conclude from a particular sign to the principal object of inquiry, namely, God's intent toward himself? The first was a question about the mind's power to know itself, the second a question about the coherence of causes and effects in regeneration.

The Order of Redemption

In Reformed orthodox divinity, God's action in regenerating was held to follow a definite order. The individual is transformed instantaneously, but several different things, regarded as causally related, were held to occur in the crucial moment. Analyzed into its components, regeneration encompasses, in order: (1) calling, in which a supernatural principle of action is infused into the soul; (2) an act of faith arising from this new principle, accepting the offer of Christ's righteousness presented in the gospel; (3) repentance, the effective turning of the person away from evil and toward true good; (4) justification, in which God, in virtue of Christ's righteousness believed in, absolves the person from the guilt of sin and from his debt of obedience to the moral law; (5) adoption, in which the person acquires the status of a "son" of God, with all the perquisites thereof; (6) sanctification, one of the perquisites, in which, by infusion of gracious habits, the person becomes himself actually holy; and (7) glorification, also one of the perquisites, in which the person experiences a foretaste of the joy and peace of heaven and hopes for fulfillment of both. At point (3), a person is said properly to be "converted," to have entered the covenant of grace, and to be in "union" with Christ, though strictly speaking "conversion" and "regeneration" begin in "calling"; at points (5) through (7) a person is said to enjoy "communion" with Christ.[9]

In the *Marrow*, Ames described the causal connections among these elements. Calling, the first act of election in respect of man himself, consists in the outward offer of the gospel and the inward receiving of it in faith; it issues in union with Christ. From union follows a change in the believer's relationship to God, namely, justification and adoption, and also a change in the believer's person, beyond that effected in calling. Justification, God's sentence of pardon, is "pronounced in actuality upon the first relationship which is created when faith is born." Faith precedes it as instrumental cause, laying hold of Christ's righteousness, which justification follows as an effect. Adoption presupposes reconciliation in justification and so presupposes faith and calling, and the witness of the Spirit of Adoption is given to believers only "after they have already believed." The change in believers themselves involves "an alteration of qualities in the man himself . . . wherein justification is manifested and its consequences . . . brought into being." Strictly, sanctification is distinguished from the initial communication of faith "as a principle of new life," being, rather, "that change in a believer in which he has righteousness and indwelling holiness imparted to him." Glorification, a change from the state of misery to that of happiness, is the actual possession of the blessedness resulting from the sentence of justification. Puritans differed in the handling of certain details of this scheme, but they generally agreed with Ames about the causal relationship among calling, faith, justification, and sanctification.[10]

It should be further noted that the order of regeneration just described, as it appears in the handbooks of divinity, is primarily a logical and a theological sequence, rather than a description of a series of events in the spiritual life of individuals. The latter, Puritans frequently noted, varies widely. Repentance, for example, may often be known before faith in the promises, the act of faith may not always be accompanied by full persuasion of the truth of the promises in one's own case, and subjective certainty of glorification is not enjoyed by all believers.[11] Essentially, the pattern outlined by Ames is an elaboration of the affirmation that the Holy Spirit, through the preaching of law and gospel, separates men from their sins and turns them redemptively toward God, with significant personal consequences for themselves as well as for their relationship to the Heavenly Father. Because the question of assurance was an urgent one for Puritans, they devoted much space to delineating steps toward, and degrees of, rebirth, which steps and degrees might be experienced in time. These gradations, however, insofar as they belong to a coherent scheme, were not understood necessarily or even primarily as a temporal sequence. Puritan discussion of the "stages" and "morphology of conversion" (in the idiom of modern interpretation), while exceedingly useful in preaching, pastoral care, and personal devotion, was chiefly a description of an order of causes and only secondarily of a series of historical events.[12]

As represented in formal Puritan divinity, the order of redemption begins with the decree of election, encompasses the spiritual rebirth of sinful human beings, and ends with the glorification of the saints in heaven. It is at once immanent in time and transcendent of time, in substance and in logic. This duality is reflected in Puritan theological discourse, where, especially in treating of the order of divine action *ad extra,* a distinction between "order of nature" and "order of time" is commonly employed as a means of discriminating between what is logically implicated in the being of a thing, on one hand, and historical occurrence and personal awareness, on the other.[13] The practical "uses" and "applications" of Puritan discourse about regeneration apply chiefly to the "order of time." In the formal order of the Puritan sermon, however, they appear as conclusions from the exposition of "doctrine," and much of what is treated under the latter head is understood to apply only "in order of nature."

This distinction between causal and temporal orders was crucial for the doctrine of assurance. Puritans accepted that regeneration of individuals remains subjectively incomplete in this life, and that, while sin ceases to reign in the saints, it does not cease to assail them. In consequence, a saint's estate in grace often seems to him very tenuous. In any case, it was evident from pastoral experience that the *marks* of regeneration were rarely experienced all together and were not likely to be experienced always in the same order. In practice, it was allowed, the moment of conversion is often difficult to determine, and sanctification, as a positive change in the individual, is more likely to be perceived than justification, which is pronounced in heaven. What is important for assurance, therefore, is not so much the order in which the gifts of grace are experienced as the order in which they are related in God's bestowing of them. Puritan divines maintained that, because of the orderliness of God's proceeding, especially as disclosed in Rom. 8:30, it is unnecessary either to know the content of God's mind directly or to have experienced the fullness of regeneration in order to be certain of salvation. Rather, since regeneration is qualitatively complete in an instant, and since the elements of it are causally related, it is needful only to be certain of any one of them in order to be assured of all the rest.[14]

In his *Cases of Conscience* Perkins offered the foregoing as a general rule for addressing the problem of personal assurance. The testimony of the Spirit, he affirmed, in certain dispositions of conformity to God's will, is a solid ground for confidence. If such testimony be wanting, the sanctification of the heart is sufficient, and if sanctification is uncertain, then the beginnings and first motions of it will suffice. "Wherever these are, there is the Spirit of God, whence they proceed. . . . One apple is sufficient to manifest the life of the tree, and one good and constant motion of grace is sufficient to manifest sanctification."[15] Whom God justifies, he also sanctifies and will surely glorify; and where sanctification is, there is the order of regeneration in its entirety. Not all Puritans were as optimistic as Perkins about the evidential value of the "first motions" of sanctification, and none believed that sanctification should remain the only ground of assurance in a Christian's life; nonetheless, most of the Puritans with whom this essay deals were sufficiently convinced of the coherence of the order of redemption to conclude confidently from the effects of saving grace in themselves to its causes, without always having consciously experienced the causes. Whether it was indeed possible to do this was one of the issues in the New England controversy.

The Power of Introspection and the "Practical Syllogism"

Reformed orthodox divines commonly taught that certainty of election is not to be sought "*a priori,* by foolish musing about the divine decree, but *a posteriori,* by a *syllogismus practicus* or *analyticus.*" Wollebius's formulation may be taken as fairly typical.

> In ascertaining our election analytically it is necessary to proceed from the means of execution to the decree, beginning from our sanctification, according to the following syllogism: Whoever perceives in himself the gift of sanctification, by which we die to sin and live to righteousness, is justified, called or endued with true faith, and elect. But by the grace of God I perceive this. Therefore, I am justified, called and elect.[16]

Calvin had preferred to rest assurance on the act of faith itself and on the subjective certainty of divine favor that faith carries with it, as prior to and independent of the fruits of faith, which provide only secondary evidence. Later Reformed theologians tended to emphasize the evidential significance of gracious works over the subjective assurance of faith itself, without, however, discounting the latter.[17]

Among English Puritans both these emphases appear, sometimes in ambiguous combination. Thus in Perkins's treatment of sanctification as a witness of the Spirit, the practical syllogism is implicit, and it is explicit in his treatment of the confidence that arises from faith. Like most Puritans he regarded assurance as in some sense ingredient in true faith, and he thought that such fiducial assurance ought to be the primary basis of a Christian's confidence. He was willing, however, to argue that the *act* of faith, essayed in hope and trust but lacking subjective confidence of fulfillment, is sufficient evidence from which to conclude to the divine intent towards oneself. Such a conclusion, he wrote, may among other ways

> be gathered, partly upon things generally revealed in the word of God, and partly upon sense, observation, and experience: the same things being revealed generally in the word, and particularly by experience. Upon this ground may we truly conclude the forgiveness of our sins, and the salvation of our souls, on this manner: He which believeth hath the forgiveness of his sins, but I believe in Christ (saith he which believeth), Therefore my sins are forgiven me. The *major* . . . is expressed in the word; the *minor* . . . is found true by experience, and by testimony of the conscience.[18]

In the same manner, Perkins admitted, a person might reason from perception in himself of other gracious acts, and on pastoral grounds he allowed that practical conclusions of this sort might constitute the beginning of assurance in particular cases.

The possibility of such reasoned conclusions about the divine favor rested on three assumptions: (a) that the order of causes and effects in the application of redemption is truly known; (b) that empirical propositions concerning qualifications given in scripture are as certain as the scriptural propositions on which they are based; and (c) that the human mind is able accurately to know its own "frame and disposition."[19] The latter point was important, for the minor proposition of the argument concerned not outward acts as such but their inward "sincerity," that is, the soundness of their motives. On scriptural and philosophical grounds, however, it was taken for granted that the mind is able to reflect knowledgeably upon itself and that this capacity is enhanced in regeneration. In the nature of the case, the mind is cognizant of its own actions. When it assents or desires or purposes, it knows itself to do each of these things, "much more being holpen by the Spirit of God, 'whom we have received . . . that we might know the things which are given unto us by God.'" Ames explained that a person may know his own estate in grace by considering his external and internal actions, and the "inclinations and dispositions" whence they flow, by exercise of "that reflex act, which is proper to man, whereby he has a power, as it were to enter into, and perceive what is in himself." This capacity of self-knowledge Ames located in the conscience, as the faculty of the understanding responsible for reviewing and judging actions. In fulfilling its office, conscience proceeds by means of a syllogism, in which the proposition (in the case of an "enlightened conscience") derives from the law of God, the assumption concerns a state of affairs empirically ascertained, and the conclusion is a judgment, arising from the state of affairs in relation to the law, and concerning the condition of the individual. Conscience, in other words, ordinarily operates via a practical syllogism.[20]

Being privy to motives, conscience is able to judge the genuineness of acts of faith, repentance, and sanctification; and on this basis the intellect, knowing the order of redemption, is able to reach a true conclusion about the individual's personal estate, and consequently about his election. The "ordinary assurance" of God's children, wrote John Ball, "is concluded by joining the light of their conscience kindled by the Holy Ghost, and ruled by the scriptures, to the immediate light of the conditions revealed in the scriptures. . . . [T]he rule by which a man discerns himself to believe, is the doctrine of God's word, declaring the quality of faith."[21] On the same basis, Perkins could frame his answer, in "a case of conscience" touching "how a man may know whether he be a child of God or not," in terms of the evidence of sanctification; and Sibbes could affirm:

> God descends down unto us from election to calling, and so to sanctification; we must ascend to him, beginning where he ends. . . .

This great secret of God's eternal love to us in Christ is hidden in his breast, and does not appear to us, until in the use of means God by his Spirit discovers the same to us. . . . The soul . . . draws [from Christ] so much virtue as changes the frame of it, and quickens it to duty, which duties are not grounds of our state in grace, but issues springing from a good estate before; and thus far they help us in judging of our condition, that though they be not to be rested in, yet as streams they lead us to the spring-head of grace from whence they arise.[22]

When the New England elders adduced works of sanctification as declarative of justification and therefore as a ground of assurance, they were in good company.

"JUSTIFYING FAITH" AND "FAITH OF ASSURANCE"

Despite wide acceptance of the practical syllogism in Reformed orthodoxy, among Puritans the precise relationship between the assurance derived from practical reasoning and the assurance ingredient in faith itself remained in a measure subject to discussion. In England in the early seventeenth century, "justifying faith" was the object of continuing dispute between "orthodox" Reformed Protestants, on one hand, and Continental Roman Catholics and Arminians and the "Arminian" party in the English Church, on the other. This dispute was chiefly about faith's relationship as a human act to justification as a divine one, though it embraced the whole content of the *locus de fide*, especially in the case of the Catholic disputants. Among Puritans, discussion focused on the nature of justifying faith itself, within the context of the Protestant conception of justification by faith alone, and, in particular, on the sense in which faith may properly be said to *be* assurance. According to one alternative, faith that justifies is essentially and primarily *fiducia*, an act of will resting on Christ for fulfillment in one's own case of the promise of redemption. According to another, faith that justifies is a full and assured persuasion that one's sins are in fact wholly forgiven. Puritan consideration of these issues was part of the larger interconfessional debate, inasmuch as Catholic controversialists charged that the Protestant conception made faith equivalent to assurance and implied that it follows justification in the order of nature as well as of time. The Puritan discussion, however, was also rooted in a degree of ambiguity about the relationship between faith and assurance that had been present in Reformed teaching since Calvin's day. Moreover, by about 1630, the notion that justifying faith is properly assurance had become an issue with elements of English nonconformity that even the more extreme Puritans regarded as excessively radical.[23] The New England antinomian dispute was, in important respects, part of the latter controversy.

Puritan divines maintained that faith occupies the crucial place in the order of redemption for individuals, in that faith is the first effect of regeneration and the instrument of union with Christ, whence all other effects derive.[24] Faith is thus the vital nexus of nature and grace in a Christian's life. This affirmation by itself, however, did not completely settle the question of the relationship between faith as the cause of justification and faith as the assurance of it, or that of the relationship of faith and justification in the causal and temporal orders. How these questions were approached depended in significant measure on the way in which the respective disputants understood the relationship between created nature and divine grace in regeneration, and on the degree of efficacy they were willing to allow to second causes in the accomplishment of regeneration. The fact that important Reformed divines emphasized on various occasions the cognitive, and on others the causal, role of faith provided scope for alternative solutions, in which "justifying faith" could be understood primarily in either causal or cognitive terms.

William Perkins is a case in point. In *A Golden Chain* he defined justifying faith as "a particular assurance of the favor of God," thereby seeming to give color to the Catholic charge; and he observed, regarding Rom. 8:16, that, besides the witness of "our spirit" in sanctification and its fruits, God's Spirit "witnesses after another manner, namely by the certainty of faith, declaring and applying the promises of God to us." At the same time, he insisted that faith justifies only as an instrument, whose proper action is to "apprehend and apply that which justifies, namely Christ and his benefits"; and he distinguished between the certainty belonging in principle to all faith and the full subjective assurance that may accompany it after long trial and experience, increasing by degrees.[25] The ambiguity of these formulations appears to have been due partly to controversial considerations. Perkins identified faith as a "particular persuasion" of divine favor in order to distinguish it from faith as general assent to revealed truth and from implicit faith in what the Catholic Church teaches. Justifying faith, rather, is the persuasion that the promises of redemption are effective for oneself; it is apprehension of God's offer of grace, not as made generally to all who believe but as made effectually to me believing. As a distinctive human act, justifying faith is, as it were, "the hand of the soul, receiving and applying the saving promises"; it is "a miraculous and supernatural faculty of the heart, apprehending Christ Jesus . . . , and receiving him to itself." Perkins also sought to counter the view that assurance is obtained in this life only by special revelation. Rather, he argued, certainty is had ordinarily by the Spirit's testimony in the use of means and by the Seal of Adoption in sanctification. Effectual apprehension of the promises under the ministry of the word he included under the "use of means," and he indicated that such apprehension implies personal assurance of their effectiveness. To apprehend Christ is thus to believe with certainty, and certainly to believe; and the act of apprehending, being the Spirit's gift, is also the Spirit's testimony.[26]

Perkins's point was that faith is not a probable hope of what one desires but may be disappointed of, but is, rather, certain knowledge of unshakeable truth. Accordingly, he placed the "seat" of faith in the intellect instead of in the will or affections, though he tended in practice to speak of faith as being in the "heart," meaning the whole soul without differentiation. At the same time, he defined "to believe in" as meaning to know, to acknowledge, and to put confidence in the object of faith, in contrast to the "merely" intellectual assent connoted by "to believe" in reference to *credenda*. The confidence or "affiance" of the soul, "embracing" and "resting in" the promises, he located in the will, ascribing it, as a fruit of faith, to the Spirit of Adoption. There is thus an implicit distinction, in Perkins's treatment, between the fiducial act of faith that unites to Christ and the assurance of faith that one is united; and it is evident from his discussion of the "degrees" of faith that a person might have the first without having very much of the second.[27]

Later Puritans, partly under the stress of controversy and partly as a reflection of the experientialism of their piety, were moved to greater precision in defining the nature of justifying faith and its relation to assurance. They seem, formally at least, to have divided the respective elements of Perkinsian ambiguity among themselves, emphasizing one or the other of them according to particular interests and occasions—and also, it appears, according to the degree to which, theologically, they subordinated the agency of created nature to that of the divine nature.

Thus, where Perkins located faith in the intellect and tended to speak of it in cognitive terms, Ames, Preston, Sibbes, and Ball insisted that faith is properly and primarily an act of the will; and they distinguished explicitly between the primary act of faith, which justifies, and a secondary act that apprehends justification already obtained. Confidence, in the sense of subjective assurance, they ascribed to the latter.[28] "Justifying faith," said Preston, is "a grace or a habit infused into the soul . . . , whereby we are enabled to believe, not only that the Messiah is offered to us, but also to take and receive him as a Lord and Saviour." The distinctive element is not persuasion of the understanding that Christ is given to me, but the further action of receiving him given. Ames observed that justifying faith is concerned not only with the truth of the promises but also with the good of the things promised, which is properly the object of the will. Faith is, therefore, "an act of choice, an act of the whole man—which is by no means a mere act of the intellect." Ball defined faith as properly *fiducia,* as a "lively and obediential affiance," in which, in addition to giving assent, a person "doth rely, cast and repose his soul upon Christ."[29]

According to these divines, justifying faith is to be classified as an "elicit act," called forth and exercised in vocation; and justification follows upon the relationship created by it. It is to be distinguished, therefore, from the subsequent "reflected act of faith" by which justification, already pronounced, is perceived by the individual.[30] Justifying faith, Ames wrote, is not "the special confidence by which we apprehend forgiveness of sins and justification itself. For justifying faith precedes justification itself, as a cause precedes its effect: but faith apprehending justification necessarily presupposes and follows justification, as an act follows the object about which it is exercised." Similarly, Preston distinguished between a "first act of faith," apprehending and taking the righteousness offered through Christ, and a "second act," by which we know that we have taken Christ. The first is "constant, and admits of no degrees," and is grounded on the faithfulness of God to perform what he promises. The second, though assisted by the Holy Spirit, "is chiefly grounded upon our own experience: for it is no more but the act of a man's own heart, reflecting upon what he has done. . . ." In the same vein, Ball distinguished between confidence as embracing Christ, which is the form of faith, and confidence as quietness of conscience, which is the effect of faith; the first he labelled "faith of adherency," the second, "faith of evidence."[31]

The context of this distinction between "faith of adherence" and "faith of assurance" was pastoral as well as controversial. It was the common observation of Preston's generation that a person may have the first act of faith and not the second, and that the latter is subject to many degrees and variations. True faith may be hidden in the heart, even while particular assurance may be lacking. "Believers," Ames noted, "do not have the same assurance of grace and favor of God, nor do the same ones have it at all times." To make justification depend on assurance, therefore, seemed to these men really to cut the ground from under true assurance, by making justification dependent on an individual's own subjective states rather than the sufficiency of God in the order of redemption. Such an interpretation, they maintained, was contrary to sound doctrine and inimical to proper care of hopeful saints. Faith, Ball observed, is necessary to salvation, but "full assurance that I do believe in that sort, is not of like necessity." God does not require full and perfect faith, but only the existence of sincere and "unfeigned" faith. Fulfillment of the promises, he insisted, depends on the thing received, Christ's righteousness, rather than on the steadfastness of the receiving.[32] If justification depends on the perfection of faith, John Downe observed, then we must despair, "for so the palsie[d] hand of faith should not receive Christ." Ames and Preston concurred. Given God's constancy in the application of redemption, where true faith is or has been, salvation is assured whether the individual is always assured of it or not.[33] Given the frailty of Christians, who, though regenerate and redeemed, wrestle with sin and weakness all their days, hope must rest finally in the divine constancy and sufficiency. From a pastoral perspective these affirmations were important, for they meant that justifying faith is compatible with the experience of subjective doubt.

Other Puritans were less confident that active faith and personal assurance were so readily distinguishable and tended to formulate the relationship between an individual's faith and his justification primarily in cognitive terms. They tended, that is, to define
active faith as "faith of assurance" rather than "faith of adherence."
They seem, also, to have been Puritans whose respect for the Protestant *sola gratia* and for the divine holiness and majesty induced
them rather emphatically to subordinate human agency in regeneration to that of the Holy Spirit. These tendencies are evident in
Cotton's identification of active, "justifying faith" as the faith that
apprehends justification, in contrast to the passive receipt of habitual faith, which unites to Christ and thereby obtains justification.
The act of faith, he insisted, is merely the act by which an individual
becomes aware of his justification already obtained, and follows it
as a "condition consequent." A similar emphasis is observable in
the writings of John Forbes, dating from 1616, and in an exchange
between Nathaniel Baxter and John Downe published in the early
1630s.[34] Both men were contemporaries of Ames; they represent,
however, an understanding rather different from his of the nature
of justifying faith and its place in the order of an individual's regeneration.

Writing in Holland during the Arminian controversy, Forbes
wished to stress the absolute gratuity of justification and its entire
dependence on God's good pleasure. To this end he made "adoption" the primary category in the order of redemption. The decree
of election comprises God's adoption of the elect as "sons," which
is effected in calling. All the benefits enjoyed by the elect, including
justification, presuppose "filiation" as the ground of their bestowal
on individuals. Forbes criticized the view that adoption follows
justification in order of nature, as implying that God's love and
grace are "not free, or freely bestowed upon us," but are contingent
on something in the persons of the elect.[35] Active faith, the instrument apprehending Christ's righteousness, is, he maintained, also
the means of apprehending adoption and is consequently the principal means of assurance.

In speaking of faith, Forbes tended to emphasize its character
as a transcendent cognition. A person's faith, he wrote, as a supernatural work of God illuminating the mind and transforming the
heart, "includes in it a particular knowledge, by the particular

revelation of God in his heart concerning himself in particular, that he is chosen and elected by God, that Christ is given for him, that in him he is redeemed, that in him he has remission of his sins, that through him he shall be glorified." As such, faith is the primary ground of assurance. "Our devotion, zeal, holiness, profession and obedience, will miserably deceive us, if we build our trust on them, for it is not they, but faith alone, that makes us sons of God, and truly justifies us, . . . even they are all sins, if faith be not their fountain." The order of knowing one's estate thus begins with faith. "Until a man believe he can have no right judgment of spiritual things. . . . Faith is the only eye of the soul, whereby it's able truly to discern the nature of all spiritual and heavenly things."[36] Effectual faith, Forbes declared, brings Christ into the soul "in such evidency" that it is impossible to be ignorant that he is there; so that a person first and only knows himself to be a child of God "when he comes to a lively feeling and clear sight that Christ is in him, all other gifts or graces being of no value or force in the least to give any assurance or true knowledge of a man's soul that he is truly and effectually called by the gospel to the estate of grace and glory." Cotton interpreted Forbes to mean that works of sanctification have evidential value only as they are seen to flow from conscious faith of Christ dwelling in oneself and that to adduce works of sanctification otherwise is to ground justification on human works, rather than on Christ and his grace.[37]

Baxter was provoked into print by a sermon on justifying faith in which the preacher took a position similar to that of Ames and Preston. Echoing Perkins in his reply, he defined faith primarily in cognitive terms and made resting on Christ an effect of it. Justifying faith, said Baxter, is "an assured knowledge or knowing assurance, by the which every one of the elected relies upon the promises of the mercy of God in Christ Jesus, firmly holding that Christ and eternal life together with all the merits of Christ, are given unto him unto righteousness and eternal salvation." He went beyond Perkins, however, in making the *form* of faith a "confident relation to all the word of God, and certainty of salvation, . . . so that believing and particular knowing [one] self to be elected are one." "Justifying faith," therefore, is so called because it apprehends election.[38] Cotton said much the same thing during the New England controversy. The faith that justifies, Baxter urged (again like Cotton), is infused and present habitually, and is effective for justification before it manifests itself actively in an individual's believing. He apparently thought that taking active faith as the condition of the covenant of grace tended toward Catholicism. Accordingly, he insisted that faith is commanded in the gospel, not as the condition of justification, but as "an encouragement to believe assuredly in Christ," and that the act of faith presupposes justification by infusion of the habit of faith.[39] Faith thus comes after justification in the order of regeneration, and its proper office is to reveal to the justified that, apart from any action of theirs, they are already justified.

For Forbes, Baxter, and Cotton, the proper object of faith was the effectiveness *pro me* of the promises of Christ's righteousness. Faith, which renders the promises effectual, is thus "particular application" of the promises and "of Christ in them" to the believer, and is therein assurance of the subject as well as of the object. All three men, accordingly, tended to minimize the distinction between order of nature or causes and order of experience in time, in considering the application of redemption. Forbes, indeed, observed that in the bestowing of adoption the two orders are the same. For Ames, Preston, Sibbes, and Ball, in contrast, faith was not so much certitude of the present effectiveness of Christ's righteousness *pro me* as present confidence in Christ's righteousness as the sole means of my justification, and it included necessarily an element of trustful hope in future fulfillment.[40] A person, accordingly, is "not pardoned by believing that he is pardoned" but is pardoned by desiring, entreating, and confidently resting on the promise of Christ's righteousness to those who believe. Justifying faith, Ball noted, is a confidence not of things already possessed "but of things promised and upon believing to be obtained, which in the order of causes, not in time, doth go before remission of sins." A person may therefore be justified in fact, and be certain of the object, while yet lacking subjective "feeling and sense of remission." Shepard and Bulkeley concurred. They also agreed with Ames and others of like mind among their English brethren in maintaining that assurance is ordinarily gathered via the practical syllogism from the effects of election in oneself, especially from fiducial faith and works of sanctification, and that "faith of assurance" is distinct in form and content from the act of faith that properly justifies.[41]

The Amesian formulation of the order of God's proceeding, in nature and in time, in the accomplishment of regeneration may be viewed as an effort to deal theologically with the practical observation that subjective certitude of salvation varies, or may even fail, in the experience of persons otherwise evidently godly. In part, his formulation provided a counterpoise to those elements in Reformed doctrine that fostered a sense of uncertainty in hopeful Christians, and here it addressed a keen pastoral problem. It may also be seen as reflecting a desire not to limit the circle of sainthood to the relatively small number of persons who might obtain "clear and lively sight" of their justification by "particular illumination," as against the greater number dependent for knowledge of their estate on the "inferior light" of conscience concluding from the effects of grace in themselves. The alternative position, which Cotton articulated in New England, by defining faith as a transcendent cognition, enabled its exponents to offer a seemingly more conclusive sort of assurance than that available through the practical syllogism. They did so, however, at the expense of restricting the number of the assured to those who were able to attain a sense of divine illumination. They also ran the risk of implying that assurance could be had without the evidence of gracious works and consequently of seeming to abandon the "third use" of the moral law. Their solution to the problem of assurance, moreover, might actually compound the problem of subjective doubt, for it tended to leave the hopeful without objective recourse should their subjective source of assurance, their "justifying faith," fail under stress.

CHAPTER 8

The Quest for Assurance: Radical Solutions and Puritan Dialectics

Forbes, Baxter (as nearly as can be determined), and Cotton, save for his more extreme utterances during the Antinomian Controversy, remained within the theological framework of Reformed orthodoxy. Other nonconformists did not. Three of the latter, John Eaton (1575?–1642?), John Traske (d. 1636?), and Tobias Crisp (1600–1643), warrant introduction here, as illustrating comparatively radical approaches to the problem of assurance that were current in England around 1635 and that resemble, in a number of respects, the views of the Hutchinsonians in New England. Collectively, the distinctive ideas of these men made up the "doctrine of free justification by Christ alone," which, in the sectarian agitation emerging in England in the early 1630s, became the banner of the more radical spirits. By 1640, ideas like theirs were routinely denominated "antinomian" by Puritan and Anglican divines.[1]

THE DOCTRINE OF "FREE JUSTIFICATION"

Eaton, Traske, and Crisp were all three deeply occupied with the problem of assurance of salvation, a concern reflected in their treatment of the order of redemption and of the relationship between justification and works of sanctification. Crisp addressed the problem primarily by exalting the gratuity of justification and the efficacy of the divine intent, entirely apart from any possible qualification in the objects of it, and by stressing the assurance of faith itself as the gracious apprehension of justification, apart from all creaturely works. Eaton sought to secure assurance by emphasizing the absolute efficacy of Christ's righteousness for the faithful and its objective attachment to them, to the point that God, literally, can see no sin in them. Especially noteworthy, all three men treated regeneration as the divine power of Christ dwelling in the justified, yet in such a way that it remains separate from the individual's corrupt human nature, which is not really regenerated at all. Because God considers only Christ's righteousness in the saints, they need not take seriously what they apprehend as their own sinfulness, nor allow it to trouble their assurance. However, because they do feel sin in themselves, they must rely wholly on faith for assurance, and not on their imperfect sanctification.

For Eaton, the fundamental theological tension lay between the purity and holiness of God and the utter filthiness of human sin, and the basic religious problem for him was attainment of assurance that this tension is overcome by removal of such filth from God's sight. The means to the latter are comprised in the "doctrine of free justification," which was Eaton's slogan. By justification he meant the occasion in which "by the power of God's imputation, [we are] so clothed with the wedding garment of Christ's own perfect righteousness, that of unjust we are made just before God: that is, all our sins are utterly abolished out of God's sight, and we are made from all spot of sin perfectly holy and righteous in the sight of God freely."[2] Eaton explicitly rejected the merely judicial conception of justification as God's acquitting from guilt and pronouncing righteous. Justification is rather the covering of human uncleanness by Christ's righteousness, such that the recipient is made, for God, actually and completely righteous himself. God's imputation, he wrote in a characteristic passage, "by a strong and powerful *real working, and effectual operation,* . . . conveys (as the sun conveys his beams into a dark house) that perfect righteousness of Christ to be . . . *in us,* and *upon us;* so powerfully that we thereby are made of unjust just before God; but how? not inherently, and actively, but objectively and passively, as the dark house is made light with the sunshine." This objective righteousness extends to the whole person of the recipient, body and soul, and to all his thoughts and deeds, civil, domestic, and religious, so that in God's sight he "shin[es] now in this life with Christ's good works, more glorious in perfect holiness and righteousness . . . than the sun shines gloriously in our eyes."[3]

This being the case, faith necessarily follows justification as an effect. It consists, Eaton maintained, in believing the free promise of justification in one's own case; and it issues in peace of conscience that only the truly justified enjoy. It is thus "faith of justification" rather than "justifying faith"; and justification is said to be "freely by faith without works" because only true faith sees and enjoys it. Faith, moreover, believes against reason and contrary to one's own sense and feeling of sin. Eaton admitted that sin persists in the justified, maintaining that God permits them to feel it in order to encourage belief in divine power. God, however, does not see such sin himself, and for the justified to take it seriously is but ignorance and denial of the power of God, who is able to cover sin from his sight. Accordingly, Eaton explained the petition for forgiveness in the Lord's Prayer as only a prayer of weak faith for greater assurance.[4] In the Old Testament, he allowed, God did see sin in his children, but not in the time of the New Testament. To stumble, therefore, over a sense of one's own transgression and corruption is a serious mistake, which results from "want of discerning and rightly distinguishing between the voice of the law and the voice of the gospel, between the voice of God's children judging themselves in their temptations according to their sense and feeling, and their voice of faith." The former "voice" is "merely legal" and describes man's misery "in the state of nature and by the law." For Christians, however, the Danielic prophecy about the coming of everlasting righteousness and the end of sin is now fulfilled; and, Eaton declared, "cursed therefore is the man who shall say that Christ has not utterly abolished all the sins of the faithful." From God's viewpoint there simply is no longer any sin in believers or in the church. On this ground Eaton firmly rejected the common Protestant notion that the justified are simultaneously sinners and righteous in God's eyes. By implication, when the justified sin, they do so in their own "sense and apprehension," not in God's sight, and faith consists either in suppressing such apprehension or in not being bothered by it.[5]

Eaton admitted that justification produces sanctification as its effect, in the form of zeal for obedient walking in God's commandments, but God does not regard such obedience as holy. Sanctification remains spotted by sin and imperfect, and so is to God "as filthy, menstruous, stained rags" and therefore damnable. Christ's righteousness, however, which the justified possess "objectively," obscures this foulness from the divine gaze and renders them as perfectly righteous in God's eyes as Christ himself. Nonetheless, the justified are not themselves positively or subjectively regenerated, and the conception of the renovation of human faculties by infusion of gracious habits is absent from Eaton's discussion. A Christian, rather, leads a sort of double existence, expressed figuratively as the operation in him of two "souls," a "material" one, in which he lives only to the world, and "his soul as he is in Christ," which substantially is Christ's own righteousness and which causes him to live a godly life.[6]

Eaton allowed that sanctification, though in itself repulsive to God, does serve to justify Christians declaratively before men, being a fruit of justification and therefore an evidence of it. He denied, however, that sanctification is such an evidence *to the justified,* who rely for their assurance solely on the persuasion that the "main proposition of the gospel" is effective for them. To seek assurance in works of sanctification and the performance of holy duties is to return ignorantly or willfully to the legal teaching of the Old Testament, thereby obscuring the doctrine of free justification. To urge such a way of assurance upon people is to promote "a constrained hireling sanctity" and a "hypocritical legal holiness," and to preach a "blind, zealous, dead faith."[7] "This we do," Eaton wrote, describing what he considered the outstanding ministerial failing of the time,

> because we do not first establish and root them in the assurance and joy of *Free Justification* without works; for the seeking of further assurance by works, though not as causes, but as effects, makes people set the cart before the horse, and to confound, by the violence of the light of nature, the effects with the causes; and so to labor after the supposed works of sanctification more than after faith, that should give to Christ only, the sole glory of our assurance; therefore they should first have assurance, and then do, that which they do, in thankfulness for their assurance.[8]

Traske, not unlike Eaton, distinguished between the respective times of law and gospel and denied that the law is to be preached to believers at all, for neither does it serve to work repentance and faith nor is it a rule for believers to walk by. Being a rule of the flesh, the law simply does not pertain to the gospel and the Spirit. The glass in which believers behold themselves is properly the glory of Christ's face, not the glory of Moses. Accordingly, Traske distinguished between "faith of conditional promises," which is legal, and "faith of free promises," which is alone evangelical.[9] He also distinguished between the certainty of a Christian's condition before God and a Christian's own sense of his condition. Since the former is secure, the true Christian is not to grieve when he falls into sin but to rejoice and to depend wholly on Christ. To doubt one's estate, indeed, is to doubt God. True believers always grow in grace and its fruits, however it may seem subjectively to them. Also like Eaton, Traske insisted that faith is to be tried only by itself, not by its effects, because such effects can be recognized only by faith. Faith is the one true and certain mark of salvation, and a person simply must rest in the persuasion of faith itself. A critic noted of Traske that "he will admit no difference between pressing duties, as fruits of faith, and preaching justification by works; whereupon he censures all such ministers (as do the former), for legalists and justiciaries."[10]

Most striking, however, is Traske's conception of regeneration, in which the duality of natures suggested in Eaton's figure of the Christian's two souls becomes explicit. "Sanctification," Traske declared,

> is not in ourselves, that is, in the flesh, but only as we are in union with Christ; and by the Spirit only, as we understand it of its operations, by mortification, or quickening these our mortal bodies, yet not so in us as mingled with uncleanness, but as distinct absolutely from the flesh, as another nature, yea a participation of the divine nature, which though it make up one person, yet is not at all of the old man, or of the old creation, but it is that New Creation, that new heart, and that Spirit of God which is bestowed upon us.[11]

The opposition between flesh and spirit here appears to be absolute, and the divine "quickening" does not consist in the actions of human faculties regenerated by the Spirit but in acts of the Spirit upon such faculties. The "new creature" or "new man," Traske observed, is not "any renovation of the old man, . . . born of the flesh, the fallen man," but a "new creation from nothing." The faculties of the "old man" remain unaltered, and from them the new understanding, will, and affections of the regenerate are qualitatively different. Such faculties "are gifts from heaven, and must of necessity be perfect, without any defect or superfluity, for our first generation is totally fallen, and cannot be recovered here; but our regeneration is wholly perfect, and can never be corrupted, or sin again."[12]

Sanctification, accordingly, is not in the godly themselves as part of their nature but is properly and perfectly in Christ, who, as the "new creature," is in them. Correctly speaking, Traske maintained, sanctification is the "life of Jesus" dwelling immediately in the sanctified.[13] The bestowal of the Spirit, he declared,

> yields no new habits in the flesh, as if that were changed or renewed, but is subsisting of itself, that it is of power to manifest itself by acts of quickening, and renewing, and enabling this mortal flesh, as the life of Jesus in it . . . , neither is it the sanctified person that has any habit of grace in his flesh, but the Lord Jesus dwelling in him, doth put forth the bright beams of his glory, in such virtues as do befit the time and place in which he lives.[14]

Two natures, in effect, subsist unmingled in the godly, a divine one, which does not and cannot sin, "although not in manifestation," and the old fallen nature, still "as imperfect as ever it was." Traske's critic observed that he seemed to make no distinction between the attributes of God and the created qualities in men's hearts that are the effects of God's Spirit in them.[15] Traske might have replied that he did so distinguish, but that he placed the difference in the minds of the godly themselves.

Tobias Crisp was said to have begun his career as an Arminian and then overreacted in the opposite direction. He was concerned above all to defend the free grace of Christ from the "work-mungers" and "buyers of Christ, that would bring something with them to partake of [him]"; and he bluntly declared that Christ justifies not the righteous but the ungodly, and does so while they are entirely ungodly.[16] In the covenant of grace, he maintained, God freely unites himself to his people without reference to anything in them. In contrast to God's other covenants with mankind, this one requires no antecedent conditions whatsoever. There is nothing in a person capable of inducing God to bestow Christ upon him, nor anything, however vile, that can exclude him from the covenant of grace. Herein lies the covenant's gratuity, which is the great proclamation of the gospel and the only foundation of assurance. To introduce conditions into it, therefore, derogates from the freeness of grace. Prior to union with Christ, there is nothing at all in a person that is relevant, positively or negatively, to his entry into the new covenant. In any case, Crisp averred, God is properly said to justify the *ungodly,* which implies unbelief.[17]

Justifying faith, accordingly, follows justification in the order of regeneration and is in substance equivalent to what Puritan divines ordinarily termed "faith of assurance." Crisp allowed that in a sense no one is saved until he believes, but this qualification applies only to the apprehension of salvation, not to the act of believing as a condition of it. As a human act, faith is a work, and the covenant of grace does not depend upon a work. To those who say that "faith justifies the ungodly" Crisp replied that after a person is justified he does believe; yet "it is not the faith of the person that does simply and properly justify, but it is the Christ in whom he doth believe. . . . Justification is an act of Christ, it is not an act of faith. . . . He is first justified before he believes, then he believes that he is justified."[18] Otherwise, he believes a falsehood.

It was the common observation of Reformed orthodoxy that it is Christ believed in, rather than the human act of believing, that is the efficient cause of justification. Crisp's conclusion about the relationship of faith and justification, however, was extreme. Faith, he insisted, merely apprehends justification previously accomplished, and by it a person comes to recognize justification as his own. To this extent faith may be called "our justification," in that "we are, in regard of our own hearts, and our own spirits, justified by faith." For entry into the covenant and justification before God, however, it is not faith that justifies but Christ alone, wherefore union with Christ precedes faith.[19] To say, as do some divines, that the soul must have "hands" to receive and take Christ freely given is simply false. God, rather, bestows Christ on the soul even as a compassionate person places a garment on a cripple who lacks a tongue to request help and hands to receive it. Christ, he declared, "comes . . . to a person, whiles he is in the stubbornness of his own heart, being froward and cross, and the Father doth force open the

spirit of that person, and pours in his Son in spite of the receiver."
After Christ has thus entered the ungodly, he begins to break and
tame the soul and to acquaint it with his beauty and excellence, and
thereupon the soul begins to embrace him actively. In the first receiving of Christ, however, we are utterly passive. If we are justified
by faith as a human act, Crisp remarked, then Christ needs a part-
ner, as David needed a sling and a stone when he slew Goliath.[20]

Crisp's concern with eliminating all creaturely activity from
regeneration is reflected also in his treatment of the graces of the
regenerate. The word "grace," he insisted, properly refers to the
Father's love itself, not to anything in Christians, so that so-called
Christian graces are more correctly termed "fruits of grace."[21] With
this qualification, faith, which is wrought first, may be said to be
the "radical grace of all graces," whence they flow. Faith and sanctification, however, as the life of divine grace, are in a person only
as "Christ is in the soul of every believer, and animates and acts
the believer in all things whatsoever." Crisp likened Christ to a
lodestone imparting virtue to the soul, suggesting that the power
of grace is not in the soul but in the "stone"; by implication, "gracious qualifications" do not really inhere in the regenerate. Like
Eaton, Crisp seemed to imply that there is a duality of natures in
the redeemed.[22] Speaking of sin in the justified, he remarked that
persons who receive Christ in truth, nonetheless "themselves can
do nothing but commit sin. If a person that is a believer has any
thing in the world, he has received that, if he does anything that is
good, it is the Spirit of God that does it, not he, therefore he himself
does nothing but sin, his soul is a mint of sin."[23] Though God is
aware of such sin, and though it is to him as filthy as a "menstruous
cloth," he does not trouble himself about it, for it is covered entirely
by Christ's righteousness.[24] Although Crisp allowed that Christ
does by his Spirit empower the justified to holy zeal and obedience,
he so emphasized the priority of divine activity in sanctification as
to suggest that the justified are not really altered in their own
human nature at all; and he so stressed the completeness of justification as to imply that sanctification has nothing to do with God's
apprehension of a Christian.

Crisp also suggested that a Christian's apprehension of himself
may differ seriously from God's apprehension of him. This, indeed,
was his chief answer to the problem of assurance. Since, he argued,

Christ took away all the sins of the world, the Christian stands before God entirely without fault and perfectly righteous, regardless of how he may feel at the moment. The believer who is properly in the "way of Christ" does not worry about his imperfect sanctification but knows only gladness, joy, and "no mourning for sin." The "way of Christ" in this connection includes assurance of faith, which, Crisp insisted, is the only admissible assurance. Christ being the fount of all grace, it is false and a denial of Christ's preeminence to go to any "creature" for help and strength in time of trial. By "creature" Crisp understood "any grace, or any temper of spirit in you, or any qualifications or any performances you can tender"— things that, from another viewpoint, might be considered to be effects of created graces infused.[25] Zeal for God, accordingly, does not prove that a person is a child of God, nor does serving God "night and day in that way, he calls me out unto."

Crisp admitted a difference, discernible in the ends of their respective endeavors, between the zeal of believers and that of those who have not "submitted to the righteousness of God." Like Cotton, however, he held that in outward activity and obedience there is scarcely any visible distinction. "To be zealous, that is to say, to be cordial, hearty, real, and that with fervency, and earnestness of spirit, towards obedience to the commandments of God, and to have an eye in such obedience unto God himself, to seek him in such obedience"—all this is common to both redeemed and recalcitrant. No assurance, therefore, is to be had from any of these things, and to turn to them as a way of assurance is purely legal.[26]

In consequence, Crisp insisted, the only adequate ground of assurance is faith in Christ, and there is no sounder way to know one's portion in Christ than "upon the general tender of the Gospel, to conclude absolutely [that] he is yours, and so, without any more ado, to take him . . . on his word; and this taking of him upon a general tender, is the greatest security in the world. . . . Set down thy rest here; . . . without seeking for further security." A person may know well enough whether he believes in this way, and whoever does "may absolutely conclude" that he indeed has Christ and his benefits. (This was very close to what Cotton meant by "taking Christ in an absolute promise.") Those people, in contrast, who start with the graciousness of their own spirits, and seek comfort therein, begin at the wrong end. They are at great pains, Crisp observed, in breaking their hearts and forsaking their sins, and they

> run to their inherent righteousness, to their qualifications, to their
> prayers, to their tears, to their humiliations, and sorrows, and
> reformations, universal obedience and the like. But is this to run
> to *free grace,* and free mercy in Christ: Nay, Christ alas, he is never
> thought of, Christ is clean forgotten, and wholly neglected. . . . No
> marvel, beloved, that you sweat and toil and moil all the day long,
> and all lies in the same case it did: There is no strength to bring
> forth, because you go in your own strength or the strength of the
> creature, and not in the strength of the Lord Jesus.[27]

For Crisp, Traske, and Eaton, the source and power of divine
grace lay by definition outside the human "creature," and they were
deeply suspicious of any suggestion that creaturely agency might
participate in regeneration. In consequence, the insistence of Puritan covenant theologians that the act of faith, as instrumental cause,
is the condition of the covenant of grace, seemed to them a serious
mistake. Similarly, the affirmation of Reformed divines that assurance of salvation may be obtained by practical reasoning from the
effects of grace inherent in oneself appeared to them erroneous.
These affirmations, they declared, made justification and assurance
the effects of creaturely "works," in contradiction of God's manner
of operation in the time of the gospel. They would not allow that
such works and the human faculties whence they spring might be
graciously renewed and might as such legitimately operate as instruments of the divine intent. Like Cotton and the Hutchinsonians
during the New England controversy, these men rejected the notion
that created being could participate in the transcendent work of
redemption and spiritual rebirth. As a result, they were forced to
seek justification, and subjective awareness of it, in works of divine
immediacy.

THE PROBLEM OF ASSURANCE

Puritan covenant theology offered troubled saints a double
source of assurance. It allowed them to plead the covenant with
God, importuning him to fulfill his part of the bargain by performing what he had promised; and it encouraged them to seek comfort
in the sufficiency of prevenient grace and in the immutability of

God's will in election, which underlay the covenant itself and their own participation in it. In both cases the individual was assumed to possess some evidence, however fragmentary, of God's favor toward him. That in practice Christians had often to plead for renewed assurance of their estate in grace was regarded by Puritan divines as sufficient evidence that the covenant did not include uninterrupted subjective assurance in this life. On this point they were quite frank. It was a commonplace of Puritan preaching, based on pastoral experience, that faith is inevitably seasoned with doubt.[28] The problem for Puritan pastors was to explain and interpret doubt positively, so as to integrate it into the Christian life and in particular to distinguish it from despair as the mark of reprobation. They accomplished this task in part by making "justifying faith," as the instrumental cause of justification, compatible with subjective doubt in the faithful, and in part by making a certain kind of earnest doubt itself a mark of blessedness.

Their method of proceeding is illustrated in the journal composed by Thomas Shepard in the early 1640s. This document evokes the full range and intensity of the spiritual anxieties to which Puritan saints were subject. Indeed, it suggests that the Protestant *sola fide,* while rescuing the individual from endlessly having to earn sufficient merit to cover his daily sins, in Puritan hands might deliver him to seemingly endless pursuit of firm evidence of his justification.[29] Shepard's case was scarcely so extreme, though the problem is evident in his reflection. His diary is of interest here chiefly as it reveals the dialectic of faith and doubt, in the context of covenantal affirmation, within which conscientious Puritans labored to make certain of their callings, amid all the troubles to which human flesh and spirit are heirs.

This dialectic is evident in the form, as well as in the content, of Shepard's meditations. They begin, characteristically, in a sense of personal unholiness before God or loss of divine favor and move to doubt about God's intent toward Shepard himself. On December 16, 1640, for example, he wrote, "I saw myself very miserable (1) because by my sin I had separated myself from God and turned my face from him; (2) that he was turned in his face from me: [1] I had no sense of his majesty, power, mercy, being; [2] no sense of his love. (3) I saw sin had shut him from me, and my unbelief when he came to me shut him out of me. Hence I saw a need of a mediator between us, and mourned." And again, on January 6, 1641 "[T]his morning in meditation and prayer I was tempted to think no promise, no, nor command, to seek the Lord or submit to him was spoken to me, but rather he had in justice forsaken me and so let me do what I please."[30] Usually, however, Shepard's meditations go on to consider God's sufficiency and mercy manifest in gracious works to him, to others, or to the elect generally and to conclude in assurance reaffirmed. The passage first quoted above, for example, proceeds immediately: "I had a glimpse of the fulness of grace in Christ, in meditation on John 1:14: like a fountain overflowing and above all my conceiving to poor sinners which came to him. And hence my heart began to be filled with lively hope and assurance." And the second continues, "But when I considered the scriptures, how that they did but manifest that acting will of a living God, revealing that secret will which is ever so set as the word reveals, my soul was quieted. . . ."

Such reflections might be occasioned by an event in private or public life that recalled to Shepard the thankfulness and obedience owed to God under the covenant and the imperfection of his own efforts to render it, or reminded him of his own transience and frailty. They might also be prompted by the emotional let-down that sometimes ended a strenuous Sunday. Occasions like these were stimuli for personal introspection and for casting up deficiencies and doubts in his spiritual life. They were also, however, pretexts for studied meditation on the divine *modus* in bestowing grace and in exercising the regenerate, and the meditation itself could become a means of overcoming momentary doubt in reaffirmation of God's benevolent intent toward the meditant. Accordingly, Shepard's meditations usually point in the direction of renewed confidence in God's benevolence toward him personally, and when they do not lead him immediately there, he is neither shattered nor terrified, but able to integrate the experience into the framework of his faith.

In this respect, Shepard's keeping of his diary was less an effort to answer the speculative question, Am I elect or not? by a species of introspective empiricism than an exercise of faith presupposing assurance of the object that it appears to seek. The pattern of its passages closely parallels the course of the soul in conversion, which begins in deadness to sin and moves through fear of hell and terror of God's wrath to humble waiting for Christ and eventual union with him in faith.[31] There is, however, a crucial substantive difference between the two movements. The doubt and despair of the soul on the way to conversion, confronting an angry God at the brink of the abyss, is absolute and shattering. It is a present sense of kindling fire and of heaven shut up against one. Persisted in, such despair is fatal and the mark of probable reprobation. In contrast, the doubt and anxiety about their estates felt periodically by saints after conversion, while genuine doubt, is not desolate. It expresses, rather, the anxiety of a Christian who experiences what Protestant theologians formulated in the paradox that the redeemed in this life are *simul iustus ac peccator*. It was the common affirmation of Puritan divines that the regenerate, as creatures of both grace and sin, are more sensible of their own imperfections than of the marks of glory in themselves. Such being the case, repeated rehearsal of God's way with his own became a means of affirming both positive and negative aspects of one's relationship with God, a probable hope of the former being the ground of the whole enterprise. Regarded in this light, the expressions of doubt recorded in Shepard's diary may fairly be said to reflect the awareness of a regenerate soul that his thankfulness is less than full and his obedience less than constant, that he is redeemed but still far from being saved and glorified.[32]

The subjective experience of a Christian's life, Puritan divines admitted, is a dialectic of faith and doubt, even as the substance of that life is a persistent tension between righteousness and corruption. For the perfection of both faith and righteousness, Shepard relied, as Puritans believed all Christians must, on the sufficiency of God's power and on the constancy of his sovereign will, mediated through the covenant. In this respect Shepard's meditations form an ellipse, whose foci are his own personal experience and Reformed affirmations about the divine nature. Formal Puritan divinity is similarly elliptical, and the individual *loci* of the theological system are referable to each focus. Practically and formally, the problem of assurance entails consideration of the doctrine of God's sovereign will, as well as of the immediate circumstances of the doubting saint. This is obvious inasmuch as the assurance being sought is assurance about the divine intent *pro me*, but it is true also in the sense that the seeking of assurance itself presupposes prior confidence of the divine will *pro me*. In the language of contemporaries, the first is "faith of assurance" and results from reflection based on particular evidence. The second is the confidence inherent in the "first act" of faith understood as adherence and dependence, that is, as *fiducia*. The object of such faith includes the divine intent, expressed in the promise of justification to believers. Its form is the taking of the promise to oneself, with the knowledge that in so doing the promise is effective for oneself, its effectiveness guaranteed by the sovereignty of the divine intent. The quest for assurance after this "first act" of faith, in logic and in time, presupposes this transcendent guarantee.

In the doctrine of divine sovereignty Puritans possessed a powerful transcendent referent capable of giving coherent meaning to a great deal of the apparent chaos of everyday experience. If all created actuality derives from God's decree and is the effect of God's power working according to his decree, then nothing, quite literally, is outside the circumference of the divine ordination.[33] This idea could provoke anxiety, for it obligated the individual to seek God's intent in particular incidents, about which he might err; and, stated generally, it only made the individual the object of God's intent without specifying whether God intends good or ill. However, to be aware of this possibility and to take it seriously—to be anxious about it—might itself be a favorable indication, in view of what was held to be known about the "ordained means." The reprobate, in any case, were held to be characteristically indifferent to these issues. At the same time, election was preached by Puritans as a comforting doctrine, not only because it took salvation out of man's palsied hands, but also because, being inscrutable, it left room for a positive presumption of the salvability of most people, in the absence of positive evidence to the contrary. No one, it was repeatedly affirmed, is precipitately to conclude that he is damned, merely because God has not yet rendered the means effectual for him, for no one knows what God may yet do in his own good time.[34] Further, and most important for the problem of assurance, those who were able, albeit tenuously, to find themselves within the circle of God's benevolence could enlist all the resources of the divine sufficiency toward their ultimate salvation, however much they might stumble in their present pilgrimage; and they could invoke the divine constancy when their own wills seemed to waver.[35] Moreover, the entire range of their temptations and trials might be accounted for positively as God's particular will for them.

At this point the ability to locate oneself within the circle of God's benevolence became crucial. According to covenant theology, however, God conveys this ability in the gift of faith of "adherence and dependence," which rests "upon the mercy of God in Christ for pardon and forgiveness"; and the acting of such faith includes the confidence that that mercy is indeed effective *pro me*.[36] In the covenant, Bulkeley declared, "God says, I will be a God unto thee to bless thee, and to do thee good: and this I require of thee, that thou trust to me, and depend upon me for all the good thou standest in need of; and faith does so, it rests itself upon God's promise." "Suppose," Shepard wrote, "you can not find yourself within any promise, and you see no reason to believe, only you have the Lord's call and command to believe; do you now, in conscience and obedience to this command, or to God's invitation and entreaty in the gospel, believe, because thou darest not dishonor God by refusing his grace? thou dost therefore accept of it. . . ."[37] Such motions of the soul are first possible only in effectual calling, and only as effects of prevenient grace. In believing, one is justified, and in believing, one also has assurance of that justification. In this sense Perkins characterized faith as a particular persuasion of the effectiveness of the promise in one's own case; other Puritans included the same persuasion in what they regarded as the fiducial character of faith.

Clearly, however, the ability to believe fiducially is given to some people and not to others; and although in habit faith, once given, is unshakable, in practice it admits of "many interruptions in act and operations." For this reason, Puritans affirmed, God provides various "stays and props" for faith, of which the practical syllogism is one, by which a person may come to the persuasion that what he sought in the promises is in fact granted. This sort of faith is distinct from *fiducia* and secondary to it. It is the subjective assurance that Perkins observed to be the gradual fruit of trial and experience and that Ames and Ball attributed to the "reflex operation" of the mind by which a soul is able to say, " 'I know in whom I have believed.' " Such "faith of assurance," attained via practical reflection, rests on the palpable evidence of particular acts of faith and obedience. To the scrupulous, Puritan ministers tirelessly affirmed that such evidence need not be perfect, but "merely" present and true.[38] The smallest grain of true faith is sufficient to justify, and the frailest obedience, if genuine, may be the ground of a reflex act of faith. Given the coherence and constancy of the order of redemption, such objective marks meant that the individual at some point has believed fiducially, even though his faith was so slight that he did not then perceive it or quickly forgot it. The evidence of sanctification, accordingly, could serve to rekindle initial *fiducia;* and in practice the individual could indeed have "first sight" of his justification and so "first assurance" via a practical syllogism. This order of events, however, was considered to be "of time" and not "of causes," and to result from the weakness of initial faith and the strength of corruption remaining, because of which imperfections the works of grace are usually perceived in the order opposite to that in which they are effected.[39]

Implicit here is the double paradox that a person may have justifying faith, which is an act of the will following a judgment of an enlightened understanding, and not know it, and that, having once come to know it, he may also come to doubt it. This admission derived from the pastoral observation that there are Christians who firmly trust, but whose sanctification appears to them so riddled with sin as to be a hindrance to subjective assurance rather than a support for it; that there are also Christians who seem to manifest the fruits of grace in outward conversation, yet whose conscious faith is weak and wavering; and that both these conditions may ebb and flow in the life of a single individual, including one who has had a classic, even datable, calling. In a pastoral perspective, the paradox may be viewed as an effort, within the framework of the divine *modus* revealed in scripture, to make the ground of assurance as comprehensive as possible. Bulkeley, for example, urged his hearers, in time of trials, doubts, and scruples, to turn confidently to the absolute promises of free grace, and in time of security and carelessness, to search themselves for the objective qualifications indicated in the conditional promises.[40] The reverse might also be true, and the conditional promises provide initial evidence of grace for a person who, overcome by his sense of imperfection, found the absolute promises seemingly inaccessible.

These variations and "seasons of faith," however, are entirely encompassed by the divine will. Because the saints are simultaneously sinners and righteous, they will inevitably find God's chastening hand appearing against them, and for good reason, even as they find God's gracious hand appearing for them.[41] There are times, Forbes wrote, when God seems utterly against us, "either when God upon the carnal presumption of our hearts, suffers us to fall in some dangerous trial, or . . . when God himself seems to become our enemy: so that the heart has to wrestle with GOD himself, under the sense of his wrath, all former feeling of his mercy then ceasing." This, he declared, is precisely the best time to discern the testimony of God's Spirit from our own, with its tendency toward wishful fancies, for the testimony of God is most evident when he "doth wrestle with us himself: . . . and in seeming to fight against us, yet doth sustain us, by his own strength in us, when our strength fails us." Forbes's remark is important for understanding Puritan teaching about assurance, for it suggests that to the faithful the experience of God's wrath, while disquieting, is not ultimately dispiriting, precisely because they perceive God's strength sustaining even while he assails; which is another way of saying that the assault is perceived in the context of the fiducial relationship already obtaining between the individual and God. Even in extreme doubts, Ball observed, faith naturally runs to God, clings to him, and calls upon him for aid, and "thus faith of adherence is stronger than faith of evidence, belief in Christ for remission, than assurance of pardon and forgiveness."[42]

The experience of God's apparent wrath, moreover, was positively referred by Puritans to God's good intent. Voicing a characteristic Puritan affirmation, Sibbes remarked that "God often works by contraries: when he means to give victory, he will suffer us to be foiled at first; when he means to comfort, he will terrify first; when he means to justify, he will condemn us first; whom he means to make glorious, he will abase first. A Christian conquers, even when he is conquered; when he is conquered by some sins, he gets victory over others more dangerous." To this extent tribulations, both external and internal, are only provisionally disturbing, and disquiet may be greeted as a normal ingredient of the Christian life. In another characteristic passage, Sibbes noted that victory of Christ's government in oneself is had only by fighting against Satan and the remnants of sin, so that even a gracious conscience is necessarily troubled. "It is therefore no sign of a good conscience to find all quiet, and nothing at odds."[43] Through external tribulation and inner disquietude, the true Christian "lives by his faith," which means not only that he is justified by faith *in foro divino* but also that his faith sustains him through the chaos of everyday experience. Such faith is not built on the "stays and props" of sense and experience but is prior to them and accordingly is not utterly dismayed by "our despairing feelings or sense." So understood, *fiducia* is entirely compatible with the subjective doubt arising from experiences to which the regenerate, as such, cannot be indifferent. Such doubt is not absolute, however, but is absorbed into *fiducia*, of which it becomes a mark.[44]

It seems important to note that assurance, for Puritans, was not so much that of certain contemporary religious radicals who allegedly declared, "We need not pray for forgiveness or fear sin, sin howsoever we can," as it was "assurance of faith" that those whom God justifies he will also glorify, however dark the present moment may seem and God however distant. The saints are afflicted, for their own and others' sins; God withdraws, to test and to chasten. Finally, though, God will perfect his own. In the meantime, life is a conscientious "living to God," thankfully, sorrowfully, hopefully. Full subjective assurance is often withheld until the moment of death. Yet the saints are not without confidence. It is not, however, the unconcerned confidence of those who have settled accounts with God once and for all and need trouble themselves no further about how God regards them. On the contrary, the saints remain always conscious of the gulf between what they do and what God requires of them, of the poverty of their own belief, and of their need for further grace. These tensions are clearly revealed in Shepard's journal, and they are also present, though less personally, in the sermons making up his pastoral classic, *The Sound Believer*. In essence they are the tensions of a distinctive type of spirituality, intense, athletic, highly dialectical, in which life is lived from moment to moment under the gaze of, and open to, God, who is righteous, sovereign, inscrutable, good, and to be prized above all things, before whom man is as smoke, and yet who leads, chastens, sustains, and intends good even to this very smoke.

AN EASIER WAY

Successful practice of this sort of piety required a degree of emotional stamina, a balance between presumption and scrupulosity, and a tolerance of ambiguity, not equally distributed in Puritan congregations. Puritan ministers, while striving to stir their hearers to new pitches of expectation, regularly qualified themselves, explaining that God works quietly, by degrees and by contraries, that the Spirit, while sometimes witnessing with intuitive certainty and ineffable sweetness, more usually witnesses through the power of gracious obedience, and that, while grace creates a disposition toward universal obedience to God's will, this disposition is most often perceived in weakness and is much mixed with sin. Such qualifications, however, were in some cases inadequate to the expectations raised. And they exhibited a dialectical subtlety not always appreciated by the unsophisticated, some of whom perceived the qualifications as flatly contradictory or as an attempt to deprive them of the benefits of the gospel. The minister, it appeared, took away what he had seemed previously to offer in the same sermon, and assurance seemed to be very elusive after all.

Objections arose. One sort came from people who, as Hooker characterized them, judged according to their own sense of things rather than the biblical promises and expected Christ to come to them with great fanfare and striking effect. They were unhappy at being told that he comes quietly, in unexpected ways, and may be missed by the unwary. Some people, said Hooker, tend to think that when they are first united to Christ "some extraordinary sweetness . . . should be in [them]. . . . Every sinner sets up a fancy in his own imagination, that if Christ comes, strange matters will be wrought. . . . Were Christ in me [they say], then I should have such and such sufficiency. . . . You will not believe the king is come, unless he hug you in his bosom." Another, not unrelated, objection was raised by certain English "antinomians," who complained that the "legalistic" preachers could give them no settled assurance of free salvation but set them to endless learning of obedience, which left them forever troubled in conscience because of their seemingly insurmountable imperfections.[45] These problems, which sprang partly from over-literal construction of sermons and partly from inability to perceive the prescribed effects of grace in the self, created pressure in Puritan congregations toward an easier, more direct route to assurance than that offered by "standard" Puritan divines.

This pressure is traceable in the various religious radicalisms emerging in and around the Puritan movement in the 1620s and

1630s.[46] Theologically, it was exerted at three points in the Reformed system that posed special difficulties for hopeful Christians: (1) at the affirmation that the regenerate are simultaneously sinners and righteous in God's sight, (2) at the use of the moral law as the rule of Christian obedience, and (3) at the practical syllogism as the way to assurance. Objections at all three of these points were voiced by Crisp and Eaton and in varying combination by the "antinomians" who claimed both men as their heritage. In each case, the theoretical ground of objection was a strict subordination of created nature to divine grace and power in the work of redemption. This subordination, the objectors claimed, by definition excluded from a gracious estate any reliance on law or works. It also had the effect of rendering human frailty and imperfection inconsequential in God's sight.[47]

In order to cope with doubts occasioned by failure in duties of obedience, dissenters of the Eatonian-Crispian persuasion sought to divorce assurance from sanctification, in three ways primarily. First, they rejected the law as the glass of righteousness in which Christians are to examine themselves, claiming that the law pertains only to the time before the gospel was revealed and that legal scrupulosity is now no longer required. On this ground they argued that such scrupulosity is a mark of unfaith, and they opposed as false teachers ministers who urged sanctification as evidence of justification. Thereby they earned for themselves the label "antinomian." When the Hutchinsonians in Massachusetts rejected the declarative use of conditional promises as "legal," they were giving expression to this tendency. Second, Etonians and Crispians asserted that God does not see the imperfections of his justified children and consequently that failure of obedience is irrelevant to their relationship to God. Since they are already his children, and therefore justified and saved, whatever they may do or fail to do respecting the law is really not pertinent. Thus, one of them observed, God sees everything through the same green glasses, and so everything appears green to him. Failure of obedience, accordingly, need not trouble a Christian's assurance. Third, "antinomians" of this sort tended to make a person's own estate in grace the proper object of his faith, rather than Christ's righteousness promised, and to make the task of faith equivalent to achieving subjective certitude of election. Accordingly, they urged doubtful Christians to abandon the search for seemingly elusive marks of grace in themselves, and bid them simply to believe firmly that they were justified. To divines who were the objects of their criticism, these dissenters seemed to be saying that the elect are justified before faith, that justifying faith is assurance, that assurance cannot be had from works, and, at the most extreme, that "the careless Christian is the choicest believer, because he depends wholly on Christ" and not on "creatures."[48]

To the problems raised by persistence of the sense of sin, Eatonian-Crispian dissenters sought to reduce the seriousness of sin in the justified, availing themselves primarily of three possibilities. First, they suggested that God does not punish sin in his children but only in unbelievers, though he may permit his own to suffer trials for other reasons. The sins of the justified, therefore, do not seriously affect their relationship to God and need not be a source of doubt or anxiety. Second, they endeavored to distinguish between an individual's own sense of sin and God's absolute blindness to it. Accordingly, they argued, while the justified may be said to sin in their own apprehension, this apprehension, contrasted with their purity in God's sight, is but error and ignorance. Third, and more radically, they sought to distinguish between the divine life of Christ dwelling in the regenerate and the corrupt life of the old man dwelling side by side with it, and they asserted that only the former pertains to a Christian's salvation. In this sense the regenerate cannot sin—a notion that earned its exponents the title "libertines." In any case, they argued, because the natural faculties of fallen man remain imperfect and corrupt, they are incapable of perceiving spiritual things, or of concluding from creaturely works to assurance of a blessed estate. The practical syllogism, therefore, is useless as a way to assurance. To their opponents, these people appeared to say that to doubt one's estate because of sin, or to mourn for sin, is to doubt God and so is worse than sin, and that a person cannot trust his own sense or conscience at all but must believe contrary to both.[49]

In order to assist tender consciences who could never be sufficiently certain of their "gracious qualifications" and for whom the practical syllogism was in consequence unworkable, Eatonian-Crispian radicals turned to the transcendent, ineffable seal of the Spirit, which they tended to formulate as an immediate divine illumination or direct verbal testimony. Such "spiritual sealing," they maintained, is wholly superior to a testimony merely mediated through created faculties operating on the data provided by scripture and by personal acts of faith and obedience. This tendency is apparent in Cotton's insistence that first assurance may be had only in "spiritual sight" of one's own justification, by the Spirit's testimony and without reference to any creaturely works. It is reflected, also, in the alleged claim of certain Hutchinsonians that "they have their assurance by revelation, seeing the very book of life unsealed and opened unto them, so that they may see and read their own names written in it." Of such persons Bulkeley observed that "it is too low a work for them to descend into themselves, and to examine how it is with them *within*, whether they be in the faith or no."[50] The persons in question might have responded that what they found in such introspective descent, being creaturely, was insufficient ground for settled assurance or even irrelevant to it.

All of the above formulations appear to have originated, in one degree or another, in the desire of earnest spirits for a more positive, not to say graphic, assurance that all the benefits of the covenant of grace are presently possessed than they were able to find in the dialectical propositions of the "legalist" ministers. They also reflect a degree of impatience with the element of trustful hope in future confirmation and consummation that Reformed divines included within the notion of fiducial faith.[51] The formulations fostered by this impatience appeared radical and even dangerous to more "orthodox" contemporaries, because they seemed to absolve Christians from obedience to the moral law and because they seemed to dissolve the qualitative difference between Creator and creature in regeneration; and they did in fact tend to upset the balance of nature and grace in the Christian life that covenant theology sought to maintain.

The affirmations here reviewed also appeared radical to contemporaries in that they tended to deprive Christians of what Reformed divines ordinarily regarded as objective ground of assurance, casting the hopeful instead onto wholly subjective ground. Followers of Eaton and Crisp seemed to say that a Christian should pay no heed to the order of redemption disclosed in scripture or the conditional promises offered there, or to observable effects of grace in himself, but only to what, more often than not, were likely to be the fancies of a distraught heart or an overheated imagination.

Puritan pastors argued that, apart from the evidence of biblical word and gracious work, assurance by intuitive "revelations" is only as sure as the particular intuition or fancy, which will almost certainly wane, to be replaced once again by doubt.[52] To make this sort of "assurance" equivalent to justifying faith, as certain "antinomians" seemed to, was to make faith and doubt fundamentally antagonistic and to risk condemning the weak or unstable Christian to an agonizing oscillation between momentary feelings of joy and profound despair. Furthermore, identification of assurance with justifying faith also undercut the comfort that Reformed theologians usually derived from the Protestant *sola fide,* in the context of the doctrine of divine sovereignty. For if "justifying faith" was really "faith of justification," then its failure not only left troubled Christians without subjective support but also called into question the *objective* truth of their justification in heaven. The Puritan Henry Burton raised this issue with the Eatonians: "What if true faith, while during the time of some temptation the exercise of it is suspended, [and we] do not see, nor enjoy the fruit of justification? Must we therefore pass sentence upon ourselves, that we are not justified?"[53] Here Burton identified the critical practical difficulty in the radicals' solution to the problem of assurance. He answered his own question with an emphatic negative and with the affirmation that justification, once obtained, is secure and remains unshaken, though the act of faith may fail intermittently.

CHAPTER 9

The Nature of New England Antinomianism

Antinomianism has a long history as a characteristic form of Christian dissent. It is evident in the New Testament, and it enjoyed its latest and perhaps greatest flowering on the Continent and in England during the Reformation era. The label "antinomianism" derives from the syndrome's distinctive mark, namely the denial of the relevance of the moral law to true Christians because of the ability claimed for the Holy Spirit to separate persons directly and radically from the obligations of ordinary worldly existence. The New Testament notions of the work and witness of the Spirit and of liberation through spiritual rebirth, and especially the Pauline antitheses of law and gospel and of works and faith, contain the seeds of antinomianism, and during the sixteenth and seventeenth centuries it sprang up wherever free grace and spiritual conversion were vigorously preached.[1]

Formally at least, there are two sorts of antinomianism, one affirming that the moral law delivered in the Old Testament has nothing to do with justification, the other asserting that the justified have nothing to do with the law. The first is concerned primarily with the means of conversion and justification, the second with the grounds of Christian conduct and assurance. In the *Sektengeschichte* of the Reformation both forms appear, separately and in combination. The former, in the name of free justification and the power of the preached gospel, denied the preparatory function of the law, as a "schoolmaster," to drive men to Christ through fear of sin; and it was hostile to any suggestion of causal relationship between law, works, or human agency, and justification.[2] The second variety denied that the law pertains to the relationship between God and the justified, either because God no longer regards sin in them or because the Spirit so dwells in them that they are incapable of sinning; and it was opposed to the urging of duties of obedience upon Christians and to seeking marks of election in such obedience, as confusing legal works and free grace.[3] The debacle of the Kingdom of Münster, in 1532, linked antinomianism inseparably with flagrant libertinism, and the connection was regularly exploited thereafter for polemical purposes; though, apart from Münster, sufficient instances of excess and aberrance could be found in the period in question to give color to the charge that antinomianism inevitably led to moral license.[4] It was possible, however, to hold antinomian doctrines without in practice committing or condoning moral excess, and not everyone who might technically be labeled "antinomian" ended in libertinism.

Antinomian ideas, nonetheless, could issue in hostility toward established order in church and state; and, indeed, antinomianism's impact was felt primarily at this point, the issue of moral laxity being perceived as an aspect of the assault upon authority. This disruptive potential, moreover, lay less in antinomianism's conclusions about the uses of the law than in its premises about the work of the Holy Spirit. Both forms of the syndrome exalted the unconditioned, unmediated operation of the Spirit in the application of redemption, to the point of seriously minimizing, if not altogether overruling, the Christian's continuing rootedness in the ontological and moral orders of creation. From the antinomian perspective the agency and instrumentality of creatures are incidental to the Spirit's gracious work, which renders the Christian, morally and ontologically, a veritable "new being." Reformed orthodox theologians conceived of regeneration as the infusion into man of supernatural principles, empowering him to new understanding and new obedience, but without altering his condition as a creature or freeing him from earnest struggle with the remnants of sinfulness in himself. Antinomians, in contrast, tended to regard regeneration as a spiritual transformation, elevating the individual above the moral ambiguities of creaturely existence and freeing him from the canons of "common," "earthly," merely "legal" morality. Thus the Dutch sectary Henrik Niclaes could affirm of himself that "he is godded with God and co-deified with him, and that God is hominified with him"; and a Swiss enthusiast could declare that he had attained a condition of perfect submission to the Spirit and was accordingly undefiled by sin, so that whatever he did, including decapitating his brother, was God working in him. In a less extreme form, an English "familist" maintained that through Christ he was accepted by God as perfect, that perfection may be obtained in this world, that "Christ dwelling in a believer, and being his guider and disposer, he may say, 'Repentance is hid from mine eyes,' " and, referring to believers, that " 'He that is born of God sinneth not.' "[5] New England antinomianism, which was more restrained, belonged mainly to the second variety identified above and expressed itself chiefly in rejection of sanctification as evidence of election and opposition to ministers who urged recourse to such evidence.

"ANTINOMIANS" AND "FAMILISTS"

The contemporary association of New England antinomians with the horrors of Münster was highly imaginative. Anne Hutchinson flatly and frankly rejected alleged "libertine" notions, and she and her followers were much regarded for their godly living (charity toward opponents and respect for magistrates excepted).[6] New England antinomianism was theological and political, rather than libertine. Officially, the Hutchinsonians were disciplined for the public consequences of their opinions, being formally charged with fostering disunity in the colony, showing disrespect of constituted authority, and making slanderous remarks. One of them, protesting to the General Court that he was being punished for his judgment, was bluntly told: Not for his judgment, but for not keeping it to himself, and so disturbing the public peace. This distinction was not entirely casuistical. The authorities of the Bay Colony were genuinely reluctant to prosecute for opinion's sake alone and were earnest in their efforts to reason the principal dissenters out of their "errors" before proceeding to legal measures.[7] The Hutchinsonians' opinions, however, were such as to set them seriously at odds with the established order, and their public behavior reflected a characteristic sectarian striving for heavenly purity and a corresponding disinclination to compromise with merely worldly imperatives. Insofar as this striving threatened the cohesiveness required by the safety of a new plantation and upset the balance between living in the world and being a holy people, which was to be the peculiar estate of Massachusetts, the Hutchinsonians became a concern of the civil government, and Winthrop strove earnestly to check them.[8] Insofar as Hutchinsonian tenets threatened the balance that the Reformed theological tradition sought to maintain between created instrumentality and increated power in the work of regeneration, and insofar as the Hutchinsonians espoused heretical notions and extreme opinions concurrently abroad in old England, the ministers of the Bay reasoned with them, debated them, and strove to refute them.

Winthrop, in the *Short Story*, labeled his antagonists "antinomians" and "familists," and Weld, in his preface to the 1644 edition, observed that the opinions appearing in Boston in 1636 had come, along with certain immigrants, from England.[9] The latter observation was partly apologetic—Weld wished to locate the source of the disturbance outside the circumference of the New England "way"—but it was also factually accurate. The appearance of Burton's *The Law and the Gospel Reconciled* indicates that John Eaton had established himself in London by 1631 and that his activities were causing problems for Puritan clergymen; and there is sufficient similarity between the Newtown synod's list of errors and the expressions associated with Eaton to suggest that the former did not all originate in New England.[10] The use of "antinomian" and "familist," too, while obviously pejorative, was also in a measure descriptive. By the early 1630s both tags had acquired fairly definite meaning in English ecclesiastical circles, as denoting diffuse but identifiable sectarianisms whose representatives had attracted official attention intermittently since the turn of the century. Familists were distinguished by their emphasis on personal union between Spirit and believer, antinomians by their rejection of the moral law as the rule of Christian obedience. Together they shared ideas that appear, explicitly or implicitly, in the utterances of Eaton, Crisp, and Traske.[11]

There apparently existed in England, from the reign of Edward VI at least, a continuous if unspectacular tradition of sectarian nonconformity, diffuse in its origins and composition, sustained by *Winkelprediger*, self-styled prophets, and clerics of dubious orthodoxy, and susceptible to the same enthusiasms for ecclesiastical purity and spiritual experience that animated Puritans.[12] In this tradition the echo of Niclaes may be perceived and through him, of elements of the Dutch and Low-German sectarianism of the middle third of the sixteenth century. This English sectarian current participated in the surge of religious excitement of which Puritanism was the principal vehicle; and the Puritan movement, while generating plenteous sectaries of its own, served also as a haven and nursery for individuals whose religious radicalism reflects other sources. Notions derived from the latter, interacting with characteristic emphases of Puritan preaching, helped to produce a variety of subtle and not-so-subtle corruptions of the theological dialectic of Reformed orthodoxy.[13] By the early 1630s, tension within the English Church was mounting not only between Puritans and Laudians but, at the opposite end of the ecclesiological and theological scale, between Puritans who, while denouncing the bishops as anti-Christian, insisted that law and gospel are inseparable and that the Spirit works mediately through created things, and still more radical souls who would enjoy both gospel and Spirit independently of all mediation. Participants in the latter controversy were calling each other "legalists" and "antinomians" in 1632.[14] The Boston affair of 1636–38 indicates that when God opened Massachusetts to Puritans as a refuge from the bishops, some of the "antinomians" went also, intent, like their fellow dissenters, on enjoying the gospel freely and more purely.

Hutchinson appears to have been one of these more radical spirits. At her trial before the Boston church, she was alleged to hold:

> "That sanctification can be no evidence of a good estate in no wise."
> "That the first thing we receive for our assurance is our election."
> "That union to Christ Jesus is not by faith."
> "That there be no created graces in the human nature of Christ nor in believers after union.
> "That we have no grace in ourselves but all is in Christ and there is no inherent righteousness in us.
> "That an hypocrite may have the righteousness of Adam and perish."[15]

There is considerable continuity between these expressions and Cotton's views about the order and nature of justifying faith, justification, and sanctification and about the evidential significance of gracious works. On these issues, moreover, both Cotton and Hutchinson reveal marked affinity with the religious radicalism that found expression in Eaton and Crisp.[16] The same may be said of Hutchinson's more striking views on direct revelations, the soul and the resurrection, the relationship between the letter and spirit of scripture, and the true ministry of the gospel.[17] The last two deserve particular mention here.

During her examination before the General Court, Hutchinson charged that the New England elders "were not able ministers of the New Testament" because they "had not the seal of the Spirit" and so were like the apostles before the resurrection—that is, were "ministers of the letter and not the spirit" and therefore able to preach only a covenant of works.[18] This allegation she based on 2 Cor. 3:6, identifying the "letter" that "kills" with the "letter of the gospel," rather than with the "letter of the law"; and she implied that the Spirit's testimony, as distinct from the biblical word, is the superior authority.[19] This sort of antithesis between spirit and letter was common enough in Reformation sectarianism. Niclaes, for example, held that "the Bible was not the word of God, but a signification thereof; and that it was but ink and paper: but the word of God was spirit and life." Similarly, Eaton distinguished between literal and spiritual knowledge, the one consisting "in the word and doctrine from heaven," the other in "a joyful spiritual feeling knowledge of the excellency of free justification." Whoever have the latter "see after a spiritual manner the things freely given of God," using "the similitudes and human representations in the scripture, as an help to their weak capacities; yet they stick not in them, but ascend by them . . . to the high working of God above all human representations and earthly excellencies." In the English sectarianism of the first half of the seventeenth century this contrast between letter and spirit may readily be traced, along with corresponding antitheses of law and gospel, Old and New Testaments, bondage and liberty, flesh and spirit, old and new covenants, works and grace, Moses and Abraham, Hagar and Sarah, false preachers of legalism and dead faith and true ministers of the gospel of free grace.[20] In response to detractors, Eaton noted that, in the world's present state, Ishmael will persecute Isaac, and whoever will preach Christ truly "and confess him [alone] to be our righteousness" must expect taunts and calumnies from the Ishmaelites who excel only in "literal learning and in . . . legal zeal."[21]

In the course of her personal confession, which brought the Court's proceedings to an abrupt conclusion, Hutchinson remarked that when, in England, the Lord had discovered to her the true ministry of the New Testament, "he left me to distinguish between the voice of my beloved and the voice of Moses, the voice of John the Baptist and the voice of antichrist."[22] This distinction of voices, together with the suggestion that the apostles, not yet being "sealed" by the Spirit, preached a covenant of works until they were given the Spirit at Christ's ascension, reflects a dispensationalist manner of thinking that also appears among contemporary English sectarianism. Eaton characteristically opposed the respective "voices" of law and gospel and also distinguished three "times" of the church, those of the Law, of John the Baptist, and of the Gospel. The first was the time of legal rigor and the Old Testament, showing that nothing pleases God but perfect righteousness and driving men, by the burden of the law, to long for the Messiah. There followed the time of John the Baptist, who "revealed sin terribly by the law," yet, by "pointing to the Messiah now come and present, he did not only preach and seal by baptism a fuller exhibiting of the glory of free justification; but thereby also the former legal severity that then lay upon the children of God . . . began to slack and cease." John, however, only pointed the way. In the time of the Gospel, which began with Christ's death, the pedagogy of the law is entirely ended for those who are "by faith grown to full age." God's people now partake of free justification by the righteousness of Christ, making them "perfectly holy and righteous from all spot of sin in the sight of God freely." The "voice of Christ" Eaton identified with the preaching of the "doctrine of free justification" in the time of the Gospel.[23]

Parallels between notions associated with Eatonian "antinomians" and the views of Anne Hutchinson and John Cotton seem noteworthy. In Hutchinson's case they suggest that certain of her ideas were not directly deduced from the tenets of Reformed orthodoxy as articulated by Puritan clergy but had roots, as the elders of the Bay Colony were not unaware, in the substratum of popular English heresy.[24] In Cotton's case such parallels suggest that the more extreme views he advanced around 1637 were not solely the result of his own nightly musings on Calvin but were part of current controversy along the radical edge of English nonconformity.[25] This observation is neither startling nor novel. To make it seems important, however, in view of the impression occasionally left by modern interpretation that New England antinomianism was largely a local phenomenon, generated by the combination of Cotton's preaching of free grace and the stress of life in the wilderness, and that Hutchinson was Cotton's over-eager pupil, who carried his essentially Protestant doctrines to extreme and therein excessive conclusions. It is not improbable that conditions in Boston were such in 1636 that Cotton's preaching could spark an antinomian outburst. Other ingredients, however, seem to have been present in the critical mixture besides anxiety about spiritual estates, physical privation, and Hutchinson's alleged ability to follow a doctrine to its logical conclusion.[26] Among these ingredients, it appears, were the doctrines and temper of contemporary English sectarianism, which members of the Boston congregation imported, along with other commodities, into the City on the Hill.

The founding of Massachusetts, while liberating Puritans to institutionalize their version of Reformed piety more fully, also tapped a reservoir of popular heresy in old England, conducting a measure of it westward to America. London and the eastern counties were long regarded as the principal habitat of English sectaries; there were more London and Lincolnshire people in Boston than elsewhere in the Bay Colony, and it seems scarcely accidental that New England antinomianism was concentrated in the Boston church.[27] Whether Cotton's presence emboldened the Boston extremists to public expression of their views, or whether the presence of Hutchinson's brand of piety prompted Cotton to preach as he did, is impossible to determine. It is apparent that on certain points of doctrine, as well as in the flavor of their piety, the two were in agreement, though Cotton was more refined. Cotton later said that he was taken in by the Hutchinsonians, though this assertion seems odd, since he had apparently known some of them personally for years.[28] It may have been that he was thinking much the same thoughts as they and so failed to notice the differences separating them. It seems unnecessary, in any case, to derive the content of New England antinomianism from Cotton's version of Puritanism, save in a formal sense, or to trace the outburst of 1636–38 to Cot ton's preaching, save in a local and occasional sense. In the larger context, both Cotton and the Hutchinsonians may be considered an expression of a radical strain of English nonconformity already evident by 1630, which cannot unqualifiedly be identified with "Puritanism."[29]

"A FAIRE AND EASIE WAY"

In a letter written toward the spring of 1638, Cotton attributed his behavior during the Antinomian Controversy to his concern with the problem of assurance. "God has so often exercised me," he wrote, "with recurrent fears . . . about mine own spiritual estate, and the estates of some others depending on me, that I could not rest mine own spirit upon any sign thereof (though otherwise good in itself)." In consequence, he said, he had been "forced, not to seek out new ways of peace," but to seek ways clearly more direct and therefore more reliable than that provided in the practical syllogism.[30] For Cotton, as for Shepard, assurance was an intensely urgent matter. Once, they had agreed on the means to it. During his English ministry, Cotton devoted a sermon-series to the subject, taking as his text 1 John 5:12: "He that hath the Son hath life; and he that hath not the Son of God hath not life." At this point in his career, he was able to affirm that Christ's presence could be known from observation of its effects in behavior and disposition and that Christians could argue from such signs to "the truth of our spiritual life, and from thence to the truth of our fellowship with Christ." By 1636, however, Cotton appears to have despaired of the ability of the godly to perceive the life of grace in themselves and to have resorted to the directness of the Spirit's own testimony, insisting that only prior apprehension of the Son's presence could validate the life of grace. In his "Rejoynder" to his colleagues, he declared that knowledge of justification begins with God's testimony "in a word of free grace only without works," which the Spirit then confirms by acting the believer in gracious works, though these works can be known as gracious only by the Spirit's further testimony.[31]

Here lay the immediate issue in the New England controversy: what could be known objectively, without transcending the orders of creation, about the Spirit's regenerating of an individual? Was assurance the work of a gracious human spirit, reflecting on personal behavior and motives in light of the rule of obedience and the conditional promises given in scripture, and so a human work? Or was assurance a work of the Spirit himself, "speaking peace" directly to the soul, and thus a divine work? Shepard and Bulkeley, in harmony with Reformed orthodoxy generally, maintained the former. Sanctification, they believed, inheres in the regenerate; all the relevant data for trying one's estate fall within the scope of the natural human capacity for perception and reflection; and conscience, instructed by the Spirit in the word, is competent to draw the appropriate conclusions, wholly within the moral and ontological orders of creation. Cotton, Hutchinson, and their mutual admirers, in contrast, would not admit human works, however "good" or gracious they might be in themselves and however well attested in scripture, as ground for assurance; nor would they permit human faculties, however enlightened by regenerating grace, to mediate the cognition that confirms and "seals" a gracious estate.

Created and Increated Grace

At this point a more basic issue than the means to assurance is evident in the controversy, namely, the issue of the relationship between divine grace and created being in the regeneration of particular human beings.

Before the Boston church Hutchinson was charged with maintaining that "the first thing we receive for our assurance is our election," in the sense of a direct testimony of the Spirit. The Newtown synod condemned the notions that "no created work can be a manifest sign of God's love," taken as referring to such created graces as love to the brethren, and that "nothing but Christ is an evidence of my good estate," understood in reference to the opposition between Christ "manifesting himself in works of holiness" and "Christ nakedly revealing himself to faith." In his fast-day sermon, Wheelwright declared of justification and knowledge of it by faith that "none other doctrine under heaven is able to justify any, but merely the revelation of the Lord Jesus Christ," and that Christ must do and act all for us "when all is taken away from the creature and given . . . to Christ." In a similar vein, Cotton held that "justifying faith" is the assurance of estate that comes to the elect as an effect of their justification, in particular as the result of a divine testimony.[32] All of these expressions concern the means to assurance, but they also imply something about the *nature* of those means. Some people in Massachusetts apparently suggested that the Spirit works "in hypocrites, by gifts and graces, but in God's children immediately," and that "all graces, even in the truly regenerate, are mortal and fading." Hutchinson allegedly held that there are "no created graces in the human nature of Christ nor in believers after union." Cotton maintained that the agency, instrumentality, and activity of creatures, including gracious habits, are incidental to the Spirit's work in regeneration.[33] These formulations, taken together, suggest that for Cotton and the Hutchinsonians, the basic theological antithesis lay not so much between "nature" and "supernature" (in a modern sense), or between "corrupt nature" (of fallen mankind) and saving grace (in the contemporary Protestant sense), as between created being as such and the increated being of the Trinity.

Commenting on Cotton's conception of faith, Bulkeley identified the fundamental theological issue in the New England dispute:

> This is some of that new light which the old age of the Church has brought forth; which what it tends unto, I know not, unless it be to this, that a man should not look at any habitual grace in himself, whether sanctification or faith, or any other, in as much as these avail nothing (according to them) to a man's justification, seeing as we are justified before faith: They would have a man to see nothing in himself, because (as they think) *the grace which is seen is temporal, that grace which is not seen is eternal.*[34]

In other words, for the New England dissenters, grace that is subject to empirical observation, as something belonging to the created order, is qualitatively different from grace that is dispensed immediately by the Holy Spirit in his own person and therefore does not belong to regeneration at all.

The key to the issue lies in Hutchinson's alleged reference to "created graces," in Cotton's antithesis (noted in Chapter 3) between the "created light" of human cognition and the "immediate light" of "spiritual" knowing, and in Bulkeley's contrast between "temporal" and "eternal" grace. Implicit in these antitheses is a distinction between created and increated nature commonly employed by Reformed divines to discriminate between the being and activity of God, which are necessary, and the contingent being and activity of everything else, including heaven, earth, animate and inanimate beings, the biblical word, the preaching of law and gospel, and the habits of faith and sanctification. Such habits, which God gratuitously infuses into the soul, are distinctive in that they are contrary to fallen human nature and beyond the attainment of natural human capacities. They cannot, like a carpenter's skill, be acquired through practice, nor does corrupt man think to acquire them. Inasmuch, however, as gracious habits are contingent in both existence and activity, being gifts of God distinct from himself, they belong to the *created* order.[35] In this sense the grace bestowed in regeneration, though "supernatural," is also "created" and "temporal." Reformed orthodox divines insisted that salvation is "by grace alone," but they also maintained that God in effecting salvation works mediately, through such created instruments as infused habits. Cotton and the Hutchinsonians, on the contrary, held that the phrase "by grace alone" excludes created means and that the Spirit must act upon, or simply "act," individuals directly; and they tended to minimize severely, if not actually to deny, the instrumentality of created things in the salvific transformation. In accomplishing and in revealing regeneration, they claimed, the Spirit operates directly upon the individual's mind and will; they strongly implied that regeneration does not consist in gifts of grace empowering the mind to new insight and the will to new obedience, but in the indwelling in the believer of divine being itself.

In one form or another this antithesis between created and increated grace in spiritual rebirth appeared regularly along the sectarian fringe of English nonconformity in the early seventeenth century and is perhaps diagnostic of that fringe. Thus, for Traske, the "new creature" in believers did not consist in gracious habits infused but in Christ's divine power inhabiting. "Familists," according to one observer, were distinguished by their apparent refusal to separate "the attributes of the Almighty" from the "effects of his Spirit in men." Crisp's chief disciple, Robert Lancaster, was reported to have said that faith and repentance are as much graces as are food, money, and clothes, the only true graces being the Spirit's testimonies of God's love.[36] For Crisp himself, Christ and his "own" are united prior to and independently of the act of faith, and works of sanctification are really Christ's acts "in" his own. For Eaton, the holy works of the justified are not really holy in God's sight. For neither Crisp nor Eaton could works of sanctification be evidence of justification and ground for assurance, apart from prior "sight" of justification "by faith." They repeatedly suggested, when they did not explicitly declare, that creaturely action as such, gracious as well as "merely" natural, is incompatible with divine grace and consequently is to be excluded from rebirth, or at best admitted as something adventitious to it.

To exclude creaturely action from rebirth, however, from the Reformed orthodox perspective, was to suggest that the beneficiaries of saving grace are not actually transformed in their own persons but only experience a transient change under the Spirit's influence. It was to suggest, indeed, that there is no real difference between the acts of saints and those of hypocrites. Cotton and Crisp accepted this proposition and accordingly would not allow sanctification as evidence of justification. For this reason also they made no distinction between the causal and evidential significance of "works" relative to justification but considered both relationships "legal" and therefore illegitimate. To the New England elders such notions were absurd, being "clean contrary" to scripture and to experience.

The experientialism of Puritan piety included the affirmations not only that the individual may be taught by the Spirit in the word and moved by the Spirit in calling but also that the Spirit effects a permanent, positive change in the individual's person. To suggest that Christians should do and see nothing in themselves, but should leave all to Christ and the Spirit, was to imply that the saint's regeneration does not touch him fundamentally in his own being and that when the saint perceives Christ to withdraw from him, Christ actually does withdraw, taking all his graces with him. To this suggestion Shepard replied, "Do you think the Holy Ghost comes on a man as on Balaam, by immediate acting, and then leaves him, and then he has nothing? Yes beloved, know you that Christ is in you . . . as well as out of you; in you, comforting, dwelling, sanctifying, preparing the heart for himself."[37] Unlike Balaam, who prophesied only when the Lord put words in his mouth, the Christian experiences God's regenerating work as an indelible alteration of his nature, which includes the perceptible "healing" of his mind and will. For this reason, the New England elders believed, the saints may be held to Christian obedience, and they also have within themselves objective ground for comfort when their subjective sense of Christ's presence fails. To the Hutchinsonians, however, Shepard's affirmation suggested an illegitimate mingling of the created and the increated.[38] For them, created grace, as created, remained on the "near" side of the infinite qualitative difference—to borrow the idiom of a later era—separating the realm of creatures from the increated being and power of the Trinity.

Historical Affiliations

These observations have implications not only for analysis of the Antinomian Controversy itself, but also for locating its principals in the history of New England theology and of Protestant theology as well. John Cotton and Anne Hutchinson have sometimes been represented, and Cotton represented himself, as champions of true "Reformation principles" against doctrinally illegitimate exaltation of human activity in regeneration. Cotton sprinkled his writings with morsels of Calvin, even as John Eaton cribbed freely, though much less astutely, from Luther on Galatians. On the basis of his critique of the other elders, Cotton has in the twentieth century come to be classed with those New England preachers, including Jonathan Edwards, who asserted the principles of divine omnipotence, human impotence, and free justification against a creeping Arminianism among American Puritans. On similar ground, the elders whom Cotton opposed have been represented as crypto-Arminians, effectively if not deliberately undercutting divine sovereignty in regeneration in their desire to make a place for human activity.[39]

There are several problems with this assessment. Association of Cotton and Edwards as representatives of a thorough Reformed Protestantism is not incorrect, yet between them lay significant differences qualifying the relationship. In particular, Edwards did not share the emphasis on the Spirit's immediate operation that distinguished Cotton's position in 1636–38, nor did he share Cotton's views about the evidential value of sanctification. On the contrary, amid the excitement of the Great Awakening, Edwards accepted the criteria advanced by Shepard and Bulkeley for discerning the truly regenerate—not, that is, on their own testimony of an immediate word of the Spirit to their hearts, but by universal obedience, in conscience and conversation, to the will of God revealed in scripture.[40] The suggestion that Cotton's colleagues were departing from normative Reformed doctrine and that Cotton and Hutchinson were not is scarcely correct. It is rooted, apparently, in misreading or neglect of three important distinctions in formal Puritan divinity, noted above: (1) between God's decree considered in itself, as free and unconditioned, and the manner of God's execution of his decree under the conditions of the created world; (2) between the natural ability of man, as man, to will and to act and the "natural" inability of man, as fallen and corrupt, to will well; and (3) between the created being of graces infused and the increated being of God who infuses.

The New England clergy in the seventeenth century were in general influenced less by the specific formulations of the Swiss Reformers than by the scholastic divines of the orthodox period. These theologians, despite the academic character of their labors, were no less convinced than Calvin of the absolute sovereignty of God and no less devoted to the *sola gratia*. They were moved, however, to reflect in greater systematic detail upon the *way* in which the sovereign God freely bestows grace; and they were led by the scholastic tradition and by their own intellectual temper to insist that the created order, including man's nature as rational agent, is not violated by the divine omnipotence. This insistence found expression in the affirmation of federal theology that the application of redemption is essentially covenantal in character. By so affirming, however, covenant theologians did not liberate fallen man from moral impotence or bring about any "enlargement of his innate capacities."[41] Calvin was quite convinced that human beings, as such, act and that even the unregenerate, when they obey the godly laws of Geneva, do God's will. They do not obey from a good will, however, and their obedience does not and cannot contribute to their justification. In this respect, Ames's understanding of the innate capacities and moral impotence of mankind was essentially the same as Calvin's. In developing the covenant-motif, Ames sought to deal with the further questions how, in regeneration, grace is related to natural capacity and how, concretely, the divine decree is administered—questions not excluded in advance by the doctrines of unconditional election and total depravity. They were questions, moreover, to which the scholastic tradition offered resources for an answer, in the concept of infused habits and in the doctrine of multiple causality.

Puritan divines, impelled by the experientialism of their piety and by their desire for a disciplined and godly church membership, refined Reformed orthodoxy's systematic elaboration of the "application of redemption" according to their own experience; and they exploited the result for its homiletical and pastoral utility. They did so, however, without abandoning either the Reformed doctrine of depravity or orthodoxy's desire to uphold the integrity of the created order. Calvin's categorical assertion of human helplessness in salvation and of God's unconditioned operation in regeneration was especially congenial to Cotton; and in debate with his colleagues he drew on the Reformer to show that works have nothing to do with justification, including the evidencing of it.[42] It should be noted, however, that the issue under discussion in Massachusetts was not so much the meriting of justification, or the fulfillment of required conditions before conversion, as whether human works are compatible with justification at all. Cotton answered in the negative and tended to conflate the two problems, either for the sake of rhetorical advantage or because he honestly saw no difference between them. His rejection of human activity matched his exaltation of the Trinity's operation, which, from the perspective of the received theological tradition, appeared as an illegitimate subordination of created nature to increated being. In its full scope, Cotton's negative to human activity undercut the concept of the covenantal dispensation of grace and, with it, the integrity of the ontological and moral orders of creation that covenant theology sought to uphold.

It may be argued that, in dealing with Cotton and the Hutchinsonians, the New England elders were asserting what they conscientiously regarded as proper Reformed doctrine, in the face of what they correctly perceived to be sectarian tendencies. In England, by the 1630s, the phrase "free justification by grace alone," with its variants, was becoming something of a party slogan. Often it appears less as a conscientious appeal to the cardinal principles of the Reformation than as the rallying cry of assorted nonconformists whose common characteristic was unusual intimacy with the Holy Spirit, to the ultimate subordination of creaturely activity, created works, and biblical word, and with these a tendency toward rejection of both the second and the third uses of the moral law.[43] In New England, in 1636–38, the phrase "free justification" served (though not in all instances) as the positive polemical counterpart to the charge of "preaching," "being under," or "going aside to" a covenant of works. Protestations about "free grace" may serve, however, to conceal incipient sectarianism as well as to evidence doctrinal purity; and this ambiguity, together with the usage of the phrase in contemporary English controversy, suggests that claims for the normative Protestantism of the New England dissenters should be accepted with reservation. In any case, neither Luther nor Calvin understood the *sola gratia* to mean that God, in acting graciously, violates the ontological and moral orders established at creation; and both Reformers actively opposed those who, in the name of "free grace," would dissolve the infinite qualitative difference between creatures and the Persons of the Trinity.

Examined in the context of contemporary Reformed divinity, the theological evidence suggests less that the elders of the Bay Colony were crypto-Arminians, undermining the *sola gratia* by slight concessions to unregenerate human agency, than that Cotton, in 1636, was a crypto-sectary, perilously close to invalidating creaturely agency altogether, of both biblical word and regenerate work, in the name of the unconditioned, increated agency of the Trinity. If in fact the elders were exalting human activity at the expense of divine grace, it was in the qualified sense of advancing works of sanctification as legitimate first evidence of justification, and they had ample ground in the Reformed theological tradition on which to rest their appeal to the practical syllogism. They did not, in any case, suggest that the evidence of sanctification was particularly easy to obtain, or that practical assurance of sanctification, once obtained, was casually to be "rested in." Nor did they maintain that practical assurance was the only assurance.[44] To people who complained that they doubted of their estate because they had not been conclusively sealed with the Spirit in an immediate testimony, Shepard replied, in effect: You have the promises of the gospel; go then to Christ in them, trusting to him who makes them and believing that they are made to you. In believing, you are justified;

and in believing, you have assurance.[45] In this appeal to the confidence of faith there is an echo of Perkins, and behind him of Calvin.

Cotton offered his hearers a more direct route to assurance than either the practical syllogism or the confidence inherent in *fiducia*. In order to do so, he reversed the relationship of faith and justification in the order of redemption, and he severely subordinated created nature to increated being. In both respects his position, from the viewpoint of Reformed orthodoxy, was theologically questionable. It was also susceptible to distortion. Thus John Underhill, sometime captain of the Boston militia and a supporter of Hutchinson, was cited before the Court in September 1638 for saying that "he had lain under a spirit of bondage and legal way five years, and could get no assurance, till at length, as he was taking a pipe of tobacco, the Spirit set home an absolute promise of free grace with such assurance and joy, as he never since doubted his good estate, neither should he, though he should fall into sin."[46] Whether intended seriously or in jest, the remark fairly suggests what Cotton's position on assurance might imply. Cotton, to whom it had since been revealed where things in Boston stood, rebuked Underhill, observing that God never sends "such a spirit of comfort but in an ordinance . . . , and ergo advised him well to examine the revelation and joy which he had." Two years earlier, also, Cotton had been unwilling to say that the Spirit's revealing is above, or independent of, or contrary to the biblical word or other ordained means of grace. By so much he had remained orthodox.

The Covenantal Dialectic

Theology being for Puritans the "doctrine of living to God," the theological task began for them with elucidation of the divine will disclosed in scripture, nature, and events, and culminated in application of the resulting theologoumena to the religious and ethical life of the congregation. In this respect, the end of theological reflection was that "observance" which Ames considered the substance of the Christian life. Underlying and supporting this practical emphasis was a series of more strictly theological convictions concerning the ground, nature, and end of "observance." The universal obedience that was the ideal of Puritan piety and the object of Puritan preaching was acknowledged to be necessarily the fruit of a regenerate heart; and sanctification in this life was held to presuppose an order of causes flowing from God's intention to glorify himself in the creation, just reprobation, and merciful redemption of men. The will of God presented as injunction thus leads necessarily to the will of God considered as absolute volition; and theology, which addresses human vitality in the present moment, leads forward and backward, like the being of the present moment, to the being of God who is Alpha and Omega, from whom and to whom are all things. "All creatures in the world," wrote Shepard, "are of God, and for God, so that, being of him, they receive their being from him as their first efficient, and being for him, are therefore preserved and governed by him as their utmost end." The creature, in both its being and the ends it serves, is thus a coming from and a "reflux and return" back to God, who is Uncaused Cause, Pure Act, Necessary Being, and, in relation to all outside himself, preeminently Absolute Will.[47] The creation and its history, including the order of redemption and within that order God's covenant with mankind, Puritans referred to a divine volition that in its nature is consistent with the divine nature and in its content is suited to human nature.

Precisely at this point—at the affirmation of the covenantal character of the dispensation of grace according to God's ordinate power—the issues raised by the New England antinomians impinged. According to Puritan covenant theology, under the terms of the covenant of works mankind incurred an invarying obligation to fulfill the divine will as it concerns human action. In this obligation man's place was fixed in the moral order instituted at creation. In entering into a mutual agreement with man, to which man willingly consented, God acted in accordance with man's created nature as a "cause by counsel." In this divine self-accommodation, the ontological order of creation was affirmed and respected. God's institution of the covenant of grace, moreover, did not alter his determination to uphold the orders of being and morality established at the beginning of the world. Though God graciously enables the elect to consent to the covenant and to believe the promises, he also requires that they actually consent and believe. Their faith is to be their own. The same is the case with sanctified obedience to the law as the rule of Christian life. Christ in his mediatoral office, Shepard noted, "did not believe and repent, and perform duties of thankfulness for us"; these actions are "personally required" of us.[48] Human beings are not stones but active, moral creatures, and God—paraphrasing Dort—does not work upon them as upon blocks and brutes that lack such capacities.[49]

Fundamentally at issue between elders and dissenters in Massachusetts Bay was the extent to which God, in translating human beings to the life of heaven, respects and employs the orders of being and morality that comprise the substance and rule of earthly life. Cotton and the Hutchinsonians, for whom created nature and the Spirit's operation were mutually antagonistic, considered the covenants of works and grace to be mutually exclusive, and they challenged the other elders accordingly. In so doing, however, they called into question that respect for the created order which Reformed federal theology sought to secure by making the covenant of works the paradigm of God's salvific activity. In rejecting the evidential value of works of sanctification, Cotton and the Hutchinsonians appeared to question the continued validity of the moral law for the regenerate, in effect introducing a dichotomy into the moral order to which Reformed Protestantism was characteristically hostile. If in fact the objective holiness of the saints is so tenuous that it can be discerned only by the Spirit's testimony, and if *Christ* must "act" sanctifying graces for believers, then in what sense, Puritan divines inquired, may the regenerate be required to obey the moral law? The antinomian tendency, indeed, was to reject all human activity in conversion, before, during, and after, and in consequence to reject the pedagogical function of the moral law before conversion and its regulative use after it.[50] Insofar as Cotton and the Hutchinsonians insisted that God's treatment of man in the covenant of grace is quite different from that in the covenant of works, they appeared dangerously close to serious theological error. Their opponents argued that, although the Hutchinsonians claimed to be exalting God's freedom, they were in fact pretentiously disregarding the revealed order of redemption, so that they might appear religious themselves and keep their own carnal pleasures in the bargain, an attitude characteristic of the unregenerate, who by definition remain under the full force of the covenant of works.[51]

It was in this sense that antinomians on both sides of the Atlantic were said to open up a "fair and easy way to heaven," a charge that, like other things said of them, was in a measure descriptive as well as pejorative.[52] A woman who accosted Edward Johnson as he debarked at Boston told him that Anne Hutchinson preached "better gospel" than any of the university-trained "blackcoats." Johnson found subsequently that this "better gospel" meant that he must "take a naked Christ," unmediated through the ministry of the law and the ordinances of the gospel, and that he must look to nothing in himself as evidence that he had in fact taken Christ.[53] To Johnson this teaching was profoundly disturbing, for it seemed to preclude him "from partaking with the divine nature of Christ, in that mystical union of his . . . Spirit creating, and continuing his graces in the soul"—in other words, it threatened that he personally might not become regenerate at all. For others whose capacity for dialectical tension was smaller than Johnson's, the free and ample gospel of a "naked" Christ seemed to reduce the ambiguity of the Christian life as understood by Puritans, with its cycles of triumph and lapse, of faith and doubt. That such ambiguity was a source of stress is apparent from Puritan devotional literature, from personal journals like Shepard's, and from the acts of desperation, contemplated or carried out, sprinkling the records of Puritan piety. For people to whom fiducial confidence was not given, or who were temperamentally incapable of encompassing the dialectic of faith and doubt, a gospel seeming conclusively to overcome that dialectic might have great appeal.

Put more positively, there was in the Pauline dichotomies of law and gospel, flesh and spirit, and works and faith—shorn of Paul's qualifications, unencumbered by school divinity, and fertilized by triumphalist language like that of Niclaes—a message of liberation not only from the demands of "legal righteousness" but from the mediation of creatures as well. From the antinomian perspective, indeed, these were the same thing. If spiritual rebirth is essentially a matter between an individual and the Third Person of the Trinity and is accomplished wholly by the latter's increated power, which comes to possess the regenerate, then the individual is quite independent of created instruments. He need not rely upon the word of scripture in order to learn the will and ways of God, for the Spirit teaches him directly and more clearly. He need not come to Christ through earnest and sometimes agonizing attendance upon the preaching of law and gospel, for Christ has nothing to do with the law, and he has Christ in his heart immediately by the power of the Spirit. He need not evidence his good estate by doing good deeds, for the Spirit in his heart tells him of his good condition, and good deeds only "justify" him "to manward." Indeed, he need not fear sin or the law, for whatever he does is done by the Spirit acting in him, or if not, then God does not see the act. From this point of view it readily appeared that ministers who held up the law as the mirror of Christian righteousness and who could offer no more settled assurance than the "endless learning" of obedience and repentance were but "work-mongers" and "legalists."

To Puritan ministers in the orthodox tradition, the antinomian position seemed offensively casual, in conception as well as in implication, not only because it was often stated with flippancy to people accustomed to respectful address but also because it seemed to reflect gross oversimplification of the conditions of imperfection and anticipation under which, they believed, the Christian life is lived. Traske complained that ministers who pressed obedience and repentance as the way of Christians fostered despair rather than comfort, and he countered that grieving over sin and doubting God's favor are evidence of weak faith, rather than of the presence of the "new creature." For the true believer, he suggested, it is easier to believe that sins are remitted than it is to confess them. His Puritan critic entered the customary response that, since regeneration is not perfect in this life, some doubt is to be expected, especially in the event of moral lapse, and that, since conscience is more privy to the mixed condition of the heart than to God's mind, confession is easier than belief of remission. Traske, he implied, had never really struggled with the ambiguities of the Christian life that the doctrines of *simul iustus ac peccator* and fiducial faith sought to address. "All is easy to this man, who has found an easier way to heaven (if we may believe him) than was ever known before, or is safe to follow now."[54] The fact that Traske made justifying faith persuasion of one's justification seemed proof that he did not understand the stresses to which faith may be subject. Traske in his own way appears to have understood the stresses, but he sought somehow to eliminate them in advance from his conception of faith, rather than to encompass them within it. Sibbes, in contrast, recommended Ball's *Treatise of Faith* because he knew Ball had been much "put to it, to know by experience what it is to *live by faith.*"[55] What Sibbes meant is embodied in the alternations of subjective confidence and doubt recorded in Shepard's journal, which are sustained, in their earnestness and intensity, by a species of confidence that neither Traske nor Hutchinson seems to have enjoyed.

Certain of the Caroline Anglican divines, it has been observed, "lowered the market" for salvation by including moral endeavor within the formal cause of justification.[56] Much the same may be said of contemporary English antinomians, in the sense that they seemed to ease the way to heaven by freeing saints-presumptive from the obligation of attendance upon ordinances and hopeful saints from the obligation to test their callings by their obedience. Given the suppositions about the nature of God with which Reformed orthodoxy began, however, there is no possibility of overcoming the ontological and moral distinction between Creator and creature to the extent that antinomians implied, not even in the state of glory, where the saints "enjoy" God directly but are not dissolved into him. Having created mankind as rational agents, and having promulgated a rule by which they are to be governed, God is bound by his nature to deal with them accordingly and not as he might with lesser creatures who have neither understanding nor volition. To say without qualification that the Spirit "acts" believers was to suggest that believers do not act themselves, implying either that their human nature is overwhelmed or that a Person of the Trinity has assumed human nature in them. To the New England elders, the first implication seemed plainly erroneous, the second simply blasphemous. To assert flatly that believers are "not under the law" or are "not to act from a command" was to suggest that the law, given at creation as the rule of God's dealings with men, is abrogated or fundamentally altered, implying that believers are freed from the moral obligations incumbent on men as men or that the rule governing the saints in heaven differs essentially from that laid down at the beginning of the world. These implications, too, seemed erroneous. God being what he is, and having done in creation what he has done, he is constrained to act thereafter, even to glorification of the saints in heaven, in a manner essentially continuous and also essentially covenantal. So conceived, grace is free, but man is not freed from responsibility; he cannot be, without ceasing to be human. Antinomians seemed to say that grace is simply free.

CHAPTER 10

Epilogue

On the stage of seventeenth-century English history, the New England Antinomian Controversy was a minor, provincial flurry. It was important for the subsequent history of Massachusetts Bay because its outcome assured the ascendancy there of the strain of Puritan piety and thought represented by Winthrop, Bulkeley, and Shepard, and because it helped to stimulate further clarification of New England ecclesiology. Its historic magnitude aside, however, the New England dispute involved a major theological issue, an issue as old as Christianity and one to which Puritans were especially sensitive. The relationship of nature and grace is among the perennial problems of Christian faith and practice, which must find some way of dealing with the juxtaposition of heavenly and earthly orders in the lives of individual Christians. How sweeping are the consequences for worldly existence, in family, market, school, state, and church, of the new order brought about by the intervention in a person's life of divine grace? Is there an utterly unbridgeable gulf between the new creation into which the regenerate are taken up and the old creation in which, up to that point, they lived, moved, and had their being? Or does participation in the new order only alter a person's relationship to the old, without completely dissolving his ties with it, and enable him to order earthly life in new ways? Upon the answer to these questions hangs a series of answers to others, concerning ecclesiology, ethics, the practice of piety, and the shape of Christian society.

For Puritans the problem of relating old and new creation was made acute by their peculiar self-consciousness and by their historical situation. Regarding themselves as the latest and perhaps final stage of the Protestant Reformation, they increasingly felt a divine obligation to achieve in England a nation of godly churches, as against churches of merely baptised persons. In doing so, however, they had somehow to remain godly and pure without becoming otherworldly or amoral, and they had to uphold the freedom of God in giving and the freedom of man in receiving grace, without making salvation a consequence of human action and therein denying the distinctive Protestant doctrines. The intellectual devices by which they endeavored to sustain and to contain this tension were mainly theologoumena asserting a mutual relationship between created nature and divine grace and tending to balance the thrust toward the transcendent by affirmation of the created order. In proportion as Puritans were hounded and hindered in their task of furthering godliness in England, however, their sense of urgency increased, and with it the difficulty of maintaining proper balance between old order and new, and between nature and grace. Under stress, alternative solutions emerged that tended to simplify the dialectic in one direction or the other.

These solutions involved not only technical theology but ecclesiology and personal piety as well. At one end of the Puritan spectrum, by 1645, there had emerged an extreme separatism seeking to withdraw from ecclesiastical or worldly impurity, and a theological extremism asserting that the Holy Spirit dwells substantially in the reborn, at the expense of creaturely integrity, and drawing an absolute distinction between law and gospel and between works and faith. Toward the other extreme lay varying degrees of compromise with the ecclesiastical and political kingdoms of this world, and a theology that tended to make the decree of election contingent upon foreknown faith or to make its effectiveness depend upon motions of the human will. To the Hutchinsonians, who participated in the former tendency, regeneration was a "miracle" pure-and-simple, in which God overrules created nature and elevates it above the common moral order. For the New England elders, who stopped well short of the latter tendency, regeneration was also a miracle, but one achieved mediately, "naturally," and in accordance with the moral order established at creation. For them the covenant of grace was necessarily of the same form as the covenant of works, requiring consent and obedience from man. For the

Hutchinsonians, in whose estimation mankind could not properly covenant with God at all, exhortations to human activity respecting justification and its evidencing implied covert reliance on the covenant of works, at the expense of the purity, gratuity, and sovereignty of saving grace. Although the elders felt themselves to be architects of an outpost of the new, divine order, their society was, in practice, as broad as the heterogeneous population of Massachusetts. The Hutchinsonians implied that they would prefer not to do business with "enemies of Christ."

On Tuesday, January 30, 1649, Charles I of England stepped through the middle window of the Banqueting House at Whitehall onto the scaffold from which, at four minutes after two, he passed into history. The execution of the king, reflecting the rise in power of the army radicals, was symbolic of the rending of a considerable consensus of faith and practice built up within the Puritan "center" during the first forty years of the century, when Puritans constituted the increasingly constrained religious and political opposition in England. The death of Charles marked a seemingly absolute break with the old order. By 1649, however, the new Puritan order, in any coherent and comprehensive sense, was powerless to be born. Puritanism's sense of newness, expressed in the doctrine of the Holy Spirit's activity in the regenerate and in the Reformed conviction of the utter equality of men in their need for grace and in their dependence upon the divine sovereignty, was conducive to a potentially divisive individualism. In the end, this individualism overtook the Puritan sense of order. Once the unity enforced by persecution and warfare was removed, fission occurred, especially but not exclusively at the point of ecclesiology—a phenomenon that Cromwell might in a measure contain but could scarcely overcome. The most positive result of the splintering of the Puritan movement was increasing insistence, among a widening variety of nonconformists, on the principle of toleration. Its negative result was the ultimate collapse of the Puritan program for establishing a godly commonwealth in Britain. Partly in response to the flowering of the sects, and partly as a vehicle of internecine politics, heresiography became in the 1640s a significant genre in Puritan literature, and Puritan polemicists, until the end of the century, tilted their swords less against Roman Catholics and Arminians than against members of their own party.

In debate with sectaries during Commonwealth and Protectorate, and in exchanges between less radical nonconformists beginning in the early 1650s and continuing into the 1690s, issues involving the relationship of nature and grace in regeneration continued to occupy an important place. Prominent among them was the question of the nature of the covenant of grace and of the parties to it—in particular whether the covenant is actually made with human beings, or only with Christ, mankind partaking of it only as they are united to Christ by the Spirit. At the hands of "orthodox" divines the covenant-motif underwent further elaboration. Between covenant of grace and covenant of works an intratrinitarian covenant emerged, frequently designated the "covenant of redemption," in which Christ was held to have contracted with God for fulfillment of the covenant of works. The covenant of grace is founded upon this covenant of redemption, in which salvation has been obtained for mankind. Salvation, however, is applied to the elect in the covenant of grace, which is necessarily made with individuals.[1] The more radical element tended to absorb the covenant of grace into the intratrinitarian covenant, lest the gratuity of redemption be compromised by a transaction involving human consent. The covenant of grace is made with Christ alone, its benefits becoming available to individuals only as they are first "in" Christ. In controversy over these issues, after the Restoration, New England divines tended to maintain the position articulated in the 1630s and 1640s by Shepard, Bulkeley, and Norton, arguing that the freeness of justification may consist with a covenant made with particular persons, without compromising the Protestant principles of *sola gratia* and *sola fide*.[2]

In their faithfulness to the teachings of the first generation, New England Puritans represented something of an exception. After 1660 English nonconformity entered upon different paths from those that had led to Westminster, and intellectual and religious currents flowed in channels often remote from the shores of Massachusetts Bay. New England, founded as a beacon to guide the further reformation of the English Church—which reformation the Westminster Assembly had been summoned to carry out, and which had eventuated, ironically, in the Act of Toleration—became one of the more distant provinces of the "first" English empire. Toleration was, in a sense, the inevitable outcome of the

Puritan tendency to split into subgroups, each enamored of its own relative ecclesiological, doctrinal, or moral purity; and it also reflected a gradual relaxation of sectarian intensity after the striving and exhaustion of the Cromwellian period. Either way, it was perceived initially in Massachusetts as the end of the campaign for a new order, and New England Puritans turned to the task of carrying on the tradition in the face of an indefinitely postponed eschaton.

In a measure, both the sectarian zeal of Puritans and its subsequent cooling can be related to Puritan formal theology, at least in the sense of legitimating ideology. Classic Puritan divinity sought to embrace, in taut harmony, divine activity and created nature, religious individualism and ecclesiastical order, emotional piety and intellectual precision, Plum Island and New Jerusalem. For those able to encompass it, this dialectic provided a conceptual framework in which to order a considerable range of personal experience; and in this measure it conferred upon the believer a certain resiliency in the face of events. One man's dialectic, however, may be another's antinomy. The theological and pastoral formulations articulated by the founding generation of New England divines implied a degree of intellectual and emotional sophistication and a tolerance of ambiguity that were not equally present in individual churchgoers. In practice, dialectical balance could be lost or in individual cases never attained, and without it, aberration was possible at any point between Plum Island and New Jerusalem. Once the mutual tension between nature and grace was dissolved, a Puritan could become a Yankee or a Unitarian as readily as he could become a Baptist or a Quaker. Either way, Puritan divinity offered cognitive resources for coping with changing circumstances, or for challenging a succession of standing orders.

Historians are sometimes inclined to see in the experientialism of English Puritans the beginnings of the broad, international pietistic impulse represented variously by Philip Jacob Spener, John Wesley, and Jonathan Edwards. The "natural" side of the Puritan dialectic of nature and grace had similar importance for subsequent Anglo-American religious and intellectual history.

Whatever Puritans may have thought of God's sovereignty and power, their view of man, considered as a creature, was frankly flattering. The affirmations of the integrity of second causes, of the natural liberty of man's will, of the ability of human reason to derive knowledge of God from his effects in creation, and of the importance of rational "method" in theologizing, far from being submerged in pious feeling, were premises, both for the practice of piety and for the exposition of articles of faith. The order of redemption formulated in the Puritan theological scheme presupposed an inherent capacity in human nature to receive and to exercise gracious power and also presupposed the "eviternity" of the distinctively human faculties of reason and will. Though created with him in time, these faculties belong to an individual's immortal soul and are in fact what fit him for eternal felicity, understood as intuitive intellectual apprehension of the divine essence and complete conformity of will with the divine will. Puritanism shared these affirmations with Protestant orthodoxy and with the scholastic tradition generally. Fallen man, his will corrupted, is a despicable creature; but man considered in himself is truly but little lower than the angels. For this reason, it may be suggested, the way from Perkins's *Golden Chain* to Locke's *Reasonableness of Christianity*, while not direct, is nonetheless continuous; and while there is an immediate connection between Shepard's *Parable of the Ten Virgins* and Edwards's *Religious Affections*, there is also a connection, though less direct, between Norton's *Orthodox Evangelist* and Cotton Mather's *Christian Philosopher*.

As the seventeenth century gave way to the eighteenth, the rationalism and naturalism of Protestant orthodoxy were absorbed into the characteristic preoccupations of the Enlightened, for whom natural reason was the distinguishing, cardinal—and sovereign—human capacity. The orthodox theologian's concern for the liberty and integrity of second causes appears, much altered, in the Newtonian world-machine, in which second causes are for practical purposes sovereign. Much later, in Thomas Jefferson's versions of the "life and morals" of Jesus, one may perceive orthodoxy's respect for the powers of human reason and human conscience—now unqualified by doctrinal norms and made into the chief principles of biblical and theological criticism.[3] In response to a changing climate of opinion, a substantial segment of Anglo-American nonconformity abandoned the rational and natural realms to philosophers, taking refuge in varieties of institutionalized piety, fortified by increasingly rigid biblicism and theological dogmatism. In the process the weight of Christian truth-claims came to rest unduly on the alleged miraculousness of the biblical miracles, and articles of faith came to be regarded as divinely authored in proportion as they were intellectually offensive. This situation persisted, in some areas of Reformed Protestantism, into the twentieth century.

In the New England tradition, Edwards remained fully cognizant of the work of his theological forebears, which he reaffirmed in the philosophical idiom of his own era. His notion of the "new spiritual sense" created by the Holy Spirit in the regenerate was a restatement, in terms of Lockeian empiricism rather than scholastic metaphysics, of Reformed orthodoxy's insistence that grace qualitatively enhances the power of human faculties, without destroying their nature; and behind his identification of true religion with "holy affections" lies Shepard's insistence that the Spirit is present in the saints in and through infused graces disposing man's natural faculties to new actions. Edwards's pupil, Samuel Hopkins, readily adopted a "moral government" theory of the atonement, partly because he lived in a time of self-conscious constitutionalism but also because the Reformed tradition, from the early seventeenth century, was replete with references to the moral law as the form of God's government of reasonable creatures. In his formulation of the doctrine of divine sovereignty, Hopkins seemed severely to reduce the natural agency of second causes; yet in his separation of "regeneration," as God's action, from "conversion," as man's action in virtue of God's, he pointedly affirmed the respective integrity of divine and human efficiency. In both cases, in thought and sometimes in expression, Hopkins echoed Norton. Charles Finney, whose primary commitment, as a child of the Second Awakening, was to experientialism, refused to allow the distinction between order of nature and order of time that was implicit in Hopkins's treatment of calling. "Regeneration" and "conversion," he insisted, are the same act, and the act is man's act. In Finney's emphasis on the calculated employment of "means" in the production of conversion experiences there is an echo of the earlier Puritan understanding of the instrumentality of second causes. In his forceful advocacy of "new measures," however, and in his doctrine of conversion, Finney made divine agency practically coincident, in nature and in time, with human agency.[4]

With Finney's generation, also, came the "temperance" movement and other manifestations of a tendency within evangelical

Protestantism on both sides of the Atlantic to locate sanctification in outward acts of quite specific obedience, rather than in an inward disposition to universal obedience and benevolence, as Shepard, Edwards, and Hopkins had done. By this time, much of the resiliency conferred by its original dialectical balance had gone out of the Puritan tradition, and with it much of the creative tension between nature and grace and between newness and order, from which seventeenth-century Puritans derived both vitality and stamina. Also lost was the dialectic of pious worldliness, which regarded a spiritual, heavenly calling as incomplete without a material, earthly one, and vice versa. The more self-conscious heirs of Puritans—those who strove according to their lights to continue the tradition—found it increasingly difficult to hold together reason and faith in their religion, and also increasingly difficult to embrace the fullness of the world with a good conscience.

"Preparation for Salvation"

Perry Miller initially introduced New England "preparationism" as an interpretive category in the context of the national moral reformation prescribed by the "Reforming Synod" of 1679, which met to address the problem of maintaining a godly commonwealth in the Bay Colony.[1] The founding generation had committed Massachusetts to a "national covenant" with God, in which divine favor was contingent upon the colony's external obedience in moral and religious duties. Such obedience, not requiring personal regeneration, could be enforced by a godly minority ruling through the agency of the civil law. As the unregenerate majority increased, however, so did the problem of enforcing the obligations of the national covenant. The New England clergy, Miller argued, in response to what they regarded as a diluting of the impulse to public and private piety, fastened upon the notion that there are preparatory conditions antecedent to conversion, in the pursuit of which would-be saints are required to exercise themselves. From their pulpits, the ministers conducted a hortatory campaign, urging their hearers to preparatory moral endeavor, with the incidental but desirable effect that, in striving to discern and avoid their sins, they would perforce fulfill the terms of the national covenant. Well before 1679, Miller observed, there existed a distinctive New England doctrine of "preparation," Hooker being its chief spokesman, which affirmed the ability of the unregenerate to act in ways significantly related to conversion. In 1636–38, exhortations to earnest moral endeavor and to attendance on ordinances by regenerate and unregenerate were common in New England pulpits, with appropriate social consequences; the "preparationist" Hooker played a prominent role in the Newtown synod; and the Hutchinsonians were vociferous against human activity before and after conversion, with negative implications for moral and religious endeavor. In view of the tradition about Cotton's devotion to Calvin, and in light of Miller's own view of the Reformed attitude toward human activity, "preparation," understood as crypto-Arminianism, appeared to be the fundamental issue in the Antinomian Controversy.

It may be suggested, however, that there are a number of difficulties with this formulation.

1. In the chief documentary sources for the Antinomian Controversy, explicit concern with moral endeavor prior to conversion, as a point of contention, is relatively inconspicuous. Noting this circumstance, Miller characterized preparation as "the hidden issue" in the controversy, on the grounds that it was not yet a "consolidated doctrine" and therefore "figured deceptively as an incidental term in the technical disputations" and that, being suggestive of Arminianism, it was so theologically loaded that "the authorities made every effort to play it down."[2] There are deficiencies, however, in both of these arguments. Among Reformed Protestants, English Puritans were peculiarly concerned about the nature of personal regeneration, largely, it may be suggested, for ecclesiological reasons. Determined to create covenanted churches of the apparently godly, if not of the actually regenerate, Puritans were inspired to elaborate in detail the order and evidences of the "application of redemption," and the pedagogical function of the law was taken under this rubric. New Englanders, especially Hooker, devoted much attention to non-saving preparations antecedent to conversion, yet they shared this concern with their English brethren; and in stressing "legal" preparation to receive Christ, they were elaborating a commonplace of Reformed divinity. Their elaboration, moreover, was well developed by the early 1630s, so that "preparation" in this sense would seem to have been current in 1636 to the point of requiring no special mention.[3]

The suggestion of censorship, during or after the controversy, is unconvincing in view of the *variety* of materials assembled by Hall. In the first half of the seventeenth century "preparation" came under discussion among Puritans in at least four somewhat different respects: (1) whether the preparatory states of compunction and humiliation are themselves evidences of election, such that if God has wrought them, he will shortly and surely work vocation; (2) whether such states are evidence of effectual calling and may be resorted to by a person who doubts his calling because of imperfect sanctification; (3) whether such states are qualitatively of the same grace as vocation and so in some sense "saving," or whether they are only "common" works of the Spirit; (4) whether works of preparation are proper conditions of vocation, which, when men perform them by their own efforts or by common grace, God must accept and reward.[4] Puritans argued about all these questions, with each other and with opponents; but these are not the issues about which Cotton, in 1636, was writing passionate though controlled letters to his colleagues, nor are they the issues upon which his colleagues wished earnestly to examine him. Those exchanges are dominated, rather, by discussion of the nature and relationship of faith, justification, and sanctification in the order of regeneration and of the means to knowledge of all three—issues quite as exciting at the time, and more comprehensive, than "preparation" in Miller's sense of the term.

2. If the fundamental issue in the Antinomian Controversy was "preparation" antecedent to conversion, Cotton's place becomes even more ambiguous. For in *The New Covenant,* comprising sermons delivered during the controversy, Cotton matter-of-factly discusses preparatory states, necessary before union with Christ, that correspond to Shepard's states of "conviction" and "compunction." God ordinarily, that is, in the normal course of his redemptive activity, works a double preparation on the elect, making them conscious, by a "spirit of bondage" under the law, of their sinfulness and, by a "spirit of burning" in the face of God's wrath, cutting them off from all hope of grace and from all comfort of their own legal works. Such preparations are not "saving," there being no saving works in the soul before union with Christ, but they are preparations. Norton made the same point in *The Orthodox Evangelist,* which Miller regarded as a theological systematizing of preparationist notions.[5] In any case, it was not unusual for Puritans, when discussing the second use of the law, to point out that such "preparations" are not saving, and it is not entirely clear whether Cotton, in doing so, was speaking to Shepard and Bulkeley, neither of whom regarded legal preparations as saving. In his discussion of

the preparatory office of the law Cotton was essentially "orthodox"; and in his "Rejoynder" to his colleagues references to works preparing and to works antecedent to faith appear in the course of discussion about discerning justification, that is, in the context of "conditions consequent" to calling (to use Cotton's phrase), rather than in the context of "stages" antecedent to it.[6]

3. The majority of the New England clergy were yet able in 1636 to distinguish comfortably between theological doctrines of predestination and irresistible grace, as they pertain to salvation, and metaphysical doctrines of determinism. As observed above, the Reformed doctrine of divine sovereignty was not regarded in the orthodox period as excluding human activity from regeneration. That a person was predestined to a certain end, and saved by grace alone, did not affect his nature as a rational, willing agent, nor did it mean that he could "do nothing" morally significant in daily life, but only that he was impotent to effect his own salvation. Denial of such efficacy to individuals, however, was not regarded as inconsistent with the assertion that human activity, in the context of the ordained means for dispensing grace, is instrumental in the application of redemption. The command to believe, Puritan divines insisted, is incumbent upon everyone, and though only the elect receive the ability to fulfill it, everyone is obliged to consider himself susceptible of regeneration and to attend diligently upon the means. The utility of these conclusions for promoting exertion in religious duties is obvious. They do not, however, necessarily indicate an "Arminian" drift, unless it is also concluded that the fallen will, of its own power, is able to consent to God's offer of forgiveness, and that this consent is the effective condition of justification —conclusions that were roundly rejected by Puritans on both sides of the Atlantic.[7]

For these reasons it seems unlikely that the issue of activity *per se* preparatory to conversion had immediate Arminian overtones in Massachusetts and was therefore something to be alluded to rather than stated, as Miller suggested. The Hutchinsonians, not averse to name-calling, tagged the elders "legalists" and "enemies" of Christ and of "free grace"—rather forceful terms of reproach in the context in which they were uttered. What they intended by "legalism" was quite close to what John Eaton meant by "legal zeal" and "zealous dead faith"; and, while Eaton and the Hutchinsonians both objected to human activity in regeneration, their objections included considerably more than the relationship between effectual calling and prior "unregenerate doings"—to borrow a phrase from later New England controversy.

4. The matter is further complicated by the fact that "preparation" in Puritan theological discourse may refer to two different things. "Preparation for conversion," that is, for translation from a state of apostasy to a state of grace, comprises the states of conviction, compunction, and humiliation by which a sinful soul is made ready to receive regenerating grace. The doctrinal *locus* is chiefly that concerning the pedagogical use of the law. Strictly taken, *salvation* refers to the glorification of the saints in heaven; "preparation for salvation" comprises a Christian's growth in grace following conversion.[8] Between the beginnings of holiness in calling and its perfection in glory lies a life of struggle with the remnants of sin, during which the converted are expected to prepare themselves, by diligent exercise of graces received, for presentation before their exalted Lord. The doctrinal *locus* is, in effect, that concerning the third use of the law. In Shepard's *Parable of the Ten Virgins,* for example, the second sense of "preparation" dominates. The sermons that make up this volume, for all their stress on attending on means and performing holy duties, are primarily eschatological in orientation. They constitute an extended exposition of the parable of the virgins in Mt. 15:1–13, some wise, some foolish, but all apparently virgins, waiting to meet the bridegroom; and they are addressed explicitly to the *church,* comprising regenerate and unregenerate, but all visibly saints, who are preparing to meet Christ at his second coming, though with differing effect. "Preparation" is a recurrent motif, but preeminently in relation to Christ's imminent coming and chiefly in the sense of exercising and therein perfecting the habits of grace infused in regeneration.[9] In the course of his exposition Shepard addresses issues relevant to the antinomian dispute, but it is not evident from his remarks that he is defending "preparation" in Miller's sense.

5. Statements by and about antinomians, both English and New English, are frequently as applicable to the place of human activity in believing, in discerning justification, and in works of sanctification—all of which have to do with the nature of regeneration itself—as they are to moral endeavor antecedent to conversion.

In the passage from Weld's preface to the *Short Story* (quoted in Chapter 1), for example, only the reference to the work of the law concerns a condition antecedent to faith. Hutchinson's hostility to human activity certainly included moral endeavor before conversion, but that this was the focus or sum of her concern is less certain. Issues equally if not more important, from theological and practical viewpoints, are raised explicitly in the rest of the passage from Weld.[11]

The same may be said of the errors and improper expressions collected by the ministerial synod in 1637. Taken at face value, the majority of these items fall, more or less, into four categories, concerning (a) the nature of justifying faith, (b) the nature of sanctification, (c) the nature of Christ's or the Spirit's indwelling in the believer, and (d) the means of knowing one's estate. This observation is confirmed by examination of the rest of the documents. The explicit issues, and those which receive most extensive treatment, concern the relationship in the order of redemption among faith, union with Christ, justification, and sanctification; and they coalesce in the question of the validity of works of sanctification as evidence of a justified estate. This question involves the matter of the activity of supernatural graces in the regenerate and the matter of the relationship of the Holy Spirit to the believer. If Cotton, in rejecting saving preparations before union with Christ, meant to include the action of infused faith, he was using "preparation" in a quite novel sense. The same is true if he wished to exclude works of sanctification as illegitimate "preparations" to active faith, which he understood as faith of assurance. Reading, in Millerian fashion, "between the lines" of the documents, one might conclude that "preparation" was a crucial issue in the controversy on the broader practical front, as part of a homiletical technique for producing conversion experiences. Explicitly for the participants in the controversy, however, the broader issue at both practical and theological levels was that of the means to knowledge and assurance of one's justified estate, an issue that turns on how the nature of regeneration is understood, not on what a person is alleged to be able to "do" to "facilitate" regeneration.

More recently, Norman Pettit, taking up certain of Miller's suggestions, also treated preparation as the principal issue in the New England controversy. In contrast to Miller, he found it explicit rather than implicit, and he defined preparation as "affective" "turning to God" prior to conversion, rather than as moral endeavor.[12] Cotton, Pettit argued, rigorously emphasized legal constraint, leading to sudden conversion of the passive soul, whereas the other elders stressed the gospel's "drawing" of the soul to Christ, during which process the soul acts "in a spiritual way" in anticipation of conversion. Cotton does in fact seem to have exalted the ministry of the law in destroying the confidence of corrupt nature over the allure of the gospel promises; whereas Shepard and Bulkeley appear to have given a more equal place to both, in the prelude to effectual calling. This difference was consistent with Cotton's tendency to diminish the place of created faculties in all phases of regeneration. It would seem a mistake, however, to reduce the Antinomian Controversy to the single issue of the subjective ability of the elect to "desire" God before regeneration is actually wrought in calling. Though a number of the "errors" collected by the Newtown synod may be construed as denying this sense of preparation, they deny much more as well, and more explicitly, as do the positions addressed in the sixteen questions put to Cotton by his fellow ministers.[13] Moreover, the doctrine of the law as *pedagogus ad Christum* entailed the notion that through the law's work the elect should come earnestly to desire Christ, though not with the holy desire that distinguishes the truly regenerate.

Cotton, as Pettit noted, regarded the resort to conditional promises as building justification on the "hay and stubble" of "works." As Cotton's colleagues pointed out, however, this proposition might mean either of two things: it could mean to build justification on works of legal righteousness, in the sense of fulfilling the condition of the covenant of works; or it could mean to seek assurance, when one's subjective sense of justification "lies prostrate," by testing one's obedience against the rule of scripture (the "third use" of the law) according to the practical syllogism. Cotton included both meanings under "hay and stubble," as did contemporary English antinomians, and on essentially the same ground, namely, that human works and the law have nothing to do with grace, either before or after its effectual operation in calling. This is a larger issue, however, than "legal constraint" versus "affective drawing."

It should be noted in this connection that Cotton rejected active faith as the condition of the covenant of grace, not only as something "preparatory" to or "anticipatory" of effectual calling but as *part of calling* itself, and that he also rejected the *act* of faith, as an act of adherence and dependence on Christ, as evidence of union with Christ.[14] He did so, it may be suggested, partly because he wished to exclude creaturely acts as such from calling, making it entirely a divine work, and also because he shared the tendency of that strain of contemporary English nonconformity that, severely subordinating created to increated being, perforce defined justifying faith as subjective assurance of justification. That Cotton did so, and was unable or unwilling to distinguish the causal from the evidential value of gracious works in ascertaining a person's estate, seems to have impressed his colleagues as being more problematic than his treatment of the relative significance of the ministries of law and gospel antecedent to calling. It seems, in any case, to have been symptomatic of a larger and more fundamental theological problem.

Notes

CHAPTER ONE

1. Samuel Sewall, *Phaenomena* (Boston, 1697), p. 59.

2. Richard Sibbes, *The Excellency of the Gospel above the Law* (London, 1639), pp. 198–200, 240 (cf. 297); Thomas Goodwin and Thomas Ball, "Epistle Dedicatory," in John Preston, *Life Eternal, or, a Treatise of the Divine Essence and Attributes* (London, 1631), sig. A7^{ro}, pp. 4–6; Preston, *The Cup of Blessing* (London, 1633), pp. 12–13; Richard Baxter, qtd. in Geoffrey Nuttall, *The Holy Spirit in Puritan Faith and Experience* (Oxford: Basil Blackwell, 1946), pp. 22, 46; Walter Craddock, qtd. in Nuttall, p. 144; John Goodwin, [*Pleroma to Pneumatikon*], *or, a Being Filled with the Spirit* (London, 1670), p. 341.

3. See, e.g., William Ames, *The Marrow of Sacred Divinity* (London, 1642), 1.1, 1.2, 1.8.17–22; cf. Robert Rollock, *A Treatise of God's Effectual Calling*, tr. Henry Holland (London, 1603), p. 182; William Perkins, "On Callings," in Edmund S. Morgan, ed., *Puritan Political Ideas, 1558–1794* (Indianapolis: Bobbs-Merrill, 1965), pp. 35–59.

4. Perkins, *A Golden Chain, or, The Description of Theology*, in *Works* (London, 1626), 1. 10; Ames, *Marrow*, 1.1.1, and *Conscience with the Power and Cases Thereof* (London, 1643); see also Ames, *Marrow*, 1.1.12, 2.1.1.

5. See William Haller, *The Rise of Puritanism* (1938; rpt. New York: Harper and Row, 1957), pp. 19–23 and ch. 4.

6. See Edmund S. Morgan, *The Puritan Dilemma: The Story of John Winthrop* (Boston: Little, Brown, 1958), ch. 1.

7. Westminster Larger Catechism, qq. 1, 2.

8. Thomas Shepard, *Theses Sabbaticae, or, The Doctrine of the Sabbath*, in John Albro, ed., *The Works of Thomas Shepard* (1851–53; rpt., New York: AMS Press, 1967), 3, pt. 1, th. 3, 4.

9. "Nature" in Puritan discourse has two senses. Strictly, it refers to what is essential to a thing as it was created. Thus it belongs to the nature of fire to rise, of a stone to sink, of a plant to grow, of an animal to move about, and

of a human being to think and to will. Loosely, and most frequently, the word refers to mankind's corrupt nature after the fall of Adam, by which human beings are rendered incapable of serving perfectly anything but sin. It is in the latter sense that the word appears in the recurrent opposition between "nature" and "grace"; and it is to "nature" as "corrupt nature" that "flesh," in the opposition "flesh" and "spirit," is to be referred. Regenerating grace is not hostile to human nature as such, but to corrupt human nature. See Perkins, *An Exposition upon the first five Chapters of . . . Galatians,* in *Works* (London, 1617), 2. 213; Ames, *Marrow,* 1.8.61–73; 1.12.35–36, 44; 1.14.21–30; Thomas Hooker, *The Unbeliever's Preparing for Christ* (London, 1638), pp. 87, 94–95; John T. McNeill, ed., *Calvin: Institutes of the Christian Religion,* tr. Ford L. Battles (Philadelphia: Westminster Press, 1960), 3.3.12.

10. James K. Hosmer, ed., *Winthrop's Journal: "History of New England,"* *1630–1649* (New York: Charles Scribner's Sons, 1908), 1. 195–96. "Justification" here refers to the judicial transaction in which the believer is counted righteous in God's eyes and is absolved *in foro divino* from the guilt of sin, although he remains in himself a sinner. "Sanctification" refers primarily to the moral transformation in which, by infusion of graces by the Holy Spirit, the individual himself is rendered actually holy. This double transformation of the regenerate corresponds to the double plight of fallen man, who is alienated from a righteous God by the guilt of sin and is himself depraved, i.e., morally incapable of rendering obedience to God freely. Derivatively, "sanctification" refers to the holy acts put forth by the regenerate. See Ames, *Marrow,* 1.27, 1.29.

11. See, e.g., Winthrop, *Journal,* 1. 211.

12. Weld's edition was entitled *A Short Story of the Rise, reign and ruine of the Antinomians, Familists & Libertines that infected the Churches of New England* (London, 1644); see David D. Hall, ed., *The Antinomian Controversy, 1636–1638: A Documentary History* (Middletown: Wesleyan University Press, 1968), pp. 199–200.

13. Weld, in Winthrop, *Short Story,* in Hall, *Antinomian Controversy,* pp. 203–4. In quotations from sixteenth- and seventeenth-century sources, spelling and punctuation have in general been modernized.

14. Their own formulations often seemed excessively facile; see below, Chapter 8.

15. Thomas Shepard, *The Parable of the Ten Virgins Opened and Applied* (London, 1659), in *Works,* 2. 59, 191–92, 203–6 (cf. 401–2), and *The Sound Believer: A Treatise of Evangelical Conversion* (London, 1645), in *Works,* 1. 213.

16. Perry Miller, "The Marrow of Puritan Divinity," *Publications of the Colonial Society of Massachusetts,* 32 (1937), 254, 278, 284–86, 289 (cf. 273, 285), " 'Preparation for Salvation' in Seventeenth-Century New England," *Journal of the History of Ideas,* 4 (June 1943), 259–62, 266–76, 278–79, and *The New England Mind,* 2: *From Colony to Province* (1953; rpt. Boston: Beacon Press, 1961), ch. 4.

17. See, e.g., Miller, "Marrow," pp. 248–56, 263, 271, 280, 283–84, and " 'Preparation,' " pp. 253–62, 278–79; cf. Miller, *The New England Mind,* 1:

The Seventeenth Century (1954; rpt. Boston: Beacon Press, 1961), p. 200. Edmund Morgan, for example, considered Cotton a self-conscious defender of the Protestant principles of human helplessness and divine omnipotence in the face of Arminian-like tendencies among the other elders; Cotton precipitated the controversy when he "warned his listeners away from the specious comfort of preparation and re-emphasized the covenant of grace as something in which God acted alone and unassisted" (*Puritan Dilemma*, pp. 134–40). Larzer Ziff defined the controversy in terms of "legalism" and a "conditional" understanding of the covenant of grace, in contrast to absolute election and human passivity in regeneration; the issue between Cotton and his colleagues was the "extent to which ... a man contributed to his salvation" (*The Career of John Cotton: Puritanism and the American Experience* [Princeton: Princeton University Press, 1962], ch. 4). More recently, Norman Pettit developed certain of Miller's notions about preparation, with modifications, into a general interpretation of seventeenth-century New England controversy; like Miller, he identified "preparation" as the fundamental issue in 1636–38 (*The Heart Prepared: Grace and Conversion in Puritan Spiritual Life* [New Haven: Yale University Press, 1966], esp. ch. 5). Any criticism aside, one must readily acknowledge the substantial debt owed Professor Miller by anyone concerned today with the study of American Puritanism: see Edmund S. Morgan's appreciation in "Perry Miller and the Historians," *Harvard Review*, 2 (1964), 52–59.

18. The chief documentary sources for the controversy are here taken as the exchanges between Cotton and his colleagues, published in Hall, *Antinomian Controversy;* Anne Hutchinson's testimony in the General Court and the Boston church, in ibid.; Cotton's sermons, published in *The New Covenant, or a Treatise unfolding the order and manner of the giving and receiving of the Covenant of Grace* (London, 1654); Peter Bulkeley's sermons in *The Gospel Covenant, or the Covenant of Grace Opened* (London, 1646); Thomas Shepard's sermons in *The Parable of the Ten Virgins;* and the "catalogue of ... erroneous opinions" in John Winthrop's *Short Story,* in Hall, *Antinomian Controversy.*

19. The question is partly one of confessional norms (see, e.g., Pettit, *Heart Prepared,* p. 218). For Puritans, as *Reformed* Protestants, the canons of the Synod of Dort (1619) and the Second Helvetic Confession (1566) were, strictly speaking, more appropriate *dogmatic* standards than the dicta of the Reformers, or of any other individual theologian, however eminent. Both formularies are emphatic that faith comes to the elect wholly as a gift of grace, but there is nothing in either to require that faith must therefore come totally in despite of human powers and faculties, or that conversion is necessarily experienced as a " 'violent subjection,' " instantaneous and unanticipated (ibid., p. 218; cf. Miller, "Marrow," pp. 263, 271). Both explicitly note that grace does not rob human beings of every action, and *Helvetica posterior* indicates that faith and the life of faith both admit of "increments." See John T. McNeill, *The History and Character of Calvinism* (London: Oxford University Press, 1954; rpt. 1973), pp. 88–89; *Confessio et expositio simplex orthodoxae fidei,* art. 9, 14–16, in Wilhelm Niesel, ed., *Bekenntnisschriften und Kirchenord-*

nungen der nach Gottes Wort reformierten Kirche (2d ed.; Zollikon-Zürich: Evangelischer Verlag, 1938); "Dordrechter Canones," *Tertium et quartum doctrinae caput*, § § 12, 16, 17, in E. F. K. Müller, ed., *Die Bekenntnisschriften der Reformierten Kirche* (Leipzig: A. Deichtert'sche Verlagsbuchhandlung, 1903); cf. Calvin, *Institutes*, 3.14.21.

20. See F. Lau, "Orthodoxie, altprotestantische," *Die Religion in Geschichte und Gegenwart* (3d ed.; Tübingen: J. C. B. Mohr, 1957–), 4. 1719–30; John W. Beardslee, ed., *Reformed Dogmatics* (New York: Oxford University Press, 1965), pp. 3–25; Isaac A. Dorner, *Geschichte der protestantischen Theologie* (München: J.G. Cotta, 1867); Otto Ritschl, *Dogmengeschichte des Protestantismus* (Göttingen: Vandenhoeck und Ruprecht, 1926), vol. 3, chs. 50–55.

21. See Samuel E. Morison, *Harvard College in the Seventeenth Century* (Cambridge, Mass.: Harvard University Press, 1936), chs. 7, 8, 12, 13; cf. Paul Althaus, *Die Prinzipien der deutschen reformierten Dogmatik im Zeitalter der aristotelischen Scholastik* (1914; rpt. Darmstadt: Wissenschaftliche Buchgesellschaft, 1967).

22. For literature pertaining to Reformed orthodox and technical Puritan divinity, see the Bibliographical Note, below.

23. See, e.g., Nuttall, *Holy Spirit;* Haller, *Rise of Puritanism,* chs. 1–4; James F. Maclear, " 'The Heart of New England Rent': The Mystical Element in Early Puritan History," *Mississippi Valley Historical Review,* 42 (1956), 621–52; see also William Haller, *Liberty and Reformation in the Puritan Revolution* (New York: Columbia University Press, 1955; rpt. 1963).

24. See, e.g., John Winthrop, "A Model of Christian Charity," in Morgan, *Puritan Political Ideas,* pp. 76–93.

25. See David Little, *Religion, Order, and Law: A Study in Pre-Revolutionary England* (New York: Harper and Row, 1969), ch. 4.

26. See Roland F. Bainton, *The Reformation of the Sixteenth Century* (Boston: Beacon Press, 1959), pp. 250–55; see also, e.g., the ambivalence experienced by Winthrop, Cotton, and Shepard on emigrating to New England: Morgan, *Puritan Dilemma,* chs. 3, 4; Shepard, "Autobiography," in Michael McGiffert, ed., *God's Plot: The Paradoxes of Puritan Piety* (Amherst: University of Massachusetts Press, 1972), pp. 53–57, 61–62; Ziff, *Career of Cotton,* pp. 65–70.

CHAPTER TWO

1. Edmund S. Morgan, *Visible Saints: The History of a Puritan Idea* (Ithaca: Cornell University Press, 1963; rpt. 1966), ch. 3; cf. Haller, *Liberty and Reformation,* pp. 106–7.

2. Haller, *Rise of Puritanism,* ch. 5; Nuttall, *Holy Spirit,* chs. 1, 3.

3. Edmund Morgan, *Roger Williams: The Church and the State* (New York: Harcourt, Brace & World, 1967), p. 7; see esp. William Haller, *The Elect Nation: The Meaning and Relevance of Foxe's Book of Martyrs* (New York: Harper and Row, 1963), pp. 65, 80, 130–32, 140–42, 222–23, 245–49.

4. See Morgan, *Roger Williams,* pp. 6–10; Joy Bourne Gilsdorf, "The Puritan Apocalypse: New England Eschatology in the Seventeenth Century" (Ph.D. diss., Yale Univ., 1964); James F. Maclear, "New England and the Fifth Monarchy: The Quest for the Millennium in Early American Puritanism," *William and Mary Quarterly,* 32 (April 1975), 223–60.

5. Winthrop (1587–1649) was the son of a Puritan clothmerchant turned country gentleman. He briefly attended Trinity College, Cambridge, was for a time a member of Gray's Inn, and in 1626 became an attorney of the Court of Wards and Liveries. In October 1629 he was chosen governor of the reorganized Massachusetts Bay Company, superintending the Company's expedition in March of 1630. Winthrop devoted his life in New England to judicious exercise of the "particular calling" of civil magistrate. By extending to the freemen the privileges of the Company's charter, he achieved in Massachusetts one of the most liberal franchises then known. Cotton (1584–1652) was educated at Trinity and Emmanuel Colleges, Cambridge, and was converted by a sermon of Richard Sibbes, then lecturer at Trinity Church. His own first sermon in the "plain style" was instrumental in John Preston's conversion. In 1632, faced with arraignment before the Court of High Commission, Cotton went into hiding and then resigned his parish, sailing in June 1633 for New England, in company with Thomas Hooker and Samuel Stone. On Winthrop's role in keeping the colony to its task and preventing fragmentation, see Morgan, *Puritan Dilemma.* On Cotton's role in the formation of New England church polity, see Morgan, *Visible Saints,* pp. 80–106, and Larzer Ziff, ed., *John Cotton on the Churches of New England* (Cambridge: Harvard University Press, 1968), pp. 1–36; cf. John Norton, *Memoir of John Cotton,* ed. Enoch Pond (New York: Saxton and Miles, 1842), p. 65.

Biographical notices in this and subsequent chapters are based chiefly on articles in the *Dictionary of National Biography,* the *Dictionary of American Biography,* Cotton Mather's *Magnalia Christi Americana,* A. W. M'Clure's *Lives of the Chief Fathers of New-England* (1870), and Sprague's *Annals of the American Pulpit* (1857).

6. Winthrop, "A Model of Christian Charity," pp. 75–93.

7. Wheelwright (1592–1679) was born in Lincolnshire of a line of landholders in the fen district. He was educated at Cambridge and, in 1623, succeeded his father as vicar at Spilsby, Lincolnshire, remaining until 1631. He arrived in New England in May 1636 and was received in June, with his wife, into the Boston church. In 1641 he was formally reconciled with the Massachusetts authorities.

8. "Examination of Mrs. Anne Hutchinson at the Court in Newtown," in Hall, *Antinomian Controversy,* pp. 336–39.

9. Hall, *Antinomian Controversy,* p. 6; "Examination of Mrs. Hutchinson," in ibid., pp. 317, 322–23.

10. Hall, *Antinomian Controversy,* pp. 4, 14–16.

11. Winthrop, *Journal,* 1. 195–97, 201.

12. Hall, *Antinomian Controversy,* p. 7; "Propositions of the Church at

Boston ... at a conference with some brethren of Newtown," *Winthrop Papers* (Boston: Massachusetts Historical Society, 1929–), 3. 324–26.

13. Winthrop, *Journal*, 1. 197. Wilson (ca. 1591–1667), educated at King's College, Cambridge, was converted to the Puritan party by William Ames, resigning his fellowship thereupon. From 1618 to 1630 he was lecturer at Sudbury, Suffolk, there making the acquaintance of Winthrop, with whom he sailed to New England.

14. Winthrop, *Journal*, 1. 201–4. Vane (1613–62) was converted to Puritanism at the age of fifteen, refusing the oath of allegiance and supremacy on matriculation at Oxford. For two years, it is said, he refused the sacrament, being unable to find any who would administer it to him standing. He was active in civil and ecclesiastical politics during the Civil War; his later religious views were a puzzle to his contemporaries. Peter(s) (1598–1660), educated at Cambridge, was converted in 1620, partly by Thomas Hooker. Silenced in 1627, he eventually fled to Holland, where he became minister of the English church at Rotterdam. Dislodged by the intrigues of Archbishop Laud, he removed to New England in the fall of 1635, becoming minister at Salem.

15. Winthrop, *Journal*, 1. 204–5.

16. Ibid., 1. 204, 206; cf. "Propositions of the Church at Boston," *Winthrop Papers*, 3. 324–26.

17. Winthrop, *Journal*, 1. 208, 211; Hall, *Antinomian Controversy*, p. 7; Wheelwright, "A Fast-Day Sermon," in C. H. Bell, ed., *John Wheelwright: His Writings, Prince Society Publications*, 11 (Boston, 1876; rpt. New York: Burt Franklin [n.d.]), 153–79.

18. "Proceedings of the General Court ... [Nov. 2, 1637]," in Winthrop, *Short Story*, pp. 252–54; cf. error no. 31, in ibid., p. 227; Winthrop, *Journal*, 1. 209, 212–13, 218.

19. Winthrop, *Journal*, 1. 211.

20. Ibid., 1. 215–16, 219.

21. Hall, *Antinomian Controversy*, pp. 24–25; Winthrop, *Journal*, 1. 206–7 (cf. 203); see also John Cotton, *Sixteen Questions of Serious and Necessary Consequence*, "The Elders Reply," "Mr. Cotton's Rejoynder," and *A Conference ... Held at Boston*, all in Hall, *Antinomian Controversy*.

22. Cotton Mather, *Magnalia Christi Americana, or The Ecclesiastical History of New England* (Hartford, Conn.: Silas Andrus, 1820), 1. 348; Edward Johnson, *The Wonder-working Providence of Sion's Saviour in New England*, ed. William F. Poole (Andover, Mass.: Warren F. Draper, 1867), pp. 102–3. Shepard (1604–49), educated at Emmanuel College, was converted by Preston in 1624. From 1627 until silenced in 1630, he was lecturer at Earles-Colne, Essex. He became pastor at Newtown in the winter of 1636. His sermon series, based on the parable of the ten virgins in Mt. 25:1–13, was continued in a weekly lecture until May 1640, and his notes were published posthumously as *The Parable of the Ten Virgins Opened and Applied* (London, 1659). In 1645 he had published in London *The Sound Believer: A Treatise of Evangelical Conversion*, embodying the fruits of his pastoral experience, as a token for friends

left behind in England. The book, which became part of the Puritan *corpus* of practical divinity, was a careful analysis of conversion, following the pattern of Shepard's own, and of the estate of the regenerate. In it he addressed issues raised by antinomians on both sides of the Atlantic.

23. Bulkeley (1583–1659) attended St. John's College, Cambridge, succeeding in 1620 to the rectory of his father, also a nonconformist, at Odell, Bedfordshire, and to his father's estate, which was considerable. Silenced by Archbishop Laud in 1635, he sold out and removed to Massachusetts. His sermon series, on Zech. 9:11, was consciously in the tradition of Preston's *New Covenant* (1629). Prompted by the antinomian affair, it was repeated in weekly lecture and eventually published in London, in the context of similar controversy, as *The Gospel Covenant, or the Covenant of Grace Opened* (London, 1646), with a preface by Shepard (see sig. A4^{ro}–A5^{vo}).

24. Winthrop, *Journal*, 1. 232–35; "Catalogue of . . . erroneous opinions . . . ," in Winthrop, *Short Story*, pp. 219–47; "Examination of Mrs. Anne Hutchinson" and "A Report of the Trial of Mrs. Anne Hutchinson before the Church in Boston," in Hall, *Antinomian Controversy*, pp. 311–48, 350–88; Johnson, *Wonder-working Providence*, p. 119. Hooker (1586–1647) attended Emmanuel College, eventually becoming lecturer at Chelmsford, Essex (1626–29). Faced with arraignment before High Commission, he fled to Holland, where for a time he assisted John Forbes at Delft and subsequently William Ames at Rotterdam. In 1633 he returned to England, departing thence in July with a company of settlers from whom he gathered a church at Newtown in October. Davenport (1597–1670), since 1624 vicar at St. Stephen's, Coleman Street, London, was suspended in 1629 for his role in Puritan politics. In August 1633 he fled to Holland, returning in 1636 to lead a company of Londoners to New England, where he arrived in June 1637.

25. John Gorham Palfrey, *History of New England During the Stuart Dynasty*, vol. 1 (Boston: Little, Brown, 1859), ch. 12; Winthrop, *Journal*, 1. 239–41; "Proceedings of the General Court," in *Short Story*, pp. 248–62.

26. "Examination of Mrs. Hutchinson," pp. 311–48.

27. "Report of the Trial," pp. 349–88; Winthrop, *Journal*, 1. 260–61, 263–65.

28. Thomas Shepard, *Parable* and "To the Reader," in *Works*, 2. 8; Peter Bulkeley, *The Gospel Covenant*, sig. A4^{ro}–A5^{ro}.

CHAPTER THREE

1. Hall, *Antinomian Controversy*, pp. 4, 10–20; cf. Hall, *The Faithful Shepherd: A History of the New England Ministry in the Seventeenth Century* (Chapel Hill: University of North Carolina Press, 1972), pp. 159, 163–64.

2. See Chapters 5 and 7, below.

3. Johnson, *Wonder-working Providence*, pp. 95–96, an allusion linking theological learning with Ninevah, Babylon, and the Whore thereof (an ob-

servation for which I am indebted to Professor Ernest B. Lowrie); "Examination of Mrs. Hutchinson," pp. 333–37, 340–42, 347–48; Winthrop, *Journal*, 1. 201, 204–9, 212–13, 233.

4. See Winthrop, *Journal*, 1. 233–34; cf. Cotton, *The Way of Congregational Churches Cleared* (London, 1648), pp. 40–47. The nature of his compliance is suggested in an exchange with the other elders over justification, in which an "orthodox" interpretation is given of an essentially ambiguous statement of Cotton's ("Notes respecting justification, etc.," Mather Papers, Vol. 1, No. 9, Boston Public Library; cf. Cotton Papers, Pt. 2, No. 15, Boston Public Library); "Report of the Trial," p. 368; but cf. "Elders Reply," p. 62.

5. These were the crucial ones regarding the relationship of faith and justification, and sanctification as evidence of justification; Cotton, *Way Cleared*, pp. 43–46, 49–50; cf. Shepard, "Autobiography," p. 74, and Hall, *Antinomian Controversy*, pp. 340–42 (cf. 381).

6. Robert Baillie, *A Dissuasive from the Errors of the Time* (London, 1645), pp. 55–57. Cotton entered the lists with *The Keyes of the Kingdom of Heaven* (London, 1644); Baillie, one of the Scots Presbyterian Commissioners at Westminster, replied with *A Dissuasive*, which Cotton answered in *The Way Cleared*. Hooker's *Survey of the Summe of Church Discipline* was sent to England by the ministerial assembly of July 1645, in answer to *The Due Right of Presbyteries* (London, 1644), by Samuel Rutherford (another Scots Commissioner). About the same time, John Norton was deputed to compose a statement in behalf of Independency: *Responsio ad totam questionem syllogem a ... Guilelmo Apollonio* (London, 1648). In 1652 the General Court commissioned Norton to reply to a tract by William Pynchon on the Atonement. Norton (1606–63), educated at Cambridge, arrived in New England in October 1635, becoming teacher at Ipswich in 1638. He was the foremost systematic theologian among the first generation in New England, and he played a major role in the formulation of the "Cambridge Platform" of 1648.

7. Winthrop, *Journal*, 1. 259; Norton, *Memoir of Cotton*, pp. 68–69; Johnson, *Wonder-working Providence*, pp. 93–94; Mather, *Magnalia*, 1. 243–45; Baillie, *Dissuasive*, pp. 57–58, 68; Cotton, *Way Cleared*, pp. 39–40, 47–48, 52–53.

8. See, e.g., Emery Battis, *Saints and Sectaries: Anne Hutchinson and the Antinomian Controversy in the Massachusetts Bay Colony* (Chapel Hill: University of North Carolina Press, 1962), pp. 38–39; Ziff, *Career of Cotton*, ch. 4; Miller, *From Colony to Province*, p. 59; " 'Preparation for Salvation,' " pp. 268–71.

9. See Chapter 9, n. 17; cf. Hall, *Antinomian Controversy*, p. 18. Wheelwright also diverged from the Hutchinsonians, refusing an invitation to join them in Rhode Island as chaplain; his concern for free justification and the union between Spirit and believer stopped short of Hutchinson's extremes.

10. Winthrop, *Journal*, 1. 219; Cotton, *Way Cleared*, pp. 53–54; cf. Cotton, *New Covenant*, p. 58.

11. Cotton, *Way Cleared*, pp. 48–50.

12. Ibid., p. 47; *Winthrop Papers*, 3. 324–26.

13. Ziff, *Career of Cotton*, ch. 2; William Twisse, *A Treatise of Mr. Cot-*

ton's, ... *Concerning Predestination, with an Examination thereof* (London, 1646). Twisse (1578?–1646), trained at Oxford, was reckoned a Puritan in doctrine, though a moderate in church practice, on which ground he was elected prolocutor of the Westminster Assembly.

14. The sermon-collections attributed to Cotton's English period (see Everett H. Emerson, *John Cotton* [New York: Twayne Publishers, 1965], pp. 163–65, and Ziff, *Career of Cotton*, pp. 262–68) reveal continuities of thought and expression with his position in 1636–38, esp. regarding the Spirit's indwelling and witnessing, faith as the root of sanctification, and Christ as the source and reservoir of a Christian's graces. See, resp., Cotton, *A Practical Commentary ... upon the first Epistle General of John* (2d ed.; London, 1658), pp. 161–67, 279–83, 361–64, 370–72, *The Way of Life* (London, 1641), pp. 354–57, 359–61, and *Christ the Fountain of Life* (London, 1651), pp. 55–58. However, on the decisive issues of faith's activity in receiving Christ unto justification, the inherence of sanctification in the regenerate, the evidencing of justification by sanctification, and the conditionality of the covenant of grace, his position was essentially that of his New-English colleagues. See, resp., *Way of Life*, pp. 305–6, 311–13, 317, 334–35, and *Commentary on John*, pp. 344–45; *Way of Life*, pp. 350–51, *Christ the Fountain*, pp. 98–99, 105, and *Commentary on John*, pp. 204–5, 279–80; *Way of Life*, pp. 323–24 (but cf. 354–55), *Christ the Fountain*, Sermons 5, 8, 9, and *Commentary on John*, pp. 70–72, 206–7, 351–52; *Christ the Fountain*, Sermon 3, and *Commentary on John*, p. 152.

15. Cotton, "A Sermon Delivered at Salem," in Ziff, *Cotton on the Churches*, p. 44; cf. Cotton, *Sixteen Questions*, p. 46; Norton, *Memoir of Cotton*, pp. 63, 77; Baillie, *Dissuasive*, pp. 55–57; see also Morgan, *Visible Saints*, ch. 3; Haller, *Liberty and Reformation*, pp. 15, 255–56, 352–53.

16. Winthrop, *Journal*, 1. 179.

17. Twisse, *Treatise of Mr. Cotton's*, pp. 265, 269, cf. 271.

18. See, e.g., "Shepard-Cotton Letters" and *Sixteen Questions*, pp. 25, 46; Samuel Stone to John Cotton [March 27, 1638], Cotton Papers, Pt. 2, No. 12; "Elders Reply," p. 62.

19. Winthrop, *Journal*, 1. 233–34. The fifth was: "That Christ and his benefits may be offered and exhibited to a man under a covenant of works, but not in or by a covenant of works."

20. Shepard, *Parable*, p. 317; Bulkeley, *Gospel Covenant*, pp. 265, 289–90; "Peter Bulkeley and John Cotton on Union with Christ," in Hall, *Antinomian Controversy*, pp. 36, 39; Ames, *Marrow* (1642), 1.26; Edward Leigh, *A System or Body of Divinity* (London, 1654), pp. 490–91; John Ball, *A Treatise of Faith* (London, 1631), pp. 6, 11.

21. See Winthrop, *Journal*, 1. 233–34; Cotton, *New Covenant*, pp. 55–56 (cf. 26–28); "Cotton's Rejoynder," p. 94; "Bulkeley and Cotton on Union," pp. 37–38, 40.

22. "Bulkeley and Cotton on Union," pp. 36–38, 40; Cotton drew the same distinction respecting faith considered as an instrumental cause of union (*Way Cleared*, p. 42).

23. "Bulkeley and Cotton on Union," p. 38.

24. Frederick Copleston, *A History of Philosophy* (Garden City, N.Y.: Doubleday and Co., 1962), 2. 2. 51, 233–34.

25. "Bulkeley and Cotton on Union," pp. 38–39.

26. Ibid., pp. 39–41; Cotton, *New Covenant,* p. 15; cf. *Winthrop Papers,* 3. 324–26, prop. 1 of the 5 points, and props. 1 and 3 of the 15 points.

27. "Cotton's Rejoynder," pp. 85, 91–92, 93–95, 111; "Bulkeley and Cotton on Union," pp. 37, 40–41; Cotton, *New Covenant,* pp. 27–28, 93; cf. Cotton, *Way Cleared,* p. 49.

28. See, e.g., Ames, *Marrow,* 1.29; Wollebius, *Compendium,* 1.31.

29. Cotton, *New Covenant,* pp. 31–32; "Cotton's Rejoynder," pp. 101–2.

30. Cotton, *New Covenant,* pp. 34–35, cf. Leigh, *System of Divinity,* pp. 512, 516–17; Wollebius, *Compendium,* 1.31, sect. 13.

31. Cotton, *New Covenant,* pp. 34–35, 146–48, 158–59; "Cotton's Rejoynder," pp. 102–5, 143–44; Cotton, *Sixteen Questions,* p. 47; cf. *Winthrop Papers,* 3. 324–26, prop. 5 of the 15 points.

32. Cotton, *New Covenant,* pp. 101–2, 144–45, 147; cf. Cotton, *Sixteen Questions,* p. 51. Cotton's position here contrasts sharply with that of the "doctrinal conclusion" printed as the third item in John Cotton, *A Treatise of Faith* (Boston, 1713), pp. 9 –19, where graces of sanctification are represented as created graces, habits inherent in the regenerate, by which human faculties "are quickened and made alive unto God." The style and content of these pages is not that of Cotton in 1636–37; the point of view is that of the other ministers. It is possible, therefore, that the "doctrinal conclusion" is a brief presented by Cotton's colleagues, in debate on the third of the points considered at the Newtown synod.

33. "Report of the Trial," pp. 353, 374–75 (cf. 378); Winthrop, *Short Story,* error no. 23, "unsavory speech" no. 5 (cf. errors no. 15, 7).

34. Cotton, *Way Cleared,* p. 43; Bulkeley, *Gospel Covenant,* pp. 288–91; Shepard, *Certain Select Cases Resolved,* in *Works,* 1. 317–19.

35. "Cotton's Rejoynder," pp. 94, 105, 139–40; Cotton, *Way Cleared,* pp. 43–44, and *New Covenant,* pp. 28, 56.

36. Cotton, *New Covenant,* pp. 87–100.

37. "Cotton's Rejoynder," pp. 86, 92, 98–99, 137; Cotton, *A Conference . . . Held at Boston,* p. 186; "Elders Reply," ad q. 13 (cf. "Cotton's Rejoynder," p. 97); cf. Cotton, "Sermon at Salem," p. 53, and *New Covenant,* pp. 86, 97.

38. Cotton, *New Covenant,* pp. 43–44, 93, 103; "Cotton's Rejoynder," p. 91 (cf. 93). Shepard, taking Cotton's metaphor, replied to the remark quoted: No, but "if we should ask a woman married to [a] . . . husband, how she knows such a one is her husband, she would manifest it by those peculiar acts or works, or manifestations of a husband to her" (*Parable,* p. 214).

39. "Cotton's Rejoynder," pp. 140, 146; Cotton, *New Covenant,* pp. 59–60 (cf. 78).

40. Cotton, *New Covenant,* pp. 60–69, 70–72, 80–84. At one point in the debate on the *Sixteen Questions* (q. 9), discussion turned to the nature of the "image of God" present in the saints. The exchange contains a clue to the significance of the error charged against Hutchinson that "an hypocrite may

have the righteousness of Adam and perish" ("Report of the Trial," pp. 352, 374–75), and also a clue to the meaning of the opinion noted by Winthrop that a person might have "spiritual and continual communion with Jesus Christ" in the covenant of works "and yet be damned" (*Journal*, 1. 206). The question was whether "Christian sanctification" consists in the "immediate acting of the Spirit" or in infused habits that are "contrary to corrupt nature"—in effect, in "the image of God in Adam renewed in us." Cotton construed "image of God" as "sanctification" and maintained that "Christian sanctification" includes faith in Christ and repentance from sin, as Adam's sanctification did not, and springs from "the indwelling power of Christ by his spirit . . . to act and keep holiness in us," as Adam's did not. Technically, in Reformed orthodox divinity, the image of God in Adam consisted in the power to perceive God's will clearly and to obey it willingly, out of love for God and in virtue of a gracious power (see, for example, Shepard, *Theses Sabbaticae*, in *Works*, 3. 97; Ames, *Marrow*, 1.8.65–78; Wollebius, *Compendium*, 1.5.2; Polanus, *Syntagma*, 5. 34, qtd. in Heinrich Heppe, *Dogmatik der evangelisch-reformierten Kirche, dargestellt und aus den Quellen belegt*, ed. Ernst Bizer (2d ed.; Neukirchen: Neukirchener Verlag, 1958), pp. 175, 190. Cotton altered the terms of the question slightly and, as he interpreted it, a hypocrite might well attain to the righteousness of Adam before the fall and yet fail of that indwelling and immediate acting of Christ's power which is distinctively "Christian sanctification" (*Sixteen Questions*, p. 51; "Cotton's Rejoynder," pp. 99–104). Elsewhere, Cotton claimed that hypocrites may have true sanctification, including its root of faith, and yet fall away; that hypocrites are capable of universal obedience until death; and also that Adam's graces, though perfect, were transitory (see *New Covenant*, pp. 60–69, 70–72, 80–84, and n. 32; cf. also Twisse, *Treatise of Mr. Cotton's* pp. 269–70). All these points suggested a larger difference between the image of God in Adam before the fall and the image in the regenerate, and between the righteousness of Adam before the fall and the righteousness of saints, than was usual in Reformed divinity as received in New England. Though the image of God in Christ was regarded as the pattern of the new image in the regenerate, this view was not taken as implying an essential difference between it and the image of God in Adam.

41. "Elders Reply," p. 71; cf. "Cotton's Rejoynder," p. 148; cf. Winthrop, *Short Story*, confut. of error no. 69.

42. "Cotton's Rejoynder," p. 146.

43. Ibid., pp. 117, 119, 146–47. Captain John Underhill's account of his attainment of assurance echoes Cotton's view of the matter; see Winthrop, *Journal*, 1. 275–76. The points on evidencing that were submitted by the Boston church to the Newtown church are in substance the same as, and close in language to, Cotton's own deliverances on the subject; see above, n. 12.

44. "Cotton's Rejoynder," pp. 139–40.

45. Cotton, *New Covenant*, pp. 75–77; "Cotton's Rejoynder," pp. 113–14, cf. 87, 104. This usage of "evident" and "evident sign" was frequent with Cotton. In *Christ the Fountain* (e.g., pp. 61, 93) "evident sign" refers to an attitude or disposition of the individual soul, specified in scripture, which the

heart may know and from which a person may conclude that he has Christ—in effect, by a practical syllogism. By 1636, however, such "signs" were no longer "evident" for Cotton. "Ordinarily," in the sentence quoted, means in the course of the normal, ordained procedure by which God accomplishes regeneration, in contrast to "extraordinarily" or "miraculously."

46. "Cotton's Rejoynder," pp. 92, 94, 107; Cotton, *New Covenant,* pp. 28, 56.

47. Cf. "Cotton's Rejoynder," pp. 140–41; Winthrop, *Journal,* 1. 211; "Proceedings of the General Court . . . at Newtown," in Winthrop, *Short Story,* p. 252.

48. Cotton, *Sixteen Questions,* pp. 52–55.

49. Ibid., pp. 52–55.

50. "Elders Reply," p. 71.

51. "Cotton's Rejoynder," pp. 116–17 (cf. 95).

52. Ibid., p. 116.

53. Ibid., pp. 95, 98–99, 127 (cf. 132); cf. Winthrop, *Short Story,* error no. 67. In a sermon in March 1637 Cotton put his position positively, to the effect "that both our *justification, and the faith of our* justification must be built upon the *sight of Christ* as *our justification.*" Bulkeley professed himself puzzled at this statement, since it said nothing about how personal assurance may be obtained: "There must be some difference betwixt Christ's righteousness, and that which doth manifest it unto me as mine. But these two you seem to confound" (Bulkeley to Cotton, 1637, Cotton Papers, Pt. 2, No. 7).

54. Cotton, *Sixteen Questions,* p. 57; "Elders Reply," p. 75; "Cotton's Rejoynder," pp. 133–34, 138–42.

55. "Cotton's Rejoynder," pp. 107 (cf. 140, 142). Cf. Hutchinson's alleged assertion about assurance (above, n. 33). Cotton qualified himself: "I do not say in his election but in his effectual calling" (ibid., p. 142). This distinction was technically significant, but the position was essentially the same: assurance begins only with the Spirit's testimony that one's sins are forgiven.

56. "Cotton's Rejoynder," p. 80 (cf. 141); the "six witnesses" are the Father, Son, and Spirit, in heaven; and the water (of sanctification), the Spirit, and the blood (of Christ's atonement) on earth. Norman Pettit, in his treatment of the Antinomian Controversy in *The Heart Prepared,* suggested that for Cotton the "ultimate test of assurance" was not "interior motions of the Spirit stirring affections," but legal terrors under the ministry of the law (pp. 134–35). It seems likely, however, on the basis of the passages cited above, that in the matter of assurance, the ultimate test for Cotton was "spiritual sight" of a blessed estate, apart from any creaturely works, including works of the law, which "sight" he made the substance of "justifying faith."

57. "Cotton's Rejoynder," pp. 141–42, 149 (cf. 85, 126).

CHAPTER FOUR

1. Nathaniel Ward, qtd. in John Albro, "Life of Shepard," in *Works,* 1.

clxxxix; Shepard, "Autobiography," p. 43; "Journal," in McGiffert, *God's Plot,* pp. 163–64, 214–15.

2. Bulkeley, *Gospel Covenant,* p. 25.

3. Shepard, "To the Reader," in Bulkeley, *Gospel Covenant,* sig. A7^{vo}.

4. Cf. *Westminster Confession,* 3; Ames, *Marrow* (1642), 1.18.4; 1.25.4, 16, 23.

5. Johnson, *Wonder-working Providence,* pp. 102–3; Twisse, *Treatise of Mr. Cotton's,* pp. 264–65.

6. See Norton, *Orthodox Evangelist* (London, 1654), pp. 89, 137–39; Shepard, *Theses Sabbaticae,* 1.24–25, 99.

7. Sibbes, *The Excellency of the Gospel above the Law,* in Alexander B. Grosart, ed., *The Complete Works of Richard Sibbes* (Edinburgh: J. Nichol, 1862–), 4. 248. Sibbes (1577–1635) was trained at St. John's College, Cambridge (B.A. 1599) and was for a time (1610–15) lecturer at Holy Trinity Church. As preacher at Gray's Inn, whither he was called in 1617, and as master of St. Catherine's Hall, Cambridge (from 1626), he helped form a generation of influential Puritans, lay and clerical.

8. See Thomas Hooker, *The Unbeliever's Preparing,* pp. 94–95, 127–28, 137–39; (2d ser.) 4–5, 65; cf. Sibbes, *Excellency of the Gospel,* pp. 246–48; Shepard, *Parable,* pp. 51–52.

9. See Bulkeley, *Gospel Covenant,* p. 119; Shepard, *Theses Sabbaticae,* pp. 109–10, 127–28, and *Believer,* pp. 226–27, 231–33; Perkins, *Golden Chain,* in *Works* (1626), 1. 70–71; Thomas Hooker, *The Application of Redemption* (London, 1657), p. 309, and *The Soul's Exaltation* (London, 1638), pp. 26–29.

10. Shepard, *Parable,* 1.10.5, 1.21.2, and pp. 229–31, 505–7, *Believer,* pp. 127, 204–6, and *Theses Sabbaticae,* 1.83; Bulkeley, *Gospel Covenant,* pp. 302–10; Hooker, *Unbeliever's Preparing,* pp. 32–34, 56–58, 157, and *The Soul's Vocation or Effectual Calling to Christ* (London, 1638), pp. 327–29. Cf. Shepard's description of his own conversion in *Cases Resolved,* pp. 326–27.

11. Norton, *Orthodox Evangelist,* p. 271.

12. Cf. Shepard, *Parable,* 2.15.6, and pp. 109–11, *Believer,* p. 226, and *Theses Sabbaticae,* pp. 127–28.

13. Shepard, *Parable,* pp. 317–18, and *Theses Sabbaticae,* p. 128; Bulkeley, *Gospel Covenant,* pp. 289–90, 295–96, 321; Hooker, *Unbeliever's Preparing,* pp. 20, 168–69; Norton, *Orthodox Evangelist,* p. 326.

14. Shepard, *Parable,* p. 318 (cf. 424–25, 503); Bulkeley, *Gospel Covenant,* p. 298; Hooker, *Soul's Exaltation,* p. 36; Shepard to Winthrop, ca. Dec. 15, 1636, *Winthrop Papers,* 3. 330.

15. See, e.g., Bulkeley, *Gospel Covenant,* p. 298–300; Norton, *Orthodox Evangelist,* pp. 105–11; cf. John Preston, *The Breastplate of Faith and Love* (London, 1630), Pt. 1, p. 140, and *The New Covenant, or The Saint's Portion* (5th ed.; London, 1630), pp. 389–90; Cotton, *Way Cleared,* pp. 41–42. Norman Pettit's reading of this difference between Cotton and his colleagues seems somewhat to miss the point (*Heart Prepared,* pp. 145–47 [cf. 118–20]). The issue in question appears to have been, not whether men are capable of a "spiritual act" before "effectual conversion," but whether, *in* effectual calling,

faith unites to Christ as a gracious act receiving and resting on Christ, or as a gracious habit only, disposing the passive soul passively to receive Christ "in order of nature" (on the force of this phrase, see "The Order of Redemption" in Chapter 7 below). Cotton held the latter position (see *Way Cleared,* p. 41). The view Cotton attributes (ibid.) to certain "Schoolmen"—that the act of faith precedes the giving of the habit—is not that of Bulkeley or Shepard. They did maintain that the habit of faith is infused, in order of nature, before faith acts unto union, but they understood this infusion as part of effectual calling, not an unregenerate "preparation" for it. They distinguished, moreover, between the grace of faith and the grace of sanctification, which flows from union and which God does "increase" by degrees thereafter; and they would not have allowed—contrary to Pettit's suggestion—that graces of sanctification by "additional fertilization . . . bring about full union with Christ."

16. Bulkeley, *Gospel Covenant,* pp. 299, 301–2; cf. Norton, *Orthodox Evangelist,* p. 320.

17. Shepard, *Believer,* pp. 169–70, 238–40, and *Theses Sabbaticae,* pp. 110, 123; Bulkeley, *Gospel Covenant,* pp. 280–95; Shepard to Winthrop, *Winthrop Papers,* 3. 328.

18. Norton, *Orthodox Evangelist,* pp. 301–8 (cf. 319–22); Hooker, *Soul's Exaltation,* pp. 117–18; cf. Preston, *Breastplate,* Pt. 1, pp. 59–61. Preston (1587–1628) was educated at Cambridge and converted in 1611 by a sermon of John Cotton's. As dean and catechist of Queen's College, Cambridge, preacher at Lincoln's Inn and master of Emmanuel (both from 1622), and lecturer at Holy Trinity (1624), he, like Sibbes, trained and otherwise formed a generation of Puritans.

19. Norton, *Orthodox Evangelist,* pp. 321–23, 326; Bulkeley, *Gospel Covenant,* pp. 321–25; Shepard, *Believer,* pp. 166–67, 225–26. Cf. Winthrop, *Short Story,* "unsavory speech" no. 1: "To say that we are justified by faith is an unsafe speech, we may say we are justified by Christ."

20. Shepard, *Believer,* p. 226; cf. Bulkeley, *Gospel Covenant,* pp. 324–25.

21. Shepard, *Theses Sabbaticae,* pp. 110 (cf. 123, 127–28); cf. Norton, *Orthodox Evangelist,* p. 186.

22. Hooker, *Unbeliever's Preparing* (2d ser.), pp. 4–5; Shepard, *Believer,* pp. 256–57.

23. Norton, *Orthodox Evangelist,* p. 250; Shepard, *Believer,* p. 252, and *Parable,* pp. 268–71, 273–74.

24. Shepard, *Parable,* pp. 268–69, 277 (cf. 1.19.1–3), and *Theses Sabbaticae,* 1.94–95.

25. Shepard, *Parable,* pp. 271–73, 278, 282, 462–63.

26. Bulkeley, *Gospel Covenant,* pp. 288–91; Shepard, *Cases Resolved,* pp. 317–19.

27. Shepard, *Cases Resolved,* p. 320.

28. Bulkeley, *Gospel Covenant,* pp. 327, 335–36 (cf. 228); Shepard, *Cases Resolved,* pp. 320–21.

29. Shepard, *Cases Resolved,* pp. 320–21, *Believer,* p. 259, and *Parable,* p. 217; Bulkeley, *Gospel Covenant,* pp. 38–41, 291–93, 358–59.

30. See, e.g., Shepard to Winthrop, ca. Dec. 15, 1636, *Winthrop Papers*, 3. 329; Bulkeley to Cotton, 1637, Cotton Papers, Pt. 2, No. 7; Bulkeley, *Gospel Covenant*, pp. 167–68, 183–84, 226, 322–23; Shepard, *Believer*, p. 259, and *Parable*, p. 126.

31. Shepard, *Parable*, pp. 212–17, 222 (cf. 223).

32. Ibid., pp. 214–15; Bulkeley, *Gospel Covenant*, p. 232 (cf. 228).

33. Shepard, *Cases Resolved*, p. 320, and *Theses Sabbaticae*, pp. 132–33; cf. Norton, *Orthodox Evangelist*, p. 87.

34. Bulkeley, *Gospel Covenant*, pp. 234–35; Shepard, *Parable*, pp. 224, 464; cf. Shepard, *Theses Sabbaticae*, pp. 128–33; and *Believer*, p. 229.

35. Bulkeley, *Gospel Covenant*, pp. 232–34, 238–39; Bulkeley to Cotton, 1637, Cotton Papers, Pt. 2, No. 7.

36. Bulkeley, *Gospel Covenant*, pp. 226–27.

37. Ibid., pp. 235–40; cf. Ames, *Conscience*, 2.5.

38. Bulkeley, *Gospel Covenant*, pp. 153–54, 235–36 (cf. Shepard to Winthrop, ca. Dec. 15, 1636, *Winthrop Papers*, 3. 329); Sibbes, *The Soul's Conflict with Itself*, in *Works*, 1. 268–69; William Pemble, *Vindicia Gratiae: A Plea for Grace*, in *The Works of . . . Mr. William Pemble* (4th ed.; Oxford, 1659), pp. 137–39; Shepard, *Parable*, pp. 335–36; cf. Preston, *New Covenant*, pp. 345–48.

39. Bulkeley, *Gospel Covenant*, pp. 376–77; cf. Shepard, *Believer*, pp. 280–82.

40. Shepard, *Theses Sabbaticae*, p. 111, and *Parable*, pp. 303–4, 333–34.

41. Shepard, *Parable*, 1.5.2, and pp. 49, 203, 336–39; Bulkeley, *Gospel Covenant*, pp. 78, 154–55.

42. Shepard, *Parable*, p. 282.

43. Ibid., pp. 36–37, 100–101, 282–89; Bulkeley, *Gospel Covenant*, p. 78; Shepard, *Cases Resolved*, p. 329 (cf. Preston, *New Covenant*, p. 391).

44. Shepard, *Cases Resolved*, p. 329, and *Parable*, pp. 323–24.

45. Shepard, *Believer*, pp. 229–30, and *Parable*, pp. 78, 222; cf. Hooker, *The Soul's Ingrafting into Christ* (London, 1637), pp. 19–20.

46. Bulkeley, *Gospel Covenant*, p. 235 (cf. 292–93), echoing Perkins, *The Foundation of the Christian Religion*, in *Works* (London, 1612), 1. 6; cf. Hooker, *Application of Redemption*, p. 605.

47. See, e.g., Cotton, *New Covenant*, pp. 5–8, 17–18, 39–50. Describing God's covenant with Abraham as the original of the covenant of grace, he emphasized that there "is no express restipulation prerequired on Abraham's part" (p. 6).

CHAPTER FIVE

1. In Christian reflection the covenant-motif appears initially in the New Testament, beginning with St. Paul, where it serves to relate law to gospel and old Israel to new Church, usually in terms of God's covenant with Abraham; e.g., Mt. 26:28 = Mk. 14:24, 2 Cor. 3:6, 12–14, Gal. 4:24–27, Heb. 7:22, 8:7–9,

9:15–17, 13:20. In the later Middle Ages the concept of a *pactum* with the Church, founded in God's generosity and good pleasure, to provide for the orderly dispensing of grace appeared in the works of Duns Scotus and the nominalist theologians of the fourteenth and fifteenth centuries. In the Reformation era the concept of a divine covenant with the elect, on the model of the covenant with Abraham, appeared early, especially though not exclusively in German Switzerland and in the Rhineland. In this concept the biblical usage of the motif predominates, being joined and sometimes overshadowed in the orthodox period by a more speculative formulation reminiscent of the earlier nominalist one. See Heiko A. Obermann, *The Harvest of Medieval Theology* (1963; rev. ed., Grand Rapids: William B. Eerdmans, 1967), pp. 148, 167–74; Leonard J. Trinterud, "The Origins of Puritanism," *Church History*, 20 (1951), 35–57. For additional literature pertinent to Reformed federal theology consult the Bibliographical Note below.

2. Heinrich Bullinger, *De testamento seu foedere Dei unico et aeterno* (Zürich, 1535); Calvin, *Institutes*, 2.7.1, 6–8; 9.4; 10.1–2, 4; 11.1, 3–4, 8, 10.

3. See Althaus, *Prinzipien*, pp. 155–61; Ritschl, *Dogmengeschichte*, pp. 416–17; A. Lang, ed., *Der Heidelberger Katechismus und vier verwandte Katechismen* (1907; rpt. Darmstadt: Wissenschaftliche Buchgesellschaft, 1967), p. lxv.

4. Ursinus, "Catechesis: Summa Theologiae," art. 31, 33, 36 (cf. 10), in Quirinius Reuter, ed., *D. Zachariae Ursini . . . opera theologica* (Heidelberg, 1612), pp. 9–32. The notion of a covenant in creation was not clearly original with Ursinus. Wolfgang Musculus, theologian at Bern from 1549 until his death in 1563, distinguished (in *Loci Communes*, 1564) a temporal *foedus generale* in which God established the orders of the universe and an eternal *foedus speciale* with the elect for salvation (Gottlob Shrenk, *Gottesreich und Bund im älteren Protestantismus, vornehmlich bei Johannes Coccejus* [Gütersloh: C. Bertelmann, 1923], p. 50). Amandus Polanus (1561–1610; from 1596 Old Testament professor at Basel) appears to have given the covenant with Adam in integrity its characteristic designation as *foedus operum* (ibid., p. 65); see his *Syntagma Theologiae Christianae* (Geneva, 1617), Bk. 6, ch. 33.

5. Ursinus, "Catechesis," art. 12–15, 18.

6. Ibid., art. 10, 72–74, 132, 133, 135.

7. See Ursinus, *Explicationes Catecheseos Palatinae sive Corpus Theologiae*, in Reuter, *D. Zachariae Ursini*, qq. 18; 60, 61; 92; 12, 13; 15, 16, 17.

8. Franz Junius, *Theses Theologicae Leydensis* (1592), 25–26, in A. Kuyper, ed., *D. Francisci Junii Opuscula Theologica Selecta* (Amsterdam, 1882). Junius (1545–1602) was at Heidelberg during the years 1573–76 and 1584–92 and became theology professor at Leyden in 1592. Cf. Lucas Trelcatius Junior, *Scholastica et methodica locorum communium S. theologiae institutio* (Geneva, 1600), pp. 164–72; Franciscus Gomarus, "Oratio, De Foedere Dei," in *Francisci Gomari, Opera Theologiae Omnia*, (Amsterdam, 1664), sig. A2ʳᵒ–A3ʳᵒ.

9. A representative formulation appears in *Johannis-Alstedii Encyclopaedia: septem tomis distincta* (Herborn, 1630), Bk. 21, "Ethicae," ch. 1, 8; Bk. 25, "Theologia" 2, ch. 1, 2; "Theologia" 3, ch. 8–9, 12, 13, 16, 20–24. Alsted

systematically refers the dogmatic material respecting salvation to the two covenants, *foedus naturae* and *foedus gratiae,* which are essentially related in virtue of the unity of the divine law in both nature and gospel and which are referred back to the immutable will of God as lawgiver and governor; see Althaus, *Prinzipien,* pp. 128–37.

10. See Thomas Cartwright, *A Treatise of Christian Religion or, the Whole Body and Substance of Divinity* (2d ed.; London, 1616), chs. 12–14, 26, 27, and *A Methodical Short Catechism,* in John Dod and Robert Cleaver, *A Plain and Familiar Exposition of the Ten Commandments* (London, 1609), sigs. Aa8ᵛᵒ–Bb1ʳᵒ, Bb2ʳᵒ–Bb3ʳᵒ; Dudley Fenner, *Sacra Theologia sive Veritas quae est secundum pietatem* . . . (2d ed.; n.p., 1589), Bk. 4, ch. 1–3; Robert Rollock, *Quaestiones et responsiones aliquot de foedere Dei* (Edinburgh, 1596), sig. A3ʳᵒ–B3ᵛᵒ, B4ᵛᵒ–B6ʳᵒ, B8ᵛᵒ. Rollock (1555?–1599) was trained at St. Andrew's, becoming principal at the newly founded University of Edinburgh in 1583 and professor of divinity in 1587.

11. Perkins, *Golden Chain,* in *Works* (1626), 1, chs. 7, 9, 15, 17, 19, 20–29, 30, 31, 36; cf. Perkins, *An Exposition of the Symbol or Creed of the Apostles* (1595), in ibid., 1. 145, 152, 159, 164–65, and *An Exposition upon the first five chapters of . . . Galatians,* in *Works* (1617), 2. 205–7. Perkins (1558–1602), as fellow of Christ's College and lecturer at Gt. St. Andrew's, Cambridge, exercised great influence within the Puritan party as preacher, casuist, teacher of theology, and controversialist. In his chief systematic work, *A Golden Chain* (first published in 1590 as *Armilla Aurea*), he did not explicitly refer the covenant of works to the state of integrity, mentioning it in an exposition of the decalogue that concludes with a discussion of the uses of the law *post lapsum.* However, the terms of the covenant of works, as he defined them, presuppose Adam's integrity; and he spoke of Christ, in his mediatoral office between God and man respecting the law, as "the knot and bond of both covenants."

12. Ames, *Marrow,* 1.8.61–80; cf. Ames, *Medulla Theologica* (3d ed.; Amsterdam, 1628), 1.8.61–80. Ames was fellow of Christ's College, Cambridge (1607–9), and chaplain to the English community in the Hague (1611–18); in 1619 he was called to the newly founded University of Franeker as professor of divinity. In 1632 he joined Hugh Peter in ministering to the Independent congregation at Rotterdam (where Thomas Hooker also was residing), intending to remove shortly to New England. He was prevented by untimely death, though his wife made the journey, and part of his library also, which became the nucleus of the library of Harvard College. The *Medulla Theologica,* intended as a handbook for students and laymen, was first published in 1623 in Amsterdam, enjoying wide circulation in England and on the Continent; an English translation was published in 1642 by order of the House of Commons. A casuist and controversialist, as well as a theology professor, Ames may be reckoned the most influential Puritan theologian of the early seventeenth century, especially in New England. See John D. Eusden, ed. *The Marrow of Theology: William Ames, 1576–1633* (Boston: Pilgrim Press, 1968), pp. 1–11.

13. Ames, *Marrow,* 1.9.1, 5–6; 1.10.1, 2, 4, 9–11, 13; 1.39.9.

14. Ibid., 1.10.25, 29, 32–33; 1.24.17, 19–20.

15. Ibid., 1.11.1, 4–5, 8; 1.19.11; 1.21.16–17, 23; 1.22.1, 5; 1.28–29.

16. Ibid., 1.24.10–22; 1.25.1–2; 1.38.1–2, 14.

17. E.g., Preston, *New Covenant*, and *Breastplate*, Pt. 1; Richard Sibbes, *The Faithful Covenanter*, in *Works*, 6. 1–25; John Ball, *A Treatise of the Covenant of Grace* (London, 1645); James Usher, *A Body of Divinity* (3d ed.; London, 1648); Leigh, *System of Divinity* and *A Treatise of the Divine Promises* (London, 1633); Westminster Confession, 6.2–6; cf. Westminster Larger Catechism, qq. 20, 22, 30–35.

18. Norton, *Orthodox Evangelist*, pp. 2–9, 51, 91–92.

19. See ibid., pp. 18, 53–54; cf. Preston, *Life Eternal*, Pt. 2, pp. 181–82.

20. See, e.g., Ames, *Medulla*, 1.6.18; Perkins, *Golden Chain*, p. 13.

21. Norton, *Orthodox Evangelist*, pp. 15, 19, 51, 139; cf. Ames, *Marrow* (1642), 1.6.16–20; cf. Shepard, *Theses Sabbaticae*, Pt. 1, th. 18, 28.

22. Norton, *Orthodox Evangelist*, pp. 51–52, 56–57, 101, 126; cf. Preston, *Life Eternal*, pp. 180–81; Hooker, *Soul's Vocation*, pp. 62–63.

23. John Forbes, *A Treatise Tending to Clear the Doctrine of Justification* (Middelburg, 1616), p. 12.

24. Ames, *Marrow*, 1.18.4; 1.25.4, 16, 32; Perkins, *Golden Chain*, pp. 16–17, 24; Alsted, *Encyclopaedia*, "Theologia" 3, "Didactica," pp. 1586, 1588; Norton, *Orthodox Evangelist*, pp. 56–57.

25. Ames, *Medulla*, 1.10; Norton, *Orthodox Evangelist*, pp. 102–3, 104, 78–79, 82–83; cf. Ames, *Marrow* (1642), 1.9, 10.

26. That is, knowing it fully and being empowered by superadded graces to perform it; see Shepard, *Theses Sabbaticae*, 1.21.

27. See, e.g., Shepard, *Parable*, p. 125; Norton, *Orthodox Evangelist*, pp. 14–15; Bulkeley, *Gospel Covenant*, pp. 369–70.

28. Ames, *Marrow*, 1.9–10; Shepard, *Theses Sabbaticae*, 1.17, 19, 30, 90, 91, 99, 102, 110; Norton, *Orthodox Evangelist*, pp. 14–15, 80–81, 104, 115–18 (cf. 92), and *The Sufferings of Christ* (London, 1653), pp. 177–79, 180–83; Bulkeley, *Gospel Covenant*, pp. 58, 294–95, 328–29.

29. Shepard, *Parable*, pp. 125–27, and *Theses Sabbaticae*, 1.33–40 (cf. 15–17, 94); Norton, *Sufferings of Christ*, pp. 177–78, 180–83, 188–89. Puritans held that the gospel includes a command to believe, in which respect the "law of faith" is continuous with the law *qua* law; see, e.g., Bulkeley, *Gospel Covenant*, p. 101; Shepard, *Parable*, p. 136; cf. William Pemble, *Vindicia Gratiae*, pp. 132–33.

30. Norton, *Sufferings of Christ*, pp. 179, 183–84; Bulkeley, *Gospel Covenant*, pp. 57–58; Shepard, *Theses Sabbaticae*, 1.108.

31. The "third use" of the moral law, introduced by Melanchthon, was emphasized by Calvin as its principal use and as applicable only to the faithful (*Institutes*, 2.7.12–13); see François Wendel, *Calvin: The Origins and Development of his Religious Thought*, tr. Philip Mairet (1963; rpt. London: William Collins, 1965), pp. 196–203.

32. See Shepard, *Believer*, p. 118, *Parable*, p. 82, and *Theses Sabbaticae*, 1.81, 83, 90, 93, 98–99, 105–6, 108; Norton, *Orthodox Evangelist*, pp. 104, 211, and *Sufferings of Christ*, pp. 177, 188; cf. Bulkeley, *Gospel Covenant*, p. 101.

33. Norton, *Sufferings of Christ,* p. 190; Shepard, *Parable,* pp. 17–18.

34. Norton, *Orthodox Evangelist,* pp. 14–15, 42–43; cf. Norton, *Sufferings of Christ,* p. 4; Hooker, *Application of Redemption,* pp. 305–6.

35. Norton, *Sufferings of Christ,* pp. 2–10, 196–97, 221–22, 238–40.

36. Insistence on the necessarily double obedience of Christ was generally characteristic of Reformed orthodoxy, Johannes Piscator being the notable exception (Ritschl, *Dogmengeschichte,* p. 289).

37. Norton, *Sufferings of Christ,* pp. 140–41.

38. Norton, *Orthodox Evangelist,* pp. 211, 301–3, and *Sufferings of Christ,* pp. 186–87, 190–91, 198–99, 238–40, 243–45.

39. Bulkeley, *Gospel Covenant,* p. 369 (cf. 51, 97); Norton, *Sufferings of Christ,* p. 192.

CHAPTER SIX

1. Shepard, "To the Reader," in Bulkeley, *Gospel Covenant,* sig. A7^{vo}; Norton, *Orthodox Evangelist,* p. 86; Ames, *Marrow,* 1.9.5, 6; 1.10; Bulkeley, *Gospel Covenant,* p. 76.

2. Bulkeley, *Gospel Covenant,* pp. 27, 50, 281–83, 285; cf. Preston, *Breastplate,* Pt. 1, pp. 38–41.

3. Bulkeley, *Gospel Covenant,* pp. 279–80, 287.

4. See, e.g., Heppe, *Dogmatik,* p. 226; on the relationship of faith and justification, see John Ball, *Treatise of Faith,* pp. 2, 143–44; Sibbes, in ibid., sig. [A]2ro; Ezekiel Culverwell, *A Treatise of Faith* (7th ed.; London, 1633), p. 152; Hooker, *Soul's Exaltation,* pp. 116–20.

5. Bulkeley, *Gospel Covenant,* pp. 73–74, 286; Norton, *Orthodox Evangelist,* pp. 85–89.

6. Shepard, *Cases Resolved,* p. 309; Norton, *Orthodox Evangelist,* pp. 85, 88; Shepard, *Believer,* p. 195, and *Parable,* pp. 424–25; Bulkeley, *Gospel Covenant,* pp. 73–74, 369–70; cf. Sibbes, *Christ's Exaltation Purchased by Humiliation,* in *Works,* 5. 342, and *Excellency of the Gospel,* in *Works,* 4. 219; Preston, *Life Eternal,* Pt. 2, pp. 86–87, and *Breastplate,* Pt. 1, pp. 25–26.

7. Bulkeley, *Gospel Covenant,* pp. 286–87, and Sibbes, preface to John Smith, *An Exposition of the Creed* (London, 1632), in Grosart, "Memoir of Sibbes," in *Works,* 1. civ.

8. Norton, *Orthodox Evangelist,* pp. 89, 93 (cf. 78–79, 82–83, and Preston, *New Covenant,* pp. 389–90); John Forbes, *Treatise of Justification,* pp. 4–7, 9; Shepard to Winthrop, ca. Dec. 15, 1636, *Winthrop Papers,* 3. 329–30. In a similar vein, Culverwell noted that all the free, gracious promises of the gospel involve conditions, express or implied (*Treatise of Faith,* pp. 150–52).

9. Norton, *Orthodox Evangelist,* p. 86; cf. Bulkeley, *Gospel Covenant,* pp. 26–28, 42–43; Ames, *Marrow,* 1.10.2.

10. William Perkins, *A Treatise of God's Free Grace and Man's Free Will,* in *Works* (1626), 1. 731. "Natural man" here refers to man after the fall; a "morally good" work is an act of obedience to the moral law, performed out

of love and honor towards God. Cf. Perkins, *Golden Chain,* p. 20; Preston, *Life Eternal,* Pt. 1, pp. 15–16.

11. Perkins, *God's Free Grace,* p. 731 (cf. 722–23); cf. Pemble, *Vindicia Gratiae,* pp. 110–12; Ames, *Marrow,* 1.10.2, 1.12.44; Norton, *Orthodox Evangelist,* pp. 74–77, 114–15; Hooker, *Unbeliever's Preparing,* pp. 101–2.

12. Perkins, *God's Free Grace,* pp. 722–23, 727; cf. Norton, *Orthodox Evangelist,* pp. 74, 76; Ames, *Conscience,* 3.19.1–4.

13. Perkins, *God's Free Grace,* pp. 722–23, 729; cf. Hooker, *Application of Redemption,* pp. 142–43.

14. Norton, *Orthodox Evangelist,* p. 114 (cf. 137); cf. Sibbes, *Soul's Conflict,* 1. 205–6.

15. Sibbes, *Soul's Conflict,* pp. 205–6; Norton, *Orthodox Evangelist,* p. 76.

16. Miller, " 'Preparation,' " p. 261. In this connection it may be noted that the doctrine of divine sovereignty as held by sixteenth- and seventeenth-century Reformed divines, Continental and English, does not appear to have required an understanding of conversion as an instantaneous, convulsive, lightening-bolt-on-the-Damascus-Road sort of experience (cf. Pettit, *Heart Prepared,* pp. 2, 7, 10–11, 15–16; see Chapter 1, n. 17). This conception seems more reminiscent of a Cane Ridge meeting than of a Swiss or early Puritan congregation and perhaps represents a reading-back of the familiar image of the nineteenth-century frontier revival (see, e.g., Miller, "Marrow," p. 280). Zwingli, in his sermon "On the Clarity and Certainty or Power of the Word of God," enumerated twelve ways "to come to . . . a personal experience that you are taught of God" (tr. G.W. Bromiley, *Library of Christian Classics,* [Philadelphia: Westminster Press, 1953], 24. 93–95). Only one of them suggests that conversion may in some sense be violent; the rest indicate that Zwingli regarded it as anything but a "blinding flash" or an instantaneous, complete, unmistakable experience.

For the orthodox period, Heppe's *locus* on vocation indicates much the same (*Dogmatik,* pp. 404–31). His citations suggest that Continental Reformed divines did not generally regard conversion as total, believing rather that sin remains to be struggled against and that consequently assurance must be re-affirmed throughout a saint's life. Nor was the subjective *sense* of conversion regarded as being given in an instant, or as always experienced in the same way (pp. 404–5, 407–8, 411, 421). There is, rather, an implicit distinction between the effectual infusion of regenerating grace, which is instantaneous, and the gradual manifestation of it, understood as the actualization of gracious habits.

17. Preston, *New Covenant,* pp. 118–19; Shepard, *Theses Sabbaticae,* 1.99.

18. Norton, *Orthodox Evangelist,* pp. 75–76, 105, 108–10, 113–14; see also Pemble, *Vindicia Gratiae,* p. 29; Leigh, *System of Divinity,* p. 493; Richard Hollinworth, qtd. in Nuttall, *Holy Spirit,* p. 70.

19. Sibbes, *Excellency of the Gospel,* p. 258; Bulkeley, *Gospel Covenant,* pp. 299–303, 309–10. Cf. Culverwell, *Treatise of Faith,* p. 46; Ball, *Treatise of Faith,* p. 142; Usher, *Body of Divinity,* pp. 196, 199; Leigh, *System of Divinity,* pp. 501–2; Preston, *Breastplate,* Pt. 1, pp. 55–59; Ames, *Marrow,* 1.27.

20. Preston, *New Covenant*, pp. 322–25.

21. Ames, *Marrow* (Eusden), 1.9.5, 6 (see also 1.10.2).

22. Perkins, *God's Free Grace*, p. 730.

23. Ibid., p. 738.

24. Hooker, *Unbeliever's Preparing*, pp. 2–3, 26–29, and *Soul's Vocation*, pp. 283–84; Sibbes, *Excellency of the Gospel*, pp. 258–59; Ames, *Marrow* (Eusden), 1.3.2, 3, 19; cf. Leigh, *System of Divinity*, p. 502; Preston, *Breastplate*, Pt. 1, pp. 55–59 (cf. 18–20, 21–22); see also Heppe, *Dogmatik*, pp. 409–10.

25. Hooker, *Unbeliever's Preparing*, pp. 56–57.

26. Thomas Bakewell, *The Antinomians' Christ Confounded* (London, 1644), pp. 9, 11; cf. Ball, *Treatise of Faith*, p. 6.

27. Norton, *Orthodox Evangelist*, pp. 111–12.

28. Ibid., pp. 112–13.

29. See Miller, "Marrow," pp. 269, 273, 283–88, and Chapter 1, nn. 16, 17, above; Pettit, *Heart Prepared*, pp. vii, 2, 7, 15–18, 41, 104–5, 112–13, 126–28, 217–19.

30. See, e.g., Pemble, *Vindicia Gratiae*, pp. 158–67; Perkins, *Golden Chain*, in *Works* (1612), 1. 95–105, and *Exposition upon Galatians*, in *Works* (1617), 2. 220, 237; Forbes, *Treatise of Justification*, pp. 70–73; George Downame, *A Treatise of Justification* (London, 1633), p. 5.

31. See E.A. Burtt, *The Metaphysical Foundations of Modern Science* (2d ed., 1932; rpt. Garden City, N.Y.: Doubleday and Co., 1954), pp. 303–10.

32. Thus Norton, for example, observed that repentance is wrought by God efficiently and by man formally. The formal effect of the second cause in man is the effect of the first cause, essentially depending on the first cause in all respects and therein proclaiming, rather than diminishing, the all-efficiency of the first cause. At the same time, works wrought by God efficiently are ascribed to man, "because man (God not for want of power, but out of abundance of goodness being so far pleased to make use of him) co-worketh with God therein" and because "man is the next formal efficient cause, viz. in respect of the order of the ascent, and descent of the causes" (*Orthodox Evangelist*, pp. 113–14). The man, not God, repents. Cf. Calvin, *Institutes*, 3.15.17, 21; Ball, *Treatise of Faith*, pp. 9–10, 12–13; Hooker, *Soul's Exaltation*, pp. 29–32.

33. Synod of Dort, *Tert. et quart. doct. caput*, §§ 9–15, in Müller, *Bekenntnisschriften;* cf. Ball, *Treatise of Faith*, pp. 7–9.

34. Synod of Dort, *Tert. et quart. doct. caput*, § 16.

35. Cf. Pettit, *Heart Prepared*, pp. 10–11.

36. Ritschl, *Dogmengeschichte*, pp. 302–3, 307–8, 430–31; Calvin, *Institutes*, 3.15.21; see Chapter 5, n. 9, above.

37. Heppe, *Dogmatik*, pp. 50, 53, 107, 120–22, and Loc. 6, 8, citing esp. Polanus and also Braun, Wollebius, Mastricht, Heidegger, Alsted, Keckermann, and Wendelin.

38. In his "Marrow of Puritan Divinity," Miller pointed out the high estimate of human capacities in Puritan theology (pp. 274–77) and the prominence given both to the activity of second causes in the accomplishment of God's gracious purposes (pp. 266–68) and to the conception of regeneration as renewal of human faculties (p. 280). He tended, however, to regard these

as Puritan innovations and as departures from the proper Reformed position (e.g., pp. 274–75, 278–80, 293–94).

39. See Synod of Dort, *Tert. et quart. doct. caput,* § § 16, 17, on the relationship of God's "almighty work" to the "mediators" through which God exercises his power, and on the manifestation of grace in the performance of holy duties. Cf. Heppe, *Dogmatik,* pp. 108, 117, 200–202, 209–10, 405 n. 6, 407–8; Calvin, *Institutes,* 3.15.21; Ritschl, *Dogmengeschichte,* pp. 268–69; Ball, *Treatise of Faith,* p. 14.

40. See Norton, *Orthodox Evangelist,* p. 166; Hooker, *Application of Redemption,* pp. 301–4. These "states," which are not infrequently the subject of Puritan pastoral discourse, represent a conceptual filling-out of the common Protestant notion that God, before he converts a sinner, first humbles him in order to apprise him of his need for grace, this humbling being chiefly the work of the law in its "second use." Shepard, for example, distinguished three such states, "in order of nature": (1) "conviction" for sin, in which God, through the Spirit, by means of the preaching of the law, works upon the sinner's understanding until he perceives the truth of his sinfulness; (2) "compunction" for sin, in which the sinner, in his will and affections, is moved to feel the seriousness of his sinfulness and to seek to renounce it; (3) "humiliation," in which the sinner, knowing his impotence to save himself and his utter want of grace, is made willing to cast himself upon Christ's mercy, to be done with as Christ wills. See Shepard, *Believer,* pp. 116–59, 174–84; cf. Ames, *Marrow,* 1.26.12–15; Sibbes, *A Bruised Reed and a Smoking Flax,* in *Works,* 1. 44–47, and *The Riches of Mercy,* in *Works,* 6 (1863), 522–23; Preston, *New Covenant,* p. 397.

41. See Shepard, *Parable,* 2.14, 15; Hooker, *Application of Redemption,* pp. 142–43, 285–86 (cf. 306–7), and *Unbeliever's Preparing,* pp. 120–23. Cf. Ball, *Treatise of Faith,* pp. 2, 7, 13–14, 16–17; Sibbes, *Excellency of the Gospel,* p. 234; Perkins, *God's Free Grace,* p. 738.

42. See Heppe, *Dogmatik,* p. 406, n. 10; Hooker, *Application of Redemption,* pp. 283–86, 291–99, 309, and *Soul's Vocation,* pp. 312–13; Bulkeley, *Gospel Covenant,* pp. 299–300; John Rogers, *Doctrine of Faith* (London, 1629), pp. 66–67, 125–26. Despite his positive estimate of the evidential significance of "preparatory" works of law and gospel, Rogers cautioned that assurance of true faith was to be based properly upon the evidence of antecedents and fruits of faith *together;* and he was careful to point out that union with Christ and works pleasing to God are entirely contingent on faith and on nothing before, and that faith itself, in the order of redemption, is the first "mark of our election" (ibid., pp. 52, 125–26, 256, 341, 362–63, 379).

43. See Heppe, *Dogmatik,* pp. 409–10; cf. Ball, *Treatise of Faith,* pp. 11–13, 31–32; Preston, *New Covenant,* pp. 389–90.

44. Synod of Dort, *Tert. et quart. doct. caput,* § § 9–15; cf. Ball, *Treatise of Faith,* pp. 143–44 (cf. 6); Sibbes, in ibid., sig. [A]2ro.

45. Captain John Underhill, for example, told the Massachusetts General Court in 1638 that he had attained assurance while smoking a pipe of tobacco; Winthrop, *Journal,* 1. 275–76; see Chapter 9, nn. 42, 46, below.

46. See Heppe, *Dogmatik,* Loc. 20; cf. Synod of Dort, *Tert. et quart. doct.*

caput, § 16 (cf. 11, 12); Hooker, *Unbeliever's Preparing,* p. 131; Preston, *Breastplate,* Pt. 1, pp. 55, 57–58.

47. Hooker, *Soul's Exaltation,* pp. 36–37, and *Soul's Vocation,* pp. 312–13.

48. Bulkeley, *Gospel Covenant,* p. 338 (cf. 335–36).

49. Pemble, *Vindicia Gratiae,* pp. 164–65, 167.

50. Bulkeley, *Gospel Covenant,* pp. 298–99; Ritschl, *Dogmengeschichte,* p. 387.

CHAPTER SEVEN

1. Sibbes, *Soul's Conflict,* p. 269; Ames, *Marrow,* 1.28.22, 23.

2. Sibbes, *Yea and Amen, or Precious Promises Laid Open,* in *Works,* 4. 138–39; cf. Sibbes, *A Fountain Sealed,* in *Works,* 5. 433, where "privy seal" is used of God's secret decree before its manifestation in the Spirit's public sealing of the elect in regeneration, in which he "stamps" them with the image of God. Cf. also the discussion of "broad" and "privy" seals of the Spirit in the New England debate (Hall, *Antinomian Controversy,* pp. 48–49, 63–64, 335).

3. See Haller, *Rise of Puritanism,* esp. ch. 5; Nuttall, *Holy Spirit,* passim.

4. Nuttall considered Sibbes representative of the broader Puritan "center" (*Holy Spirit,* pp. 14, 23; see also 31–33).

5. Sibbes, *Yea and Amen,* pp. 134–36. Cf. Robert Bolton, *Some General Directions for . . . Walking with God* (2d ed.; London, 1626), p. 317; Preston, qtd. in John von Rohr, "Covenant and Assurance in Early English Puritanism," *Church History* 34 (June 1965), 197; Sibbes, *Fountain Sealed,* p. 409, and *Faithful Covenanter,* pp. 9–11; Perkins, *The Whole Treatise of the Cases of Conscience,* in *Works* (1612), 2. 18–20.

6. E.g., Sibbes, *Fountain Sealed,* pp. 413–14; Perkins, *Cases of Conscience,* pp. 18–19, and *Golden Chain,* in *Works,* 1. 104–5; Preston, *Breastplate,* Pt. 2, pp. 53–55.

7. Sibbes, *Yea and Amen,* p. 133; cf. Perkins, *Golden Chain,* pp. 100, 112–13, and *Cases of Conscience,* p. 19; cf. Perkins, *Exposition upon Galatians,* in *Works* (1617), 2. 224; Preston, *Breastplate,* Pt. 2, pp. 64–65, and *New Covenant,* pp. 417–18; Calvin, *Institutes,* 3.17.12, 3.13.18–19.

8. See Sibbes, *Excellency of the Gospel,* p. 298, *Faithful Covenanter,* pp. 12–15, and *Fountain Sealed,* pp. 437–38, 444; cf. Culverwell, *Treatise of Faith,* pp. 53–60, 235–36; Shepard, *Theses Sabbaticae,* pp. 119–21. To know God's mind towards oneself, Sibbes noted, one must begin not with God but with the Spirit's work in oneself (*Fountain Sealed,* p. 444). It was a commonplace of Puritan divinity that the eternal decree is ascertainable only by its effects. Similarly, the Spirit's witness is known primarily by its effects manifest in human behavior; see, e.g., Perkins, *Golden Chain,* pp. 111–12.

9. Ames, *Marrow,* 1.24–29; Perkins, *Golden Chain,* pp. 77–85; Wollebius, *Compendium,* 1.28–29. See also Bulkeley, *Gospel Covenant,* pp. 286, 323; Ball, *Treatise of Faith,* pp. 88–89; Hooker, *Soul's Ingrafting,* pp. 1–5, and "To the Reader," in Rogers, *The Doctrine of Faith,* sig. A10[ro-vo].

10. Ames, *Marrow*, 1.26.5; 1.27.1–3, 14–16; 1.28.4–6, 23; 1.29.1, 6, 8; 1.30.1–4. The chief differences concerned the relationship between repentance and sanctification and that between sanctification and glorification. On the principal elements of the order see Heppe, *Dogmatik*, Loc. 20–22.

11. Ames, *Marrow*, 1.26.34, 1.27.19, 1.19.13. See Perkins, *Golden Chain*, in *Works* (1626), 1. 100; Rogers, *Doctrine of Faith*, pp. 174–75, 189–91; Shepard, *Parable*, pp. 118, 224; Hooker, *Application of Redemption*, pp. 376–79.

12. For this reason "order of redemption" (or "of regeneration") seems a more apt label for the pattern than "stages of" or "process of conversion," as being both more inclusive and closer to Puritans' intent; see Ames on the "application of redemption," *Marrow*, 1.24; cf. Sibbes, *The Life of Faith*, in *Works*, 5. 385–408, and Hooker's usage in *Application of Redemption*. "Conversion," owing to connotations acquired in a later era of sudden, emotional religious transformation, seems misleading. For Puritans the word meant the turning of a person from devotion to sin to devotion to God, which occurrence was instantaneous but could be so slight initially that a person might not immediately perceive it. "Stages" and "process" are also misleading, as almost inevitably suggesting variation over time. Puritans agreed that the regenerate grow in grace and faith, God augmenting the grace he originally bestows according to his pleasure and the saints' diligence; and they maintained that conscious awareness of one's gracious estate could both increase and decrease over time. The basic qualitative change, however, from a fallen to a gracious estate, they held to be wrought in a moment, and essentially.

13. See, e.g., Perkins, *Golden Chain*, p. 101; Ball, *Treatise of Faith*, p. 89; George Downame, *The Covenant of Grace* (London, 1647), pp. 137, 368–69.

14. Rom. 8:30: "And those whom he predestined he also called; and those whom he called he also justified; and those whom he justified he also glorified." See, e.g., John Downe, *Treatise of the True Nature and Definition of Justifying Faith* (Oxford, 1635), p. 88 (cf. 126–28); Perkins, *Cases of Conscience*, pp. 18–20; Hooker, *Soul's Exaltation*, p. 28.

15. Hooker, *Soul's Exaltation*, p. 18–19.

16. Heppe, *Dogmatik*, pp. 122–23, 141; Wollebius, *Compendium*, 4.2.15, qtd. in Heppe, pp. 141–42; cf. Perkins, "A Brief Discourse Taken out of . . . H. Zanchius," in *Works* (1626), 1. 429–38; Forbes, *Treatise of Justification*, pp. 37–39; Rollock, *Treatise of Effectual Calling*, pp. 178–79; see also Hooker, *The Covenant of Grace Opened* (London, 1649), pp. 69–70; "Elders Reply," in Hall, *Antinomian Controversy*, p. 76; Cotton, *Conference Held at Boston*, in ibid., pp. 182–83; Sibbes, *Soul's Conflict*, pp. 265–66. The basis for the practical syllogism appears in Calvin's affirmation that good works are testimonies of God's benevolence toward the redeemed and of his Spirit dwelling in them and so may strengthen faith and, by implication, assurance (*Institutes*, 3.14.18).

17. Calvin, *Institutes*, 3.2.15–16, 28; 3.13.4–5; 3.14.19. See Wilhelm Niesel, "Syllogismus Practicus?" in Adolf Lauffs und Emil Schneider, eds., *Aus Theologie und Geschichte der reformierten Kirche: Festgabe für E. F. K. Müller* (Neukirchen, Kr. Mörs: Buchhandlung des Erziehungsvereins, 1933), pp. 158–79; Wendel, *Calvin*, pp. 275–77; cf. Ritschl, *Dogmengeschichte*, pp. 207–9, 211–12.

18. Perkins, *Exposition upon Galatians*, in *Works* (1617), 2. 208–9; Ball, *Treatise of Faith*, pp. 89–90; Preston, *Breastplate*, Pt. 1, p. 64; Sibbes, *Life of Faith*, pp. 390–91. See also Downame, *Covenant of Grace*, pp. 141–43, 145–49, and Sibbes, *Life of Faith*, pp. 396–97, where the syllogism is applied to faith and works together.

19. See Ball, *Treatise of Faith*, pp. 94, 98, 114–15; Preston, *Life Eternal*, Pt. 2, pp. 91, 92; Shepard, *Parable*, pp. 184, 223, 338–39; Sibbes, *Life of Faith*, p. 396.

20. Downame, *Covenant of Grace*, p. 149; cf. Preston, *New Covenant*, p. 325; Ames, *Conscience*, 1.1.1–11; 1.2.1–11; 1.7.[1,2]; 1.8.2, 4; 2.1.11–13.

21. Ball, *Treatise of Faith*, p. 95; see also Perkins, *Exposition upon Galatians*, p. 225; Hooker, *Soul's Preparation*, p. 48; Preston, *New Covenant*, pp. 460–62.

22. Sibbes, *Soul's Conflict*, pp. 137–38; see Sibbes, *Fountain Sealed*, p. 444, and *Life of Faith*, pp. 367–71; cf. Ball, *Treatise of Faith*, p. 88; Bolton, *Directions for Walking*, pp. 325–26; Preston, *Breastplate*, Pt. 2, p. 95; Culverwell, *Treatise of Faith*, pp. 235–37.

23. C. F. Allison, *The Rise of Moralism: The Proclamation of the Gospel from Hooker to Baxter* (New York: Seabury Press, 1966); see, e.g., Robert Bellarmine, qtd. in Bolton, *Directions for Walking*, p. 321; Henry Burton, *The Law and the Gospel Reconciled, in answer to . . . an Antinomian* (London, 1631).

24. Perkins, *Cases of Conscience*, p. 18; Preston, *Breastplate*, Pt. 1, p. 62; Ball, *Treatise of Faith*, pp. 88–89; Sibbes, "To the Reader," in ibid., sig. q2[ro]; Ames, *Marrow*, 1.3.1–3, 1.26.20–29, 2.5.17–19, Hooker, *Soul's Vocation*, pp. 283–84.

25. Perkins, *Golden Chain*, pp. 79–81, 100, *Foundation of the Christian Religion*, in *Works* (1612), 1. 5, and *Exposition upon Galatians*, pp. 208–10.

26. Perkins, *Exposition of the Symbol*, in *Works* (1612), 1. 124, and *Golden Chain*, pp. 79, 103–5; cf. Perkins, *Exposition upon Galatians*, pp. 208–10.

27. Perkins, *Exposition upon Galatians*, pp. 208–9, *Exposition of the Symbol*, pp. 112, 124–25, 128, and *Golden Chain*, pp. 79–80, 104–5.

28. For a full statement of the position, see Ball, *Treatise of Faith*, chs. 3, 7. Ball (1585–1640), educated at Brasenose College, Oxford (1602), was converted in 1610 and ordained, subsequently obtaining a living at Whitmore, Staffordshire. He was several times deprived and confined for non-subscription and for keeping prayer- and fast-days with other nonconformists. He was noted for his knowledge of controversial theology, especially as it pertained to the doctrine of justification. Sibbes commended Ball's *Treatise of Faith* as the most complete treatment of the topic then available in English.

29. Preston, *Breastplate*, Pt. 1, pp. 49, 56–57; Ames, *Marrow* (Eusden), 1.3.3 (cf. 13, 19), 1.17.16; Sibbes, qtd. in Grosart, "*Memoir*," 1. civ; Ball, *Treatise of Faith*, pp. 7, 25, 32, 141–42; Hooker, *Unbeliever's Preparing*, pp. 13, 26–28, 30, 40–41; Downe, *Treatise of Justifying Faith*, pp. 9–10.

30. Ames, *Marrow*, 1.26.26–28, 1.27.9; Preston, *Breastplate*, Pt. 1, pp. 62–63; Sibbes, *Yea and Amen*, p. 142, and *Life of Faith*, pp. 396–97; Downe, *Treatise of Justifying Faith*, pp. 2, 5–6; Rogers, *Doctrine of Faith*, sig. A5[vo]–A6[ro].

31. Ames, *Medulla,* 1.27.16; Preston, *Breastplate,* Pt. 1, pp. 63–64; Ball, *Treatise of Faith,* pp. 30–31, 90–91, 99–100; see also, Downe, *Treatise of Justifying Faith,* pp. 149–50; Bolton, *Directions for Walking,* pp. 321–22; cf. Bulkeley, *Gospel Covenant,* pp. 302–4.

32. Ames, *Marrow,* 1.27.19 (cf. 1.3.22); Ball, *Treatise of Faith,* pp. 84–87; cf. Downe, *Treatise of Justifying Faith,* pp. 8, 12–13, 69.

33. Downe, *Treatise of Justifying Faith,* pp. 2–3, 8; Ames, *Marrow,* 1.17.19; Preston, *Breastplate,* Pt. 1, p. 65.

34. Forbes (1568?–1634), trained at St. Andrew's, was exiled for his part in the Scottish General Assembly of 1606. He became pastor to the English congregation at Middelburg (1611) and later at Delft, until forced out by the interference of Charles I. Cotton was acquainted with his writings, and there is a degree of continuity between his position and Cotton's at certain points. Baxter (d. ca. 1634) was educated at Magdalen College, Oxford (ca. 1569), later becoming Sir Philip Sidney's tutor in Greek. In 1577 he joined with nine other nonconforming ministers in a sharp letter to Cartwright, repudiating what they regarded as the latter's temporizing on the vestments rubrics. In 1592 Baxter became warden of St. Mary's College, Youghal (apparently a sinecure); in 1601 he was preaching in Bristol and in 1602 became vicar at Troy, Monmouthshire. Downe (1570?–1631) was schooled at Emmanuel, Cambridge, where he was Fellow when he preached at Bristol, on justification by faith, in November 1601. He was incorporated at Oxford in 1600. Though a conformist in matters ecclesiastical, he retained the stamp of Emmanuel in theology and personal piety. Downe wrote the "Defense" of his sermon sometime in 1602 or 1603, in response to Baxter's manuscript "Answer" (see *Treatise of Justifying Faith,* sig. A2ro–A4ro, pp. 19, 177); he appears to have prepared it for the press before his death. Baxter's tract was apparently printed in 1633 (A. B. Grosart, *D.N.B.,* 1. 1348–49) and Downe's sermon and "Defense" (as the *Treatise*) two years later, suggesting the pertinence of both pieces to issues enjoying increasing liveliness in the 1630s among nonconformists.

35. Forbes, *Treatise of Justification,* pp. 4–7, 10–20, 26–27, 30–36, 42–45.

36. Ibid., pp. 73, 126–27, 147, 159; cf. Forbes, *A Fruitful Sermon at Delft* (Amsterdam, 1626), pp. 43–44, 54–55, 59, 90–91.

37. Ibid., pp. 43–44, 89–91; Cotton, *New Covenant,* pp. 161–62.

38. Baxter, qtd. in Downe, *Treatise of Justifying Faith,* pp. 82, 170–71 (cf. 35, 89, 145), 164–65.

39. Ibid., pp. 92, 95–98, 101, 107–12; cf. Ball, *Treatise of Faith,* pp. 82–88. Ball explicitly rejected the notion that habitual faith justifies (pp. 6, 143).

40. Forbes, *Treatise of Justification,* p. 49; see, e.g. Ball, *Treatise of Faith,* p. 88; Downe, *Treatise of Justifying Faith,* pp. 126–28; Ames, *Medulla,* 1.27.16.

41. Ball, *Treatise of Faith,* pp. 86–94.

CHAPTER EIGHT

1. Eaton proceeded B.A. at Trinity College, Oxford, in 1595, becoming vicar at Wickham Market, Suffolk, about 1604. In 1619 he was deprived by the

Court of High Commission for being an "incorrigible divulger of errors and false opinions," and he and his followers continued to attract official attention into the 1630s, especially around London. He was regarded by contemporaries as the literary founder of English antinomianism and may fairly be reckoned an authentic English version of the Reformation sectarianism long familiar on the Continent. Traske was a schoolmaster, undignified by university training, though apparently self-taught in Greek and Hebrew. He commenced troubling London congregations in the character of a messianic prophet and in 1620 was prosecuted in the Court of Star Chamber for "judaizing" in matters cere-monial. He recanted in prison but shortly fell into doctrinal extremes of an Eatonian sort, and he died in the company of the London "semi-separatists" associated with Henry Jacob. Crisp, the son of a substantial London merchant, proceeded B.A. at Cambridge and M.A. (1626) at Balliol, Oxford. In 1627 he became rector at Brinkworth, Wiltshire, whence he retired to London in 1642 to escape Royalist military operations. At Brinkworth he was suspected of "antinomianism," a suspicion that his subsequent preaching in and around London confirmed. His sermons, published posthumously in 1643 by Robert Lancaster (who also published the 1642 edition of Eaton's *Honeycomb of Free Grace*), stimulated controversy among English nonconformists for the next seventy-five years.

On Eaton see: Benjamin Brook, *The Lives of the Puritans* (London: James Black, 1813), 2. 466; Daniel Neal, *History of the Puritans* (rev. ed.; London, T. Tegg and Son, 1837), 2. 94; Ephraim Pagitt, *Heresiography, or a Description of the Hereticks and Sectaries of these Later Times* (London, 1645), p. 89; Anthony Wood, *Athenae Oxoniensis*, ed. Philip Bliss (New York: John-son Reprint Corp., 1967), 3. 21; Samuel R. Gardiner, ed., *Reports of Cases in the Courts of Star Chamber and High Commission* (Westminster: Camden Society, 1886), p. 320. On Traske: Edward Norris, *The New Gospel not the True Gospel, or a Discovery of the Life and Death, Doctrine and Doings of Mr. John Traske* (London, 1638), pp. 7–8; Champlin Burrage, *The Early Eng-lish Dissenters* (Cambridge, Mass.: Harvard University Press, 1912), 1. 326, 2. 301. On Crisp: Tobias Crisp, *Christ Alone Exalted, in Fourteen Sermons* (London, 1643), sig. A4^{vo}–A7^{vo}; John Lightfoot, *Works*, ed. John Rogers (Lon-don, 1822), 13. 9, 12–13; Brook, *Lives*, 2. 471–75.

2. John Eaton, *The Honeycomb of Free Grace by Christ Alone* (London, 1642), pp. 7, 24–27; Burton, *Law and Gospel*, pp. 11–12. The language and views of Burton's "antinomian" are essentially the same as those of Eaton in the *Honeycomb;* see also John Eaton, *The Discovery of a most dangerous Dead Faith* (London, 1641).

3. Eaton, *Honeycomb*, pp. 20–27, 74–78, 257, 321–22.

4. Ibid. sig. a4^{vo}–b1^{ro}, b2^{ro}, p. 311; Burton, *Law and Gospel*, pp. 12, 15, 20, 68; Eaton, *Honeycomb*, pp. 25, 47–48, 52, 59, 82, 148–50, 155.

5. Eaton, *Honeycomb*, pp. 41, 45, 75, 80–81, 118, 252, 380 (citing Luther in support!). See Burton, *Law and Gospel*, p. 35^2; cf. Eaton, *Honeycomb*, pp. 82–83.

6. Eaton, *Honeycomb*, sig. b2^{ro-vo}, pp. 90–91, 267, 305–6, 310–11, 321, 323.

7. Ibid., pp. 113, 169, 259, 311, 424; Burton, *Law and Gospel*, pp. 8, 22.

8. Eaton, *Honeycomb*, pp. 113–14 (ital. omit.; cf. 146–47); Burton, *Law and Gospel*, p. 69. On this point, at least, Cotton would readily have concurred; and the Hutchinsonians, with alacrity, identified as "legalism" what Eaton here rejects. Cf. Winthrop, *Short Story*, error no. 80 (cf. nos. 69, 72, 75, 77).

9. Norris, *New Gospel*, pp. 13–18; John Traske, *A Treatise of Liberty from Judaism* (London, 1620), pp. 13–14. Cf. Cotton's "faith of absolute promises" versus evidence of conditional promises; see "The Priority of Absolute Promises" in Chapter 3, above. Cf. Winthrop, *Short Story*, errors no. 38, 48.

10. Norris, *New Gospel*, pp. 14, 20–24, 29–34, 40–42, 48; cf. Winthrop, *Short Story*, error no. 67.

11. Traske, qtd. in Norris, *New Gospel*, pp. 25–26. Cf. the opinion attributed to Anne Hutchinson ("Report of the Trial," in Hall, *Antinomian Controversy*, p. 351): "That those of 1 Cor. 6:19 that are united to Christ have two bodies, Christ's and a new body and you knew not how Christ should be united to our fleshly bodies."

12. Traske, "Treatise of the Old Man and the New," qtd. in Norris, *New Gospel*, p. 27; Thomas Bakewell, *A Short View of the Antinomian Errors* (London, 1643), pp. 6, 8–11.

13. Traske, qtd. in Norris, *New Gospel*, pp. 25–26, 36–37. Cf. Winthrop, *Short Story*, error no. 11: "As Christ was once made flesh, so he is now first made flesh in us, ere we be carried to perfection."

14. Traske, qtd. in Norris, *New Gospel*, p. 26; cf. Crisp, *Christ Alone*, p. 195; Bakewell, *Antinomians' Christ*, pp. 5, 10–11. Cf. also Winthrop, *Short Story*, error no. 1: "In the conversion of a sinner, which is saving and gracious, the faculties of the soul, and workings thereof, in things pertaining to God, are destroyed and made to cease"; no. 2: "Instead of them, the Holy Ghost doth come and take place, and doth all the works of those natures, as the faculties of the human nature of Christ do"; no. 7: "The new creature, or the new man mentioned in the Gospel, is not meant of grace, but of Christ"; see also nos. 11, 15, 18, 35.

15. Norris, *New Gospel, p.* 18.

Traske's references to the "new creature" and "new man" and his affirmation that Christians do good works out of the power of love abiding in them because of their resurrection with Christ, and not as a duty or out of obedience to the law, are reminiscent of Henrik Niclaes, the founder of the "Family of Love"; and similar echoes are discernible in the views associated with Eaton and Crisp. See Traske, *Treatise of Liberty*, pp. 8–10, 35; Norris, *New Gospel*, pp. 15–18, 26–27, 36–37; Burton, *Law and Gospel*, pp. 20–22, 69; Eaton, *Honeycomb*, p. 125; Bakewell, *Short View*, sig. A1ʳᵒ, p. 18; cf. H[enrik] N[iclaes], *Evangelium Regni: A Joyful Message of the Kingdom*, tr. [C. Vittels] (Amsterdam, 1575?), ch. 12.7, 24.1–9, 33.12, 34.1, 35, and *Introductio: An Introduction to the Holy Understanding* (Amsterdam, 1575?), ch. 1.33, 2.1–8, 6.40, 9.35, 12.55–57. Niclaes (1502–ca. 1580), a mercer by trade and a religious visionary, moved from his native Münster to Holland around 1540, shortly thereafter announcing himself as the "new man" of the latter days and bearer of the perfect and spiritual gospel of the love of God, incarnate in himself. He acquired a scattered, international following, a considerable part of it in England, which he may have visited in the early 1550s. Between ca. 1555 and 1579 his views were propagated there by Christopher Vittels, a joiner from Delft, who translated several of Niclaes's writings into English. By the 1570s the Family of Love had established itself, primarily in East Anglia, and had begun to attract official attention; the sect appears to have persisted, obscurely, into the seventeenth century. See George H. Williams, *The Radical Reformation* (Philadelphia: Westminster Press, 1962), pp. 477–82, 788–90.

16. Brook, *Lives*, 2. 473, Crisp, *Christ Alone*, pp. 18, 60–63, 166, 170–71, 175–76.

17. Crisp, *Christ Alone*, pp. 64–65, 154–61, 165, 178, 190–92, 198–204, 207; cf. "Dr. Crisp's Answer to an Objector," in [Samuel Crisp], *Christ Made Sin* (London, 1691), pp. 118, 122, 132.

18. Crisp, *Christ Alone*, pp. 167–68, 170–71. Cf. Winthrop, *Short Story*, error no. 21: "To be justified by faith is to be justified by works"; no. 68: "Faith justifies an unbeliever, that is, that faith that is in Christ, justifies me that have no faith in myself"; cf. nos. 26, 27, 28.

19. Crisp, *Christ Alone*, pp. 168–70, 215–16; Bakewell, *Antinomians' Christ*, pp. 5, 7, 10–11, and *Short View*, p. 21. Cf. Winthrop, *Short Story*, "unsavory speech" no. 1: "To say that we are justified by faith is an unsafe speech, we must say we are justified by Christ"; cf. error no. 78, and no. 37: "We are completely united to Christ, before, or without any faith wrought in us by the Spirit."

20. Crisp, *Christ Alone*, p. 195; cf. Winthrop, *Short Story*, error no. 68; Bakewell, *Antinomians' Christ*, pp. 5, 10–11.

21. Crisp, *Christ Alone*, pp. 39–40. Cf. Cotton's tendency to derive sanctification from conscious faith; see "The Visibility of Saints" in Chapter 3, above.

22. Crisp, *Christ Alone*, pp. 45–47, 65, 137, 204. In this connection, Crisp also employed the analogy of the soul animating the body (pp. 146–47). Bakewell noted of Eatonian-Crispian antinomians that "they say Christ lives in them and acts and moves them as we move a stone; and they are still as an empty trunk for his spirit to move in, so that nothing is required of them but only to let the Spirit of God do his own work in them and by them, and they remain still but dead stones" (*Short View*, p. 21); cf. Winthrop, *Short Story*, error no. 14: "That Christ works in the regenerate, as in those that are dead, and not as in those that are alive ..."; see also nos. 15, 18.

23. Crisp, *Christ Alone*, p. 14; cf. Bakewell, *Antinomians' Christ*, pp. 7–9; cf. Winthrop, *Short Story*, error no. 36: "All the activity of a believer is to act to sin."

24. Crisp, *Christ Alone*, pp. 7–9, 26–29, 32–33, 337. On this point, Crisp agreed essentially with Eaton: God takes no cognizance of the sins of the justified; see ibid., pp. 325–32, and Robert Lancaster, "To the Reader," in ibid., sig. A3^{vo}.

25. Crisp, *Christ Alone*, pp. 8–12, 15, 99, 101–2, 128–29; cf. Winthrop,

Short Story, "unsavory speeches" nos. 7, 9; error no. 44: "No created work can be a manifest sign of God's love."

26. Crisp, *Christ Alone,* pp. 293–95 (cf. 90, 308). Crisp and Eaton both tended to deny any discernible difference in the graces of hypocrites and believers; cf. Cotton's difficulties with this point ("The Visibility of Saints" in Chapter 3, above), and Winthrop, *Short Story,* errors no. 16, 18, 73, 76. Crisp treated "zeal" in the context of the ground and causes of salvation—whether legal obedience or Christ's righteousness—rather than in the context of the ground of assurance or the evidence of justification. His treatment proceeds, however, as if the issue were *assurance,* without distinction between the causal and the evidential relationship of works to justification. Recourse to duties evidently implied for Crisp reliance on reward, and so seemed absolutely contrary to free grace (*Christ Alone,* pp. 293–299 [cf. 142–43, 301–2]).

27. Crisp, *Christ Alone,* pp. 210, 212–14 (cf. Lancaster, "To the Reader," in ibid., sig. A4^{ro}, A7^{ro-vo}; Bakewell, *Short View,* pp. 18, 22, 27–29; cf. Winthrop, *Short Story,* error no. 23: "We must not pray for gifts or graces, but only for Christ"; no. 45: "Nothing but Christ is an evidence of my good estate"; cf. also "unsavory speeches" nos. 2, 5.

28. Von Rohr, "Covenant and Assurance," pp. 195–203. See, e.g., Sibbes, *The Demand of a Good Conscience,* in *Works,* 7. 485; Preston, *Breastplate,* Pt. 2, pp. 21–22; Ball, *Treatise of Faith,* p. 96; Downe, *Treatise of Justifying Faith,* p. 69; cf. Calvin, *Institutes,* 3.2.23, 27; see " 'Justifying Faith' and 'Faith of Assurance' " in Chapter 7, above.

29. McGiffert, *God's Plot,* pp. 11–12, 14–15.

30. Shepard, "Journal," in ibid., pp. 83–84, 85 (cf. 91, 123, 211–13).

31. Shepard, "Autobiography," in ibid., pp. 45–46.

32. E.g., Shepard, "Journal," in ibid., pp. 85, 212–14. In his introduction to Shepard's "Autobiography" and "Journal," Michael McGiffert noted the repetition of the conversion pattern (*God's Plot,* pp. 25–26), but seemed to overlook the distinction between anxiety before and after conversion; and his suggestion that, throughout his life, Shepard "suffered the anticipatory torments of the damned" is seriously exaggerated. The *Angst* of the "Journal" seems qualitatively of a different sort than that of the undergraduate who, as "the terrors of God" break into his soul "like floods of fire," acquiesces in his apparent damnation and contemplates smashing his head against a wall in order to get on with it ("Autobiography," p. 43). In the "Journal," Shepard remains aware of the great gulf separating him, as the object of grace, from the holy and gracious God, but he does not, strictly speaking, *despair* in either an existential or a Christian sense, and he seems to regard his youthful flirtation with the "unpardonable sin" as quite past. McGiffert likened Shepard's recurrent anxiety about his estate to the "desperate seriousness," of which Paul Tillich spoke, of the person who encounters "the divine in the experience of utter separation from it" (qtd. in *God's Plot,* p. 21). Yet Shepard in the "Journal" is never "utterly" separated from God, in the same way that Shepard on the eve of conversion felt himself to be; and a more appropriate Tillichian analogue would seem to be the "doubt of faith"; see, e.g., Tillich, *Dynamics of*

Faith (New York: Harper and Row, 1958), pp. 20–22; cf. John Preston, *Breast-plate,* Pt. 2, pp. 22–34. Neither does it seem correct to say, as McGiffert did, that Shepard, as a principle of pastoral advice, "making despair do the office of delight, . . . grounded assurance on anxiety itself" to the point where he might have said to Goodman Brown, who committed suicide in terror over his estate, "The deeper the doubt, the higher the hope!" (p. 20). Shepard would hardly have maintained that the most desperate and clinically distraught souls —like the woman who put her child down a well in order to insure her own damnation and so be certain of something (Winthrop, *Journal,* 1. 230)—were therefore most surely among the elect. Reformed divines commonly distinguished between the anxiety and despair of the reprobate and the doubt of the faithful when experiencing God's momentary withdrawal. Saints may well be "anxious," but that is a different matter from "despair," which, strictly defined, implies probable reprobation; see Ames, *Marrow,* 1.16, 2.6.9–30.

33. The doctrine of divine sovereignty was not always stated so flatly by Reformed divines, and it always entailed logical difficulties, especially in the matter of theodicy. Once accepted within the circumference of personal piety, however, its power for practical theodicy could be considerable; see Peter Berger, *The Sacred Canopy: Elements of a Sociological Theory of Religion* (Garden City, N.Y.: Doubleday and Co., 1969), ch. 3.

34. See, e.g., Sibbes, *Soul's Conflict,* pp. 137, 184, 266, and *Life of Faith,* p. 403; Ames, *Marrow,* 2.6.30; Hooker, *Covenant of Grace Opened,* pp. 19–20, and *Application of Redemption,* pp. 309–10, 320–21, 605–8; cf. Hooker, *Unbeliever's Preparing,* pp. 23, 25, and (2d ser.) 38–40.

35. See, e.g., Hooker, *Soul's Vocation,* pp. 49–50, and *Application of Redemption,* pp. 283–86, 291–99; Preston, *Life Eternal,* Pt. 2, pp. 85–87; Shepard, *Believer,* p. 195, *Parable,* pp. 424–25, and *Cases Resolved,* p. 309.

36. Ball, *Treatise of Faith,* p. 82; Sibbes, *Soul's Conflict,* p. 264.

37. Bulkeley, *Gospel Covenant,* p. 315; Shepard, *Believer,* pp. 197–98 (cf. 215–16), and *Parable,* pp. 127, 140.

38. Ball, *Treatise of Faith,* pp. 36–40, 84–87, 90–91; Sibbes, *The Art of Contentment,* in *Works,* 5. 186–89; Preston, *Breastplate,* Pt. 2, pp. 21–22; Perkins, *Golden Chain,* in *Works* (1626), 1. 204, and *Exposition upon Galatians,* pp. 208–9; cf. Ames, *Marrow,* 1.29.29.

39. See, e.g., Hooker, *Application of Redemption,* pp. 376–79; Perkins, *Golden Chain,* in *Works* (1612), 1. 79–80; see also Rogers, *Doctrine of Faith,* pp. 65, 126, 174–75, 189–91; Forbes, *Doctrine of Justification,* pp. 37–39 (see also 1–2, 26); Sibbes, *Soul's Conflict,* pp. 137–38; cf. Winthrop, *Short Story,* error no. 60: "A man may not prove his election by his vocation, but his vocation by his election."

40. See, e.g., Ball, *Treatise of Faith,* pp. 86–87; Bulkeley, *Gospel Covenant,* pp. 358–59.

41. See, e.g., Perkins, *Golden Chain,* p. 104; Ames, *Marrow,* 1.29.29–37.

42. John Forbes, *A Letter Resolving the Question: How a Christian May Discern the Testimony of God's Spirit* (Middelburg, 1616), pp. 84–85, 91–92; Ball, *Treatise of Faith,* pp. 99–100; cf. Sibbes, *Soul's Conflict,* pp. 124–25.

43. Sibbes, *Bruised Reed,* pp. 85, 96–97, and *Good Conscience,* p. 485.

44. Ball, *Treatise of Faith*, pp. 34–35, 39–40, 84–85, 96–98, 183–84; Winthrop, *Short Story*, pp. 230–31; see above, n. 28.

45. Hooker, *Soul's Ingrafting*, pp. 16–20; Burton, *Law and Gospel*, pp. 8–9; cf. Johnson, *Wonder-working Providence*, pp. 94–95, 101–3.

46. Shepard, as a student, during his first "awakening," felt a similar pressure ("Autobiography," pp. 42–43); and an "error" condemned by the Newtown synod asserted that true assurance excludes all doubt (Winthrop, *Short Story*, error no. 42).

47. See Burton, *Law and Gospel*, passim; Bakewell, *Short View*, sig. A1^{vo}, and *Antinomians' Christ*, "To the Reader" and pp. 18–22.

48. See, e.g., Norris, *New Gospel*, pp. 13–17, 30, 34; Burton, *Law and Gospel*, pp. 22, 68; cf. Winthrop, *Short Story*, errors no. 4, 5, 33, 55, 56, 60; see also Bulkeley, *Gospel Covenant*, pp. 289, 292.

49. Bakewell, *Antinomians' Christ*, p. 14; Crisp, *Christ Alone*, pp. 8–9, 32–33, 99–102, 315–18, 333–42; Eaton, *Honeycomb*, pp. 47–48, 121–26; Norris, *New Gospel*, pp. 29–34, 40–42; Bakewell, *Short View*, pp. 31–32 cf. Winthrop, *Short Story*, errors no. 20, 32, 34, 64, 75, "unsavory speech" no. 3. The imperfection of faith as a human act was one ground, also, of objection to the act of faith as the instrument of apprehending and accepting Christ; see Bakewell, *Short View*, pp. 6–8.

50. See "The Seal of the Spirit" in Chapter 7, above; Bakewell, *Short View*, sig. A1^{vo}, pp. 10–11; Bulkeley, *Gospel Covenant*, p. 292; cf. Winthrop, *Short Story*, errors no. 40, 71, and 47: "The seal of the Spirit is limited only to the immediate witness of the Spirit, and doth never witness to any work of grace, or to any conclusion by a syllogism."

51. Eaton and Crisp tended to avoid the language of *fiducia* altogether and to speak of faith primarily as persuasion regarding one's estate. Cf. Downe, *Treatise of Justifying Faith*, pp. 126–28; Winthrop, *Short Story*, error no. 42.

52. See, e.g., Burton, *Law and Gospel*, sig. A1^{ro}–a2^{vo}; Norris, *New Gospel*, pp. 17–18; Hooker, *Soul's Ingrafting*, pp. 16–18; Downe, *Treatise of Justifying Faith*, pp. 2–3; Preston, *New Covenant*, pp. 400–403; Shepard, *Believer*, pp. 229–31, and *Parable*, pp. 311–12, 322–23. Shepard addressed the Eatonian-Crispian tendencies outlined above, in the context of the problem of assurance and of the evidential significance of sanctification, in *Theses Sabbaticae*, 1.116–19; cf. Shepard, *Believer*, pp. 210–16.

53. Burton, *Law and Gospel*, p. 17.

CHAPTER NINE

1. See A. H. Newman, "Antinomianism," *New Schaff-Herzog Encyclopedia of Religious Knowledge* (New York: Funk and Wagnalls, 1908), 1. 196–200.

2. This view is classically associated with Luther's pupil, Johann Agricola of Eisleben (1499–1566) (G. Kawerau, "Antinomistische Streitigkeiten," *Realenzyclopädie für protestantische Theologie und Kirche* [3d ed.; Leipzig: J. C. Hinrichs, 1896], 1. 585–90).

3. In the sixteenth century, the more extreme form of this view was

classically represented by the Netherlandish Libertines and appeared most spectacularly at Münster; see Williams, *Radical Reformation*, pp. 351–55 and ch. 13. The more moderate version was typified by the Lutheran antinomians Andreas Poach (1516–85) and Anton Otho (ca. 1505–?) (Kawerau, *Realenzyclopädie*, 1. 590–91).

4. See, e.g., Gardiner, *Reports of Cases*, pp. 310–11; John Strype, *Annals of the Reformation and Estate of Religion . . . During Queen Elizabeth's Reign* (Oxford: Clarendon Press, 1824), 2.2, pp. 189–91; Winthrop, *Journal*, 1. 282–83.

5. Qtd. of Henrik Niclaes, in Burrage, *Early English Dissenters*, 1. 213; Claus-Peter Clasen, "Medieval Heresies in the Reformation," *Church History*, 32 (1963), 394; Gardiner, *Reports of Cases*, pp. 189–90; see Thomas Wilcox, *The Unfolding of Sundry Untruths* (London, 1581), pp. 156–57; cf. Winthrop, *Journal*, 2. 41.

6. See, e.g., Winthrop, *Short Story*, pp. 207–8, 275–76; see also "Examination of Mrs. Hutchinson," in Hall, *Antinomian Controversy*, p. 343; "Report of the Trial," in ibid., pp. 362–63; Palfrey, *History of New England*, 1. 487, n. 2. However, in December 1640, "one Hugh Bewett was banished for holding publicly and maintaining that he was free from original sin and from actual also for half a year before, and that all true Christians after (blank) are enabled to live without committing actual sin" (Winthrop, *Journal*, 2. 17).

7. "Examination of Mrs. Hutchinson," pp. 312, 316, 342–43; "Report of the Trial," pp. 387–88; Winthrop, *Journal*, 1. 263–64. See Winthrop, *Short Story*, pp. 212, 259.

8. See Morgan, *Puritan Dilemma*, ch. 10.

9. Winthrop, *Short Story*, pp. 201–2.

10. Some of them can be found in scattered references as early as the second decade of Elizabeth, and in some cases earlier; see Wilcox, *Sundry Untruths;* William Wilkinson, *A Confutation of Certain Articles of the Family of Love* (London, 1579); David Wilkins, *Concilia Magnae Brittaniae* (London, 1737), 3. 729–30, 4. 39–40.

11. "Familists" were considered to be disciples of Niclaes. They were regarded as holding that the Persons of the Trinity are united to the regenerate; that the godly cannot sin and that praying for forgiveness is useless; that the Spirit, not the letter of the Bible, is the word of God; and that Adam's perfection before the fall can be attained in this life; and they were regarded as denying the immortality of the soul and the resurrection of the body. See Wilkinson, *Confutation*, sig. Aiii^{vo}–Aiiii^{ro} and ch. 28.4, *Ev. Regni;* Strype, *Annals*, 2.1, pp. 487, 559, 2.2, pp. 88, 284–87; Gardiner, *Reports of Cases*, pp. 188–89, 192–93; Stephen Denison, *The White Wolf* (London, 1627), p. 39. "Antinomians" were held to maintain that the consciences of believers are not bound by the law and that God sees no sin in Christians; that assurance, once obtained, is not to be doubted of; that justification is before faith and faith is the discovery of justification; and that sanctification is no evidence of justification. See Gardiner, *Reports of Cases*, pp. 181–83, 270–71, 316–18; cf. Strype, *Annals*, 3.1, pp. 63–65.

12. Eaton voiced the familiar objection to "Hog" preachers who preach

for their bellies' sake, are ignorant and immoral, and are indifferent to doctrine; to which he added his own characteristic objection to "Dog" preachers who mingle law and gospel, works and grace, marring both, and preach only the "zealous dead faith." Both sorts are equally inimical to the true interests of the children of God. See Burton, *Law and Gospel,* pp. 8–10; Morgan, *Visible Saints,* ch. 1.

13. There seems to be no serious reason to question the view of William Haller and others that the English sects of the 1640s, in organization, ecclesiology, and world-transforming impetus, were essentially free from Continental sectarian influence, being generated, rather, by impulses within the Puritan movement itself; see Haller, *Rise of Puritanism,* pp. 174–81, and Little, *Religion, Order, and Law,* pp. 253–54. Such influence does not seem entirely absent, however, from certain theological tendencies and related forms of piety. Formally, much of Tobias Crisp can be derived from Perkins and Ames, if certain elements in the latters' theology are highlighted and others are suppressed; and Burton refers to Eaton and his ilk as "homebred brats"—bred, that is, within the Church of England, in contrast to Continental imports (*Law and Gospel,* sig. B1^{vo}–B2^{ro}). Eaton and Crisp seem in fact, however, not to have been hatched exclusively out of English university theology, but to have emerged in a religious climate containing radical notions, often in curious combination, that seem essentially foreign to the university tradition of the Puritan "spiritual brotherhood." Some of these notions may be traced in the English sectarian underground during the reigns of Elizabeth and James and in the writings of Continental sectaries, including Niclaes. The Channel did not hinder Reformed theology professors en route to English universities, nor does it seem to have impeded Lowlanders fleeing persecution; and while the distinctive forms of Netherlandish Anabaptism do not appear to have taken root in the soil of English popular religion, the same cannot be said with certainty for other notions of Continental sectaries (see Williams, *Radical Reformation,* pp. 778–90). The issues that Shepard and Thomas Gataker raised with John Saltmarsh in the late 1640s and early 1650s, to name one instance, are continuous in certain respects with the issues Bakewell raised with Crisp and Lancaster in the early 1640s, with those Norris raised with Traske, and Burton with the Eatonians, in the 1630s, and to a degree with those Thomas Wilcox raised with the "libertine" "J. B." and those John Rogers raised with his "familist" in the late 1570s and early 1580s. See Shepard, *Theses Sabbaticae,* 1.114–17 (cf. 82–83); Thomas Gataker, *Antinomianism Discovered and Confuted* (London, 1652); Wilcox, *Sundry Untruths;* J[ohn] R[ogers], *The Displaying of an Horrible Sect* (London, 1578). It would be false to derive Saltmarsh from Niclaes in a direct, genetic sense, or to suggest that he was not, in a real sense, a child of the spiritual brotherhood; yet it would also be incorrect to overlook an echo of original familism that, much attenuated, seems still audible in 1650.

14. Samuel Torshell, *The Three Questions of Free Justification, Christian Liberty, the Use of the Law* (London, 1632).

15. "Report of the Trial," pp. 352, 374–75.

16. See Winthrop, *Journal*, 1. 259; Burton, *Law and Gospel,* passim; Shepard, *Parable,* pp. 133–34, 503, *Believer,* pp. 160–61, 212–14, and *Theses Sabbaticae,* 1.93–104; Bulkeley, *Gospel Covenant,* sig. A5^{ro} and pp. 161–62; Winthrop, *Short Story,* pp. 219–47.

17. Anne Hutchinson's claim to personal revelations places her in the company of Christian prophets, not infrequently female, who appear throughout Christian history, professing peculiar intimacy with the Holy Spirit, and places her also in the more localized company of English sectarian prophetesses and female preachers of the first half of the seventeenth century. See "Report of the Trial," p. 380; Thomas Edwards, *Gangraena: or a Catalogue and Discovery of Many of the Errors of the Sectaries* (London, 1646), 1. 84; cf. Shepard, *Parable,* p. 500; see also Nuttall, *Holy Spirit,* pp. 75–76, 88.

Hutchinson's views on the mortality of the soul and on the resurrection are also noteworthy, as placing her in a larger sectarian tradition. She apparently held that the soul naturally dies like an animal's but is made immortal by Christ's redemption, which occurs at his coming to the soul in union; and she denied that Christ is united to fleshly bodies, so that the body that dies cannot be the one that rises, which is rather a new, spiritual body received in conversion. She affirmed that the blessed shall "rise in Christ Jesus" in the sense of Rom. 6:1–7; and she construed 1 Thess. 5:23 as referring to Christ's coming into union with the soul, rather than to his coming at the last judgment. The elders concluded that she held "no other resurrection but . . . union to Christ," i.e., the experience of conversion instead of the resurrection at the last day; see "Report of the Trial," pp. 354–64. These motifs appear occasionally in reports of English sectarianism in the late sixteenth and early seventeenth centuries. In 1611 the bishop of Coventry and Litchfield tried a man who maintained "that the soul doth sleep in the sleep of the first death as well as the body, and is mortal touching the sleep of the first death as the body is" (Burrage, *Early English Dissenters,* 1. 218–219). John Traske maintained that Christ is not united to the fleshly body in regeneration but instead dwells in it as a separate spiritual entity; and he defined "Christian liberty" as the freedom, which all believers enjoy, of having been buried and raised again with Christ (Norris, *New Gospel,* pp. 26–27; Traske, *Treatise of Liberty,* p. 35). Niclaes's disciples were reported to hold that "the resurrection of the body is a rising from sin and wickedness" and that the resurrection spoken of by Paul in 1 Cor. 15 "is fulfilled in them, and they deny all other resurrection of the body to be after this life" (Pagitt, *Heresiography,* pp. 76, 78). Niclaes spoke of his conversion in terms of resurrection and divinization, as did his friend David Joris and also Menno Simons; see N[iclaes], *Evangelium Regni,* ch. 24.6–7; 25.1–7; 33–35, and *Introductio,* ch. 12; see also Williams, *Radical Reformation,* pp. 383, 392. The notion that the soul dies with the body or sleeps until the resurrection was widespread on the Continent during the Reformation era (ibid., pp. 20–24, 104–6, 580–92.

18. "Examination of Mrs. Hutchinson," pp. 317–25, 333–35; cf. "Report of the Trial," p. 353. Eaton regarded Christ as having been under the law until his death (*Honeycomb,* p. 84).

19. "Examination of Mrs. Hutchinson," pp. 325–26. Her response to questioning confirmed Thomas Dudley's suspicion that she held that "the gospel in the letter and words holds forth nothing but a covenant of works" (ibid., pp. 318–19, 324–25); cf. Winthrop, *Short Story*, error no. 9; Bulkeley, *Gospel Covenant*, sig. A4^{vo}.

20. Strype, *Annals*, 2.2, p. 289; cf. Winthrop, *Short Story*, error no. 61; see N[iclaes], *Evangelium Regni*, 4.5–6, 23.5–7, 33.8–10, and *Introductio*, 1.27, 4.29, 9.35; Eaton, *Honeycomb*, sig. A3^{vo}, pp. 215–16, 228–29 (cf. 167). See e.g., ibid., pp. 44–45, 80–81, 211–17, 224–29; Burton, *Law and Gospel*, p. 26; Norris, *New Gospel*, pp. 10, 18; Traske, *Treatise of Liberty*, p. 10; Torshell, *Three Questions*, p. 270; Wilkinson, *Confutation*, sig. Biii^{vo}; N[iclaes], *Evangelium Regni*, 8.1–13, 12.1–2, 10–11; cf. Winthrop, *Short Story*, error no. 40.

21. Eaton, *Honeycomb*, pp. 234–35; cf. Vane's remark about the children of the "bondwoman" and the "free woman" (Chapter 2, above).

22. "Examination of Mrs. Hutchinson," pp. 336–37; cf. Winthrop, *Short Story*, p. 272.

23. See, e.g., Burton, *Law and Gospel*, pp. 20–22, 63, 68; Norris, *New Gospel*, pp. 12–18; Bakewell, *Short View*, pp. 14–17, and *Antinomians' Christ*, pp. 11–12; Wilcox, *Sundry Untruths*, pp. 4, 87; Eaton, *Honeycomb*, pp. 84–85, 98–100, 102–6, 112, 427. Niclaes, similarly, wrote of a series of three "services," culminating in the "service of love," of which he was prophet and incarnation and which subsumed the earlier "services." The "service of love" he associated with life, the Spirit, inwardness, and incarnate truth, and the previous services with law, ceremonies, outward letters, and mediation; see *Evangelium Regni*, 8.12; 24.10–13; 37; and *Introductio*, 1.33, 2.2–9, 9.35, 12.2.

24. See "Shepard-Cotton Letters," in Hall, *Antinomian Controversy*, pp. 28–29; "Report of the Trial," p. 380; Winthrop, *Journal*, 1. 219.

25. Cotton Mather reported that his studious grandfather nightly "loved to sweeten his mouth with a piece of Calvin before retiring" (*Magnalia* 1. 250).

26. See, e.g., Ziff, *Career of Cotton*, ch. 4; Miller, *From Colony to Province*, pp. 58, 65, and " 'Preparation for Salvation,' " p. 268; Hall, *Antinomian Controversy*, pp. 12–20; Pettit, *Heart Prepared*, pp. 132–33, 140–41, 150; Darrett B. Rutman, *Winthrop's Boston: Portrait of a Puritan Town, 1630–1649* (Chapel Hill: University of North Carolina Press, 1965), pp. 116–20; but cf. Hall, *Faithful Shepherd*, pp. 161–63.

27. Hall, *Antinomian Controversy*, p. 16; see Battis, *Saints and Sectaries*, p. 255; Edwards, *Gangraena*, 1. 84.

28. Larzer Ziff implied that Cotton was afflicted with the intellectual's proverbial want of perception of the concrete world around him and so was slow to notice what was happening in his congregation, which is not implausible; at the same time, Vane and others of the Boston church seem to have recognized Cotton as a truly kindred spirit; see *Career of Cotton*, pp. 115, 126–27, 133–34, and *Cotton on the Churches*, p. 23.

29. When, in the excitement of the Civil War, sectarianism and heresy flourished in old England, the "antinomianism" and "familism" of New England was recalled as an early instance of the same phenomenon and as part of

a tradition lately come to full flower; see Pagitt, *Heresiography*, sig. A2^{ro-vo}, pp. 89, 101; Baillie, *Dissuasive*, pp. 61–63.

30. John Cotton to Samuel Stone, March 27, [1638], Cotton Papers, Pt. 2, No. 12.

31. Cotton, *Christ the Fountain*, pp. 88–89, 92–93, 121–25; "Cotton's Rejoynder," in Hall, *Antinomian Controversy*, p. 151.

32. "Report of the Trial," p. 352; Winthrop, *Short Story*, errors no. 44, 45; see also Peter Bulkeley to John Cotton, [1637], Cotton Papers, Pt. 2, No. 7; Wheelwright, "Fast-Day Sermon," in *Writings*, pp. 162–64; see "Bulkeley and Cotton on Union," in Hall, *Antinomian Controversy*, pp. 40–41.

33. Winthrop, *Short Story*, errors no. 18, 19; "Report of the Trial," p. 352; see "Cotton's Rejoynder," pp. 85, 87.

34. Bulkeley, *Gospel Covenant*, p. 321 (my italics).

35. See, e.g., Norton, *Orthodox Evangelist*, pp. 219–23; Shepard, *Believer*, p. 252, and *Parable*, pp. 268–72; see also Ames, *Marrow*, 1.8.5–6.

36. Norris, *New Gospel*, pp. 18, 25–27, 36–37; Bakewell, *Antinomians' Christ*, pp. 3–4.

37. Shepard, *Parable*, p. 203 (see pp. 204–6, 462); see also Hooker, *Application of Redemption*, pp. 51–52, 388–89; Culverwell, *Treatise of Faith*, pp. 53–54.

38. The same opposition between nature and grace underlay a number of the "errors" condemned by the synod; see Winthrop, *Short Story*, errors no. 7, 12, 15, 19, 25, 55 (cf. 16, 77); "Shepard-Cotton Letters," pp. 27–29, 32; "Report of the Trial," p. 352; cf. Shepard, *Believer*, p. 185, and *Theses Sabbaticae*, 1.83–88, 90.

39. Morgan, *Puritan Dilemma*, pp. 136–38; cf. Ziff, *Career of Cotton*, pp. 107–15; Miller, *From Colony to Province*, pp. 59–60; " 'Preparation for Salvation,' " pp. 260, 264, 267–68, 277–78; see Pettit, *Heart Prepared*, pp. 19–20.

40. Jonathan Edwards, *Treatise Concerning Religious Affections*, in S. Austin, ed., *The Works of President Edwards* (8th ed.; New York: Leavitt and Allen, 1856), 3. 182–83, 202–3; see Bulkeley, *Gospel Covenant*, pp. 153–55, 235–36, 376–78; Shepard, *Parable*, pp. 335–36, and *Believer*, pp. 280–82.

41. See Miller, "Marrow," pp. 283–84.

42. See, e.g., "Cotton's Rejoynder," pp. 117, 121, 129–30, 133, 145, 147.

43. Gardiner, *Reports of Cases*, pp. 184–85, 316–20; Eaton, *Honeycomb*, sig. b2^{ro}, pp. 44–45, 115, 426–27; Burton, *Law and Gospel*, pp. 6, 7; Crisp, *Christ Alone*, pp. 210–14, 301; Lancaster, "To the Reader," in ibid., sig. a2^{ro}, cf. A2^{vo}.

44. Shepard, *Parable*, pp. 27, 203–4, 181–82, and *Believer*, p. 185; cf. Sibbes, *Excellency of the Gospel*, p. 282, *Life of Faith*, p. 395, and *Good Conscience*, pp. 484–85. The seriousness with which the elders held their view of evidence from sanctification, and of the difficulty of obtaining it, is suggested by their refusal in April 1636 to permit the founding of a new church at Dorchester on account of insufficient evidence of "the work of God's grace" in the prospective members (Winthrop, *Journal*, 1. 177–78).

45. Shepard, *Believer*, pp. 197–98, 214–16, 306–15, and *Parable*, pp. 81–82; cf. Bulkeley, *Gospel Covenant*, pp. 48, 306–7; cf. Ball, *Treatise of Faith*, p. 93.

46. Winthrop, *Journal*, 1. 275–76. Underhill defended his remark the next day, which suggests that he was serious. His defense, as related by Winthrop, is in the tradition of John Eaton.

47. Shepard, *Theses Sabbaticae*, 1.3, 4.

48. Ibid., 1.97. Ziff's reading of this remark as expressing the "legalist" position in the controversy seems to miss the point (*Career of Cotton*, p. 112, n. 9).

49. See Shepard, *Theses Sabbaticae*, 1.99.

50. See "Report of the Trial," pp. 351–52; Johnson, *Wonder-working Providence*, pp. 94–95; Burton, *Law and Gospel*, pp. 3, 20; Lancaster, "To the Reader," in Crisp, *Christ Alone*, sig. A6ᵣᵒ; cf. Traske, *Treatise of Liberty*, pp. 2–9; Shepard, *Parable*, pp. 205–6, and *Believer*, pp. 275–84.

51. Shepard, *Parable*, pp. 191–92, 462 (cf. 78–79, 250–51); cf. Norton, *Orthodox Evangelist*, pp. 79–80.

52. See "Easing the Way to Heaven" in Chapter 1, above; Burton, *Law and Gospel*, p. 35[1]; Bakewell, *Short View*, p. 11, and *Antinomians' Christ*, p. 14; Crisp, *Christ Alone*, pp. 106–8; Norris, *New Gospel*, pp. 34–35; Shepard, *Parable*, p. 400.

53. Johnson, *Wonder-working Providence*, pp. 94–95, 101–3; see Shepard, *Believer*, p. 211.

54. Norris, *New Gospel*, pp. 29–35; cf. Crisp, *Christ Alone*, pp. 106–8; Bakewell, *Antinomians' Christ*, p. 14; cf. Hooker, *Soul's Exaltation*, pp. 181, 190–91.

55. Sibbes, preface to Ball, *Treatise of Faith*, sig. q2ᵛᵒ–q3ᵣᵒ.

56. Allison, *Rise of Moralism*, p. 100.

EPILOGUE

1. See the Savoy Declaration, Confession of Faith, ch. 8, in Williston Walker, *Creeds and Platforms of Congregationalism* (1893; rpt., Boston: Pilgrim Press, 1960); George Gillespie, *The Ark of the Covenant Opened* (London, 1677); Samuel Willard, *Covenant-keeping the Way to Blessedness* (Boston, 1682), and *The Doctrine of the Covenant of Redemption* (Boston, 1693); see also Leigh, *System of Divinity*, p. 513; Richard C. Greaves, "John Bunyan and Covenant Thought in the Seventeenth Century," *Church History*, 24 (June 1965), 151–69. Neither the formulation nor the problem, however, were new to the generation spanning Protectorate and Restoration. See Ames, *Marrow*, 1.19.3–5; Hooker, *Soul's Exaltation*, p. 170; Preston, *New Covenant*, p. 330; Bulkeley, *Gospel Covenant*, pp. 26–43; Norton, *Orthodox Evangelist*, pp. 40–41; see also Bryan Armstrong, *Calvin and the Amyraut Heresy: Protestant Scholasticism and Humanism in Seventeenth Century France* (Madison: University of Wisconsin Press, 1969), p. 141, n. 72; Heppe, *Dogmatik*, pp. 296–97, 305–6.

Cf. Cotton's suggestion that the covenant of grace is made with Christ, rather than with individuals (*New Covenant*, p. 86; "Cotton's Rejoynder," p. 86; "Sermon at Salem," in Ziff, *Cotton on the Churches*, p. 53; cf. *Winthrop Papers*, 3. 324–26, prop. 12; Winthrop, *Journal*, 1. 233–34, pt. 5.

2. See Ernest B. Lowrie, *The Shape of the Puritan Mind: The Thought of Samuel Willard* (New Haven: Yale University Press, 1974), chs. 5, 6, 9, 10.

3. See "The Jefferson Bible," in Andrew A. Lipscomb and Albert E. Bergh, eds., *The Writings of Thomas Jefferson* (Washington, D.C.: Thomas Jefferson Memorial Association, 1903), vol. 20; Daniel J. Boorstin, *The Lost World of Thomas Jefferson* (1948; rpt., Boston: Beacon Press, 1960), pp. 156–60.

4. See John E. Smith, ed., *Jonathan Edwards: Religious Affections,* vol. 2 of Perry Miller, ed., *The Works of Jonathan Edwards* (New Haven: Yale University Press, 1959), pp. 7–8, 17, 25–27; Frank Hugh Foster, *A Genetic History of the New England Theology* (1907; rpt. New York: Russell and Russell, 1963), pp. 167–74, 178–80, 182–84; Charles G. Finney, *Lectures on Revivals of Religion,* ed. William G. McLoughlin (Cambridge, Mass.: Harvard University Press, 1960), lects. 1, 3, and *Lectures on Systematic Theology,* ed. J. H. Fairchild (1878; rpt. Grand Rapids: William B. Eerdmans, n.d.), lect. 27.

APPENDIX

1. Miller, " 'Preparation for Salvation,' " pp. 253–86, and *From Colony to Province,* ch. 4.

2. Miller, *From Colony to Province,* p. 157, and " 'Preparation for Salvation,' " p. 266.

3. See Perkins, *Exposition upon Galatians,* 2. 213, 248–50; Ames, *Marrow,* 1.26.12. Cf. Pemble, *Vindicia Gratiae,* pp. 81–83; Sibbes, *Lydia's Conversion,* in *Works,* 6. 522–23, and *Bruised Reed,* 1. 44–45; Preston, *New Covenant,* pp. 394–95, 407–10; *Breastplate,* Pt. 2, pp. 49–52; Ames, *Conscience,* 2.4; Perkins, *Golden Chain,* in *Works* (1626), 1. 69–70, 78–79, 84–85; Hooker's position was established before he left England; see *Unbeliever's Preparing.* See also Norman Pettit's discussion of English "preparationists" (*Heart Prepared,* ch. 3).

4. See Rogers, *Doctrine of Faith,* pp. 126–41, 369–70; Hooker, *Application of Redemption,* pp. 100–102, 111–14, 372–79, and *Unbeliever's Preparing,* pp. 103–19; Shepard, *Parable,* pp. 266, 473–74.

5. Cotton, *New Covenant,* pp. 19–21, 24, 52–54; cf. Cotton, "Sermon at Salem," pp. 49, 51, 60–61; Norton, *Orthodox Evangelist,* chs. 6–8; Shepard, *Believer,* pp. 117–19, 130–57, 175–82, and *Parable,* pp. 137–40, 201.

6. "Cotton's Rejoynder," pp. 87–91; cf. Cotton, *Way of Life,* p. 405.

7. Norton, *Orthodox Evangelist,* chs. 4–5 and pp. 82–85, 166; Hooker, *Application of Redemption,* pp. 301–4; cf. Shepard, *Parable,* 1.9.3; Perkins, *Exposition of the Symbol,* in *Works* (1612), 1. 294–95.

8. On the first sense of "preparation," see Hooker's extended treatment in *Application of Redemption.* On the second, see Leigh, *System of Divinity,* p. 490; Ames, *Conscience,* 2.4; *Marrow,* 1.30; cf. Downe, *Treatise of Justifying*

Faith, pp. 69, 72; see also Preston, *Breastplate,* Pt. 2, p. 172; cf. Calvin, *Institutes,* 3.3.14. Technically, if the exhortation to "prepare" is addressed to the unconverted, the context is the "ministry of the law" in its "second use," which God by grace renders effectual; yet the grace in question is "common" rather than "saving," in that others than the elect may be thus wrought upon. If the exhortation is addressed to the converted, the context is the perfection in action of grace already infused, in particular of sanctifying grace, which is qualitatively different from "common" grace in that it presupposes conversion.

9. Where the figure of the "heart prepared" appears, it usually refers to regenerate souls preparing to meet their heavenly Lord; see Shepard, *Parable,* pp. 26–29, 70–74, 77–78, 86–87, 345 (see also pp. 68–70, 95–98, 112, 225–29, 430–31, 437–39, and 2.19).

10. Ibid., pp. 203–8, 219–26, 275–81, 401–2, 503.

11. See Miller, *From Colony to Province,* p. 57; see also Winthrop, *Short Story,* pp. 203–4; cf. Leigh, *System of Divinity,* p. 539.

12. See *Heart Prepared,* ch. 5 and esp. pp. 129–30, 137–38.

13. See Cotton, *Sixteen Questions,* in Hall, *Antinomian Controversy,* pp. 46–47.

14. See *Heart Prepared,* pp. 137, 145–46 (cf. 150).

Bibliographical Note

The literature treating Anglo-American Puritanism is voluminous, and growing daily. For the New England tradition, Perry Miller's *The New England Mind*, vol. 1, *The Seventeenth Century* (Cambridge: Harvard University Press, 1939), and vol. 2, *From Colony to Province* (Cambridge: Harvard University Press, 1953), remains fundamental, and not only because much of subsequent scholarship has followed Miller's lead or has commenced by reevaluating his work. Alan Simpson's *Puritanism in Old and New England* (Chicago: University of Chicago Press, 1955) is a brief introduction to the Puritan movement as a whole. Edmund S. Morgan, in a long list of books and articles, examines multiple facets of Puritan history, with sensitivity to the broader Puritan ethos. Elaborate primary and secondary bibliography is contained in Perry Miller and Thomas H. Johnson, eds., *The Puritans: A Sourcebook of Their Writings* (1938; rev. ed., New York: Harper and Row, 1963), 1. xxix–lix; 2. 777–818. More recent scholarship is reviewed in Michael McGiffert, "American Puritan Studies in the 1960s," *William and Mary Quarterly*, 27 (Jan. 1970), 38–67, and in David D. Hall's "Understanding the Puritans," in Herbert Bass, ed., *The State of American History* (Chicago: Quadrangle Books, 1970). Extensive bibliography pertaining to the New England Antinomian Controversy is included in Emery Battis, *Saints and Sectaries: Anne Hutchinson and the Antinomian Controversy in the Massachusetts Bay Colony* (Chapel Hill: University of North Carolina Press, 1962).

The Antinomian Controversy has had a long and variegated historiographical career, beginning with Edward Johnson's *A History of New England* (London, 1654), better known as *The Wonder-working Providence of Zion's Saviour*. Johnson regarded the Hutchinsonians as "antinomians" in the sense current among his contemporaries. Cotton Mather, in *Magnalia Christi Americana* (London, 1702), treated the affair as an irruption of heresy and sectarianism, in which the cardinal issue was whether assurance of justification might be drawn from works of sanctification. Thomas Hutchinson, in his *History of the Colony of Massachusetts Bay* (Boston, 1764), located the cause of the uproar in his great-great-grandmother's immediate revelations and treated the incident as a problem in religious toleration. John Gorham Palfrey, in his *History of New England During the Stuart Dynasty* (Boston: Little, Brown, and Co., 1865), interpreted it in terms of the authorities' need to maintain order in a time of military and diplomatic crisis. Charles Francis Adams, in *Three Episodes of Massachusetts History* (Boston: Houghton, Mifflin, and Co., 1892), disclaiming interest in Puritan theology, saw the affair as a contest between individual devotion to conscience and repressive dogmatic authority.

"Recovery" of the theological dimension began largely with Perry Miller, who focused attention on the Puritan "mind," especially on the tensions within it, making New England intellectual history—broadly conceived as cultural history—into a legitimate object of scholarship. His treatment of the controversy as a matter of covenant theology and New England "preparationism" is presented in " 'Preparation for Salvation' in Seventeenth-Century New England," *Journal of the History of Ideas*, 4 (June 1943), 259–86, and in ch. 4 of *The New England Mind*, vol. 2. In *The Career of John Cotton: Puritanism and the American Experience* (Princeton: Princeton University Press, 1962), Larzer Ziff interpreted the controversy in terms of theological "legalism" and "conditionality" as against human passivity in regeneration. In *The Heart Prepared: Grace and Conversion in Puritan Spiritual Life* (New Haven: Yale University Press, 1966), Norman Pettit also treated the controversy as a matter of "preparation," although along somewhat different lines than did Miller. Edmund Morgan, in "The Case Against Anne Hutchinson," *New England Quarterly*, 10 (1937), 635–49, and in *The Puritan Dilemma: The Story of John Winthrop* (Boston: Little, Brown, and Co., 1958), saw the affair as a contest between Anne Hutchinson's radical otherworldliness and the authorities' sense of ecclesiastical and civil order in the context of a holy commonwealth. In a similar vein, Darrett B. Rutman, in *Winthrop's Boston: Portrait of a Puritan Town, 1630–1649* (Chapel Hill: University of North Carolina Press, 1965), viewed it as a conflict between the ministers' drive for institutional order and the Hutchinsonians' spiritual individualism, which threatened the social fabric of the community as well as its theologically defined mission. David D. Hall, in his "Introduction" to *The Antinomian Controversy, 1636–1638: A Documentary History* (Middletown: Wesleyan University Press, 1968), placed the episode in the context of religious revival and decline, and material privation, on the edge of the New England wilderness, and identified the central issue as personal assurance of salvation. Emery Battis, in *Saints and Sectaries,* sought the sources of the controversy in Anne Hutchinson's allegedly abnormal psychology and in the sociology of Boston. Kai T. Erikson examined the incident, in *Wayward Puritans: A Study in the Sociology of Deviance* (New York: John Wiley and Sons, 1966), in the context of reflection about the social permission and control of divergence from social norms. Lyle Koehler, in "The Case of the American Jezebels: Anne Hutchinson and Female Agitation During the Years of Antinomian Turmoil, 1636–1640," *William and Mary Quarterly*, 31 (Jan. 1974), 55–78, viewed Hutchinson as a species of proto-feminist.

The principal printed sources generated by the Antinomian Controversy were published together in Charles F. Adams's *Antinomianism in the Colony of Massachusetts Bay, 1636–1638* (Boston: Prince Society, 1894). David Hall's *Antinomian Controversy* makes available all of the documents Adams collected, together with additional printed material and important, previously unpublished manuscript sources. Hall's bibliographical note indicates additional manuscript material. A number of works by principals in the controversy are available in modern editions. Winthrop's journal was published by James Savage as *The History of New England from 1630 to 1649. By John Winthrop,* 2 vols. (2d ed.; Boston: Little, Brown, and Co., 1853), and by James K. Hosmer as *Winthrop's Journal: "History of New England," 1630–1649,* 2 vols. (New York: Charles Scribner's Sons, 1908). The *Winthrop Papers* (Boston: Massachusetts Historical Society, 1929–42) contain in volumes 3 and 4 material pertinent to the controversy. John Cotton's *The Way of Congregational Churches Cleared* (London, 1648) and "Salem Sermon" are reprinted in Larzer Ziff, ed., *John Cotton on the Churches of New England* (Cambridge: Harvard University Press, 1968). Thomas Shepard's writings are available in John Albro, ed., *The Works of Thomas Shepard* (1851—53; rpt. New York: AMS Press, 1967). Cotton's *New Covenant* (London, 1654) and Peter Bulkeley's *Gospel Covenant* (London, 1646), both comprising sermons from the time of the controversy, await the attentions of a modern editor.

In study of Puritan theology there is no substitute for acquaintance with contemporary handbooks. Among the most important, and most readily obtainable, is William Ames's *Medulla Theologica,* translated by John D. Eusden as *The Marrow of Theology: William Ames, 1576–1633* (Boston: Pilgrim Press, 1968). The Westminster Standards embody a widely held Puritan doctrinal position formulated during the first half of the seventeenth century. For the catechisms see Thomas F. Torrance, *The School of Faith: The Catechisms of the Reformed Church* (London: J. Clarke, 1959). The confession, with its Parliamentary, Savoy, and New England modifications, is available in Williston Walker, *The Creeds and Platforms of Congregationalism* (1893; rpt. Boston: Pilgrim Press, 1960). John Norton's *The Orthodox Evangelist* (London, 1654) is the fullest systematic work published by first-generation Massachusetts Puritans. Its counterpart in the second generation is the massive *A Complete Body of Divinity* (Boston, 1727), containing Samuel Willard's lectures on the Westminster Shorter Catechism. Norton touches upon, and Willard enters at length into, the full scope of formal Puritan divinity. Edward Leigh's *A System or Body of Divinity* (London, 1654), although a compilation, is comprehensive and rich in marginal references. Among secondary works, E. Brooks Holifield's *The Covenant Sealed: The Development of Puritan Sacramental Theology in Old and New England, 1570–1720* (New Haven and London: Yale University Press, 1974), though specialized in focus, perceptively explores a substantial range of Puritan theology and practice. In *The Shape of the Puritan Mind: The Thought of Samuel Willard* (New Haven: Yale University Press, 1974), Ernest B. Lowrie offers a close and careful explication of Willard's systematic theology, which was substantially continuous with that of the first generation in Massachusetts. David D. Hall's *The Faithful Shepherd: A History of the New England Ministry in the Seventeenth Century* (Chapel Hill: University of

North Carolina Press, 1972) illuminates intellectual and institutional changes, especially in the latter half of the century

An introduction to the content and the literature of Reformed orthodoxy is available in Heinrich Heppe's *Dogmatik der evangelisch-reformierten Kirche, dargestellt und aus den Quellen belegt,* ed. Ernst Bizer (2d ed.; Neukirchen: Neukirchener Verlag, 1958), available in English as *Reformed Dogmatics,* tr. George T. Thomson (London: Allen and Unwin, 1950). The popular *Compendium Theologiae Christianae* of Johannes Wollebius is translated in John W. Beardslee, III, ed., *Reformed Dogmatics: J. Wollebius, G. Voetius, F. Turretin* (New York: Oxford University Press, 1965). Isaac A. Dorner's *Geschichte der protestantischen Theologie* (München: J. G. Cotta, 1867)—available in English as *History of Protestant Theology,* tr. George Robson and Sophia Taylor (Edinburgh: T. and T. Clark, 1871)—surveys the development of Reformed doctrine and practice. Otto Ritschl, in *Dogmengeschichte des Protestantismus* (Göttingen: Vandenhoeck und Ruprecht, 1926), vol. 3, surveys the development of Reformed theology in relationship to, and independently of, Geneva. Paul Althaus, *Die Prinzipien der deutschen reformierten Dogmatik im Zeitalter der aristotelischen Scholastik* (Leipzig: Deichert'sche Verlagsbuchhandlung, 1914), examines the methodological principles underlying Reformed orthodoxy. For particular concepts, terms, and individuals, Alan Richardson, ed., *A Dictionary of Christian Theology* (Philadelphia: Westminster Press, 1969), is helpful, as are pertinent entries in the *New Schaff-Herzog Encyclopedia of Religious Knowledge* (New York: Funk and Wagnalls, 1909–1914) and *Die Religion in Geschichte und Gegenwart* (3d ed.; Tübingen: J. C. B. Mohr, 1957–1965).

A comprehensive history of Reformed covenant theology remains to be written. Otto Ritschl, in vol. 3, ch. 55, of *Dogmengeschichte des Protestantismus,* traces the basic outlines. See also Gottlob Schrenk, *Gottesreich und Bund im älteren Protestantismus, vornehmlich bei Johannes Coccejus* (Gütersloh: C. Bertelmann, 1923). Perry Miller, in "Appendix B" of *The New England Mind,* vol. 1, lists pertinent titles by English and New English Puritans. Miller's article "The Marrow of Puritan Divinity," *Publications of the Colonial Society of Massachusetts,* 32 (1937), 247–300—reprinted in Miller, *Errand into the Wilderness* (New York: Harper and Row, 1964)—remains a classic treatment of Puritan covenant theology, though it is subject to correction in certain points. See esp. Leonard J. Trinterud, "The Origins of Puritanism," *Church History,* 20 (1951), 37–57; Jens G. Møller, "The Beginnings of Puritan Covenant Theology," *Journal of Ecclesiastical History,* 14 (April 1963), 46–67; and Everett H. Emerson, "Calvin and the Covenant Theology," *Church History,* 25 (1956), 136–44.

Index

Adoption: estate of, 123, 134; spirit of, 120, 122, 124

Agricola, Johann, 231 n. 2

Alsted, Johann, 215 n. 9

Ames, William, 74, 88, 178, 216 n. 12; agency of creatures, 105; covenant theology of, 84–86; and English sectarianism, 233 n. 13; faith, act of, 106; faith and assurance, 132, 133, 136, 152; faith, justifying, 132; *Medulla Theologica*, 15, 216 n. 12; mind's knowledge of itself, 128; and Reformed orthodoxy, 15, 175–76; regeneration, order of, 123–24; on theology, 5

Antinomian Controversy, New England, 147; assurance, issue of, 119–20, 169–70; and covenant theology, 9, 52; historical significance of, 20, 184; and justifying faith, 130; modern scholarship and, 12–13, 174; parties in, 28; "preparation" in, 192–99 passim; theological issues in, 9–11, 14, 40, 126, 169–72, 176, 180, 197; theological motivation in, 17

Antinomianism: defined, 161–62, 181–82; and assurance, 182; and covenant theology, 179–80; in England and New England, 11–12, 108, 157, 163–69 passim, 183; and Holy Spirit, work of, 162–63; human activity, view of, 181–82, 196–97; and Reformed orthodoxy, 183; regeneration, 162; and English sectarianism, 168–69, 235 n. 29

"Antinomians," 11, 138, 156–58, 164–65, 232 n. 11

Arminianism, 119, 128, 174, 193; and justification, 109, 114, 116–17

Assurance: and covenant theology, 59–60, 147–48; means to, doctrine of, 171; and Puritan doctrine of God, 147–48, 150–52; in New England Controversy, 28, 34, 169–70; New England elders on, 58–59, 70–77 passim, 175–78; Puritan doctrine of, 119, 125–26, 155, 159–60; radical approaches to, 138, 157–59; in Reformed theology, 34–35

Baillie, Robert, 36, 37–39

Bakewell, Francis, 233 n. 13, 228 n. 22

Ball, John, 224 n. 28; doubt and assurance, 154; faith and assurance, 133, 136, 152; faith, justifying, 114, 132, 133; means of assurance, 128; *Treatise of Faith*, 182